SELF LOVE AND C[...]

5000447382

University of
Hertfordshire

College Lane, Hatfield, Herts. AL10 9AB

Learning and Information Services

For renewal of Standard and One Week Loans,
please visit the web site **http://www.voyager.herts.ac.uk**

This item must be returned or the loan renewed by the due date.
The University reserves the right to recall items from loan at any time.
A fine will be charged for the late return of items.

NEW STUDIES IN CHRISTIAN ETHICS

General Editor
Robin Gill

Editorial Board
Stephen R. L. Clark, Stanley Hauerwas, Robin W. Lovin

Christian ethics has increasingly assumed a central place within academic theology. At the same time the growing power and ambiguity of modern science and the rising dissatisfaction within the social sciences about claims to value-neutrality have prompted renewed interest in ethics within the secular academic world. There is, therefore, a need for studies in Christian ethics which, as well as being concerned with the relevance of Christian ethics to the present-day secular debate, are well informed about parallel discussions in recent philosophy, science or social science. New Studies in Christian Ethics aims to provide books that do this at the highest intellectual level and demonstrate that Christian ethics can make a distinctive contribution to this debate – either in moral substance or in terms of underlying moral justifications.

SELF LOVE AND CHRISTIAN ETHICS

DARLENE FOZARD WEAVER

CAMBRIDGE
UNIVERSITY PRESS

PUBLISHED BY THE PRESS SYNDICATE OF THE UNIVERSITY OF CAMBRIDGE
The Pitt Building, Trumpington Street, Cambridge, United Kingdom

CAMBRIDGE UNIVERSITY PRESS
The Edinburgh Building, Cambridge CB2 2RU, UK
40 West 20th Street, New York, NY 10011-4211, USA
477 Williamstown Road, Port Melbourne, VIC 3207, Australia
Ruiz de Alarcón 13, 28014 Madrid, Spain
Dock House, The Waterfront, Cape Town 8001, South Africa

http://www.cambridge.org

First published 2002

Printed in the United Kingdom at the University Press, Cambridge

Typeface Baskerville Monotype 11/12.5 pt.   *System* LATEX 2$_\varepsilon$ [TB]

A catalogue record for this book is available from the British Library.

Library of Congress Cataloging in Publication data

Weaver, Darlene Fozard
Self love and Christian ethics / Darlene Fozard Weaver.
p.   cm.   (New studies in Christian ethics)
Includes bibliographical references and index.
ISBN 0 521 81781 1 (hbk)   ISBN 0 521 52097 5 (pbk)
1. Christian ethics.   2. Self-esteem – Religious aspects – Christianity.
3. Love – Religious aspects – Christianity.   I. Title.   II. Series.

BJ1278.S44   2002
241 – dc21   2002023791

ISBN 0 521 81781 1 hardback
ISBN 0 521 52097 5 paperback

John Clayton Fozard
1930–1980

how is one to put off/encounter except by puzzling the terms of
encounter/past inquiry

"Evasive Actions," A. R. Ammons

Contents

General editor's preface

This book is the twenty-third in the series New Studies in Christian Ethics. It shows extensive points of contact and critical dialogue with other books in the series. Darlene Weaver uses the influential framework provided by Susan Parsons in her *Feminism and Christian Ethics* for analyzing differing accounts of feminist ethics. She also has significant points in common with Jean Porter's *Moral Action and Christian Ethics* and with Lisa Cahill's *Sex, Gender and Christian Ethics*. However it is Stanley Rudman's *Concepts of Persons and Christian Ethics* and William Schweiker's *Responsibility and Christian Ethics* that provide her with the most sustained dialogue partners.

Both Darlene Weaver and Stanley Rudman argue that many recent philosophical understandings of selfhood are too limited. Indeed, Weaver suggests that they 'truncate the self.' Both authors are convinced that a notion of self-in-relation-to-God offers a much richer account of selfhood and personhood than any secular understanding. For Weaver it is the belief that 'the person is created to love God' that is fundamental to this richer account. In the process of arguing this, both authors have kept carefully to the two key aims of the series as a whole – namely to promote monographs in Christian ethics which engage centrally with the present secular moral debate at the highest possible intellectual level and, secondly, to encourage contributors to demonstrate that Christian ethics can make a distinctive contribution to this debate.

The original feature of this particular book is that it explores and defends the notion of 'self love.' Properly understood, Darlene Weaver maintains, self love is 'reflexive, embodied, and interpretive.' This sophisticated understanding – quite different from shallow modern notions of 'self-realization' or 'autonomy' – owes much to William Schweiker. Like him she attempts to show that a rich theological vein running through Augustine and Aquinas is still able to challenge modern assumptions. Both authors are also aware of the social dimensions of their respective understandings of 'responsibility' and 'self love.' In addition, there is an extended, albeit critical, debt to the theological writings of Karl Rahner and Paul Tillich running through the later chapters of Weaver's book.

Clearly any serious defense of self love today needs to engage in a considerable amount of intellectual clarification. The notion is vulnerable to attacks from philosophers and social scientists as well as from theologians. It can all too easily be misunderstood. Yet this book challenges the reader to make careful distinctions and to think more clearly about what love entails in a perplexing world. An extended defense of self love is welcome and overdue.

ROBIN GILL

Acknowledgments

This book is, most directly, the fruit of instruction, guidance, and support I received at Yale Divinity School and the University of Chicago Divinity School. Less directly, it is the fruit of a range of significant experiences and relationships from my childhood to the present. It is a joy (sometimes bittersweet) and an honor (ever that) for me to see traces of these environments, lessons, events, and persons on these pages.

Gene Outka introduced me to Christian ethical debates about love. In doing so he gave me the gift of a set of questions with which and conversation partners with whom I think about things that matter most to me. Margaret Farley introduced me to the theology of Karl Rahner and taught me a great deal about contemporary Roman Catholic moral theology. Both encouraged me with their patience, confidence, and kindness. At the University of Chicago Divinity School I received instruction and support from faculty, administrators, and fellow students. I thank especially my dissertation committee, Kathryn Tanner, David Tracy, and William Schweiker. I hope these revisions do more justice to what they taught me. The then-called Institute for the Advanced Study of Religion provided financial support, and my fellow Institute members as well as my dissertation group offered comments on early versions of my argument. Don Browning, Anne Carr, Franklin Gamwell, and Rick Rosengarten extended their expertise and kindness to me. I owe special thanks to William Schweiker. I benefited enormously from his erudition, his commitment to students, and his gratuitous confidence in and support for me. He showed me that Christian ethics can be a vocation. It is one he carries out with brilliance, energy, wit, and integrity. It is a privilege to learn from and work with him.

I began revising the dissertation while working at the Theology Department of Georgetown University. My colleagues there encouraged me during this process. Theresa Sanders read and commented on an early version of the prospectus. Vince Miller offered his wit and counsel on a variety of matters. Tod Linafelt held my hand during the submission process; I will regard this as altruistic even though a wager on the book's publication gave him a monetary incentive. Diane M. Yeager provided comments on some of the material when I shared it with her in another form. I have learned, though not well enough, from her editorial acumen and from her character. I had the privilege of learning from my Georgetown students as well. In particular, I enjoyed many conversations with my research assistant Elizabeth Sweeny about the material treated in Chapter Five. She shares with me one of the best blessings of academic life, a teacher–student relationship that blossoms into a friendship.

I continued to work on the book once I joined the Department of Theology and Religious Studies at Villanova University. It is a privilege to work with my colleagues here as well as with my students. They have welcomed me and supported my work in and outside the classroom. I look forward to many years as one of their number.

In and through these institutional settings, a number of conversation partners and friends afforded me stimulating exchanges, diversions, and support. In particular, I thank Pia Altieri, Reverend Mark Begly, Louis Faassen, and Heidi Gehman. They are friends, teachers, and blessings. I owe a special debt of thanks to Charles Mathewes and to William Werpehowski. Chuck Mathewes has seen this project evolve from its earliest stages as a dissertation proposal to its present form. I thank him for his critical feedback, assistance with the publishing process, wit and, above all, friendship. Bill Werpehowski read and commented on the manuscript in its entirety. His feedback has been most helpful.

I also owe a special debt to two anonymous reviewers for their comments and to Robin Gill and Kevin Taylor for their commitment to the project as I struggled to transform the manuscript from a dissertation into a book. I may have been less successful at this than they (and I) had hoped.

I could not have written this book without the help of my family. In particular, my sister Rachel Fozard and my brother-in-law Peter Kepperling (and soon my god-child, who is on the way!) share with me the many goods of family life and friendship. Their affection and humor, generosity and sacrifice delight and humble me. The same is true of my mother, Mary Ann Fozard, and exponentially so. When she first saw my dissertation, she said, "These are your words." It is clearer to me now that that they are ours. My mother models the good of embodied integrity, and the words I use here to describe it reflect the words and the Word by which she lives with strength, fidelity, grit, and beauty. It is an honor to offer this book as a testament to the life she lives and as a thanks to the life she gives me. My husband, Sean Weaver, gives me countless gifts, including the material support that enabled me to pursue graduate work, an astonishing readiness to subordinate his professional life to mine, the preparation of the index, as well as his forbearance, encouragement, and friendship. I thank him for the life we make together.

I dedicate this book to my father because it is undeniably an expression (however convoluted and over-intellectualized) of a life lived in the wake of his death. His legacy to me seems, more often than not, a series of misplaced attempts to understand and to compensate for the loss of him. Granted, his absence makes for a kind of presence, but in this presence, he remains absent. I hope to learn to recognize and welcome him in this life, and I pray that I may rejoice with him in the next.

CHAPTER I

The contemporary problem of self love

Within our (post) modern milieu lurks the problem of self love. Self love is an inescapable problem for ethics, secular, religious, and Christian, because ethics involves claims about human beings, that is, moral anthropologies. Self love is not only a local problem in ethics, it riddles (post) modern culture as a whole. Because ethics arises in response to the demand to orient and guide human life, it must finally be adequate to such a life. Ethics manifests a dialectical relation between human being and thinking about our being in the world and with others. This book explicates and structurally instantiates this dialectic of moral being and moral thinking. It crafts a moral anthropology in response to the practical moral problem of how to love oneself rightly, and argues that right self love designates a particular form of self-relation in which we understand ourselves truly and embody this in our acts and relations.

This project faces several obstacles from the outset. It is increasingly difficult in ethics to offer a normative account of selfhood. In part this is because a going currency, the language of authenticity, has become tired from over-use. Given the surge of self-help programs and products, and the growing tendency to cast religious belief and spirituality strictly in terms of self-fulfillment, the prospect of an adequate theoretical account of the self is undermined by trite exaltations and ideals of self-realization. What seems necessary, some argue, is not an argument on behalf of self love, but one that deflates our ballooning sense of our selves. Others, however, recognize that self-abnegation continues to be a problem for many, one reinforced by religious, especially Christian, suspicion of the self. What appears to be egoism and selfishness is often a desperate grasp for self-worth. Many feminists have noted as well that women too often *fail* to assert themselves, instead allowing their relations with others to define them. Moreover, women continue to be oppressed by supposedly universal accounts of women's nature that are employed to warrant gender-based inequities and injustice. What we require, from this perspective, is a rejection of selflessness, sacrifice, and obedience as moral ideals, along with the accounts of human nature that are used to apply these norms disproportionately between the sexes. Still others offer a more radical version of this challenge to normative accounts of the self, noting that the social construction of selves involves more than gender socialization. Increasingly, the notion of an authentic self is being replaced by the insight that identities are constructed socially and linguistically. For some this "de-centering" of identity requires resistance to hegemonic systems; it offers a liberating opportunity to choose and change identities, to experiment with various forms of presenting and locating oneself socially. For others it embodies the lamentable fragmentation of contemporary society, as well as our increasing capacity to separate ourselves from one another and from ourselves through the manipulation afforded by communications and Internet media, psycho-pharmacology, cosmetic surgery, and genetic technology.

Thus the complex theoretical accounts of the self that might deflate our ballooning self-estimation and lend substance to ideals of self-realization are widely thought to be philosophically untenable and morally suspect. Indeed, moral anthropological thinking has shifted in recent decades from ontological analyses to epistemological ones. And those epistemological analyses in large part concern the limitations of human knowledge. The general result in ethics is the rise of what I call the norm of self-realization. This norm refers to the dominant subjectivism of recent work in ethics in particular and contemporary culture in general, a shift toward voluntaristic and intuitionistic understandings of the moral good, in which moral values are primarily matters of personal or communal choice and moral obligations are taken to be largely situation-specific.

These challenges to normative accounts of the self, which I will treat in greater detail below, manifest and reinforce a basic moral anthropological problem: how to be a coherent self. This chapter argues that this dilemma is nothing other than the problem of self love. We require a moral anthropology that illuminates the relation between moral being and moral thinking and orients us practically, but does so in a way consonant with the insights of such challenges and free from their shortcomings. This book offers an account of self love toward that end. This chapter charts contemporary secular (academic and cultural) schizophrenia about the self and shows the need for a theological moral anthropology as the basis for a norm of right self love. First, let us turn to a constellation of problems that isolate the basic moral problem of how to be a coherent self.

THE BREAKDOWN OF THE LOVE SYNTHESIS

While classical accounts of the divine–human relation are varied and sometimes stand in tension with one another, nevertheless they agree on the commensurability of love for self and love for God. Classical accounts shared the claim that God is the highest good and the good of the human as such; this claim weds individual human flourishing to the self's relation with God. Proper self-relation and proper God-relation coincide. Classical theological ethics could be read as a kind of theological ethical egoism; notwithstanding the realities of pride and concupiscence, the self legitimately pursues her own happiness in her pursuit of God. Although a considerable amount of classical theology denigrates the self, this traditional link between the divine good and the self's good, mediated in the world, designates an idea of right self love.[1]

---

[1] The connection between denigration of the self and human flourishing is complex. In certain forms such as asceticism, for example, denigration of the self provides an instrument that contributes to the human's spiritual perfection. The connection between denigration and flourishing would be misunderstood were the two made patently incommensurable or if a causal relationship between them were naively construed. The connection touches on complicated questions about the place of sacrifice in the Christian (good) life, as well as long-standing conceptions of good selves and bad selves, debates about the relation of the individual to community, and the goodness of creation. For treatments of the relationship between asceticism and spiritual flourishing see Caroline Walker Bynum, *Holy Feast and Holy Fast: the Religious Significance of Food to Medieval Women* (Berkeley, CA: University of California Press, 1987); Maureen H. Tilly and Susan A. Ross, eds., *Broken and Whole: Essays on Religion and the Body* (Lanham, MD: University Press of America Inc., 1994); Peter Brown, *The Body and Society: Men, Women and Sexual Renunciation in Early Christianity* (New York: Columbia University Press, 1988).

At the risk of over-simplifying matters, it may be said that the classical Roman Catholic coordination of self love with love for God was unalterably challenged by Reformation theology.[2] But to argue that, historically speaking, the Christian tradition shifted from a favorable regard for self love to a negative attitude would be to read history reductively. For instance, while Protestant emphases on self-sacrifice are taken to exhibit a denigration of the self, we should note that such emphases are rooted in the ascetic spiritual thinking and practices of Catholicism.[3] To be sure, both Catholics and Protestants would only approve of *right* self love; the differences lie in whether such a love is thought possible and if so, in what it consists. Thus, it is more accurate to note that the differences between Protestant and Catholic attitudes toward self love concern the interpretation and weight given to pertinent theological claims, particularly with respect to creation, sin, and redemption.

As I noted earlier, central to traditional accounts of the divine–human relation is the claim that God is the highest good and the good of the human as such. Such accounts often opposed a concupiscible self love with caritas, God's love given to the self, by which the self properly loves God and others. In caritas, the human is given her highest good.[4] Thus, the human endeavor to love God is simultaneously the pursuit of her own good. This link receded as distinctly theological claims about the gratuity of grace and the sovereignty of God became more pronounced; while theological anthropological claims about the utter depravity of the human were by no means new, theologians re-asserted them vigorously in

---

[2] For a helpful comparative study of Protestant and Roman Catholic ethics, see James M. Gustafson, *Protestant and Roman Catholic Ethics: Prospects for Rapprochement* (Chicago: University of Chicago Press, 1978). Gustafson argues that the major difference between the two traditions historically has been the place of Scripture in ethical thought.

[3] For a historical study of Roman Catholic moral theology see John A. Gallagher, *Time Past, Time Future: a Historical Study of Catholic Moral Theology* (New York: Paulist, 1990). See also John Mahoney, *The Making of Moral Theology: a Study of the Roman Catholic Tradition* (Oxford: Oxford University Press, 1987).

[4] The work of Augustine and Thomas Aquinas is paradigmatic of this point. An insightful and subtle analysis of Augustine's thinking on this matter can be found in Oliver O'Donovan's *The Problem of Self-Love in Augustine* (New Haven and London: Yale University Press, 1980). See especially chapter six, in which O'Donovan touches upon Catholic–Protestant differences in the evaluation of self love and its relation to eudaimonism. See also Gerald W. Schlabach, *For the Joy Set Before Us: Augustine and Self-Denying Love* (Notre Dame, IN: University of Notre Dame Press, 2001).

conjunction with reformation claims about grace and freedom in such a way as to free the self from anxiety over its salvation. In light of reformation theology, portions of classical and medieval Catholic theology appeared to exalt the self unduly, such that the self's pursuit of its own beatitude instrumentalized both God and neighbor and obscured the inevitability of sin and gratuity of grace.

In short, the erotic tenor of classical and medieval accounts of the divine–human relation shifted in the Reformation to an emphasis on God's agape and subsequently, to agape as the norm for Christian life. The agapic love of God manifested in the Christ became the Christian love par excellence.[5] It differs radically from eros, the love of something for the sake of one's self, rather than for its own sake. The sovereign grace of God manifest in Christ's saving work prompted reformation theologians to separate the moral life from the person's status before God. Salvation and eternal happiness, while never purely a matter of one's own agency, were no longer thought to be formed through love.[6] Proper relation to others arose from the self's relation to God, no longer conceived in terms of love so much as faith. So the shift from erotic to agapic emphases accompanied, perhaps induced, another change: self love began to be considered not with respect to love for God, but with respect to love for the neighbor. While contemporary Catholic

---

[5] In making this claim I differ from Denis de Rougemont, who argues that Christian love prior to the Reformation was dominated by the idea of agape. See his *Love in the Western World*, trans. Montgomery Belgion (Garden City, NY: Doubleday and Company, Inc., 1957). His reading of history ignores the role caritas and eros have played. For a critique of de Rougemont on this count, see M. C. D'Arcy, *The Mind and Heart of Love* (New York: Meridian Books, 1959).

[6] For a historical study of love, see Irving Singer, *The Nature of Love*, 3 vols. (Chicago: University of Chicago Press, 1987). See especially volume 1. In my judgment, Singer misreads Augustine, Aquinas, and Luther and does all three a disservice. Indeed, his anti-metaphysical and atheistic commitments effect a reductive and biased reading of religious ideas of love. Nevertheless, the trilogy provides a helpful historical survey and an important analytic framework for love as a psychological state in terms of the appraisal or bestowal of value. See also Robert Hazo, *The Idea of Love* (New York: Frederick A. Praeger, 1967); Anders Nygren, *Agape and Eros*, trans. Philip S. Watson (London: S.P.C.K., 1957); D'Arcy, *The Mind and Heart of Love*; C. S. Lewis, *The Four Loves* (London: Geoffrey Bles, 1960); Alan Soble, *The Structure of Love* (New Haven and London: Yale University Press, 1990). As will be made clear shortly, this book moves away from an analysis of love in terms of motifs or types, and instead explores self love by means of an account of the lover, the self who is to love herself. In doing so I suggest an account of (self) love as a hermeneutical or interpretive activity/process.

accounts of love still tend to construe love as mutuality, and often draw upon Trinitarian accounts of God (versus the Christological/ soteriological emphases of Protestant accounts of love), it is fair to say that the Protestant approach largely determined the landscape for a contemporary Christian ethical inquiry into self love, and that Protestant critiques of the Catholic coordination of self love and love for God remain insights with which a contemporary account of self love must contend.

However, many contemporary ethicists, theological and philosophical, have problems with traditional accounts of the divine–human relationship. These difficulties can be schematized along theological, anthropological, and meta-ethical lines. First, theological questions challenge classical accounts of the divine–human relation and raise the problem of God. How can we know God? What is the nature of God? How can (and ought) we to speak about God? Classical mythic-agential theories of the divine have given way to highly de-anthropomorphized understandings of God, for example as absolute mystery or being-itself.[7] While Christian theology historically encompasses a variety of arguments about God's relation to the world, specifically, epistemic and agential questions raised by modernity now set the parameters within which such inquiry typically occurs. These questions do not permit any naïve return to traditional divine–human accounts. Love for God, then, along with an idea of proper self love in terms of love for God, are problematic ideas at best, and for many, altogether meaningless.

Second, shifts within moral anthropological thinking displace any general consensus regarding human nature and raise the problem of the self. Historical consciousness and the modern methodological posture of doubt moves thinkers to question radically any account of the human that claims to be universal. Appeals to abstract qualities in the human such as reason or freedom as potential foundations for ethics or for visions of human flourishing fail to satisfy many contemporary thinkers. Instead, they stress the specificity of the person as one who occupies a particular culture during

---

[7] For a recent treatment of personal language for God, see Vincent Brummer, *Speaking of a Personal God: an Essay in Philosophical Theology* (Cambridge: Cambridge University Press, 1992).

a particular historical period, with a particular ethnic and racial background, family unit, sexual orientation, and so on.[8] Or they focus on how the human subject is constructed and determined by various systems of power.[9] I will consider these alternatives more carefully in what follows. For now, note that questioning the existence and character of some universal human nature prompts thinkers to revise or reject traditional claims (e.g., the human is the *imago dei*). It is difficult not only to conceive of something universal in humans which provides a point of departure for a theory of self love; the very idea of a self is in question.

Finally, for many thinkers it is unclear whether God is necessary for an ethics. Thinkers such as Iris Murdoch, for instance, develop religious ethics without traditional theism.[10] Others argue that religion and the religious actually impair morality. It is unclear how religion and morality are or should be related. Does religion have some place in the good life? Does morality have anything to do with one's religious standing before God? Is morality restricted, for instance, to the sphere of human interpersonal relations? Some thinkers do exclude the religious relation between God and the human from the domain of ethics. Granted, for many, religion and morality have some relation, even if only a conventional, historical association, and, moreover, the character of that relation has long been a problem within ethics. But, the challenges put to traditional accounts of the divine–human relation not only serve to compartmentalize or neglect the religious dimension of the human and of the moral life, but, as Nietzsche, Freud, and others charge, contribute to an "overmoralizing" of the self. Thus, contemporary ethics grapples with the problem of God, the problem of the self, and the problem of how religion and morality are or should be

---

[8] Thinkers who stress this insight do so, of course, in varying degrees. Some simply emphasize that persons are embodied while others contend that our particularity disallows commonality altogether. See for example, respectively, Mark Johnson, *The Body in the Mind: the Bodily Basis of Meaning, Imagination, and Reason* (Chicago: University of Chicago Press, 1988); Judith Butler, *Gender Trouble: Feminism and the Subversion of Identity* (New York and London: Routledge, 1990).

[9] Texts which advance some version of this claim are manifold. For some representative works which make such an argument, see Michel Foucault, *The History of Sexuality: an Introduction*, trans. Robert Hurley (New York: Random House, 1978); Judith Butler, *Gender Trouble*.

[10] See Iris Murdoch, *Metaphysics as a Guide to Morals* (New York: Allen Lane/Penguin, 1993).

related.[11] If classical theological ethics stressed the commensurability of love for God and self love, the contemporary moral outlook asks if they are related at all. And as the two previous points suggest, the content given to each of those loves is debated.

In response to the breakdown of the love synthesis, this book will argue that love for God, self, and neighbor are dynamically inter-related. The costs of failing to note these inter-relations are high. Unduly separating them risks misconstruing them as competing objects of love. This error in turn threatens to undermine the legitimacy of love for self by fostering negative valuations of it. Further, it may encourage the self's obeisance to the divine quite apart from questions whether the object or form of that relation is morally good; that is, it threatens tyrannous or false devotion to the divine. Moreover, it may encourage unmitigated sacrifice on behalf of the neighbor, a sacrifice that mutilates the identity of the person and does a disservice to the neighbor as well. As a contemporary account of self love makes clear, to construe God, self, and neighbor as competing objects of love establishes false oppositions among them.

I do not deny that love for God, self, and neighbor can stand in tension with one another. Clearly, love for anything or anyone can become distorted and can encroach upon other morally obligatory loves. Since St. Paul lamented his divided will and Augustine complained that the loves of his heart outnumbered the hairs on his head, Christian thinkers have wrestled with the problem of how properly to order loves (the *ordo amoris*). This problem taps

---

[11] We can note a few distinctively modern (theological) ethical responses to these challenges to traditional theism. These responses include apologetic efforts which, for example, appeal to the functional value of Christian beliefs and symbols, or its metaphorical veracity. Many contemporary theologians and ethicists sift through Christian theology as an unparalleled set of resources, or as a kind of talk, for claims and symbols to re-appropriate. See, for example, Sallie McFague, *Models of God* (Philadelphia, PA: Fortress, 1987). Some responses to the deconstruction of human nature have emphasized basic, common goods and needs which all humans share, such as the need for shelter and nourishment, the (admittedly varied) kinship structures which accompany human communities, and so on. See, for example, Lisa Sowle Cahill, *Sex, Gender and Christian Ethics* (Cambridge: Cambridge University Press, 1996), especially 46–72, and Charles E. Larmore, *Patterns of Moral Complexity* (Cambridge: Cambridge University Press, 1987). Or, alternatively, they look to language and stress the conditions for communication in order to locate regulative norms for human interaction. See, for example, Seyla Benhabib, *Situating the Self: Gender, Community and Postmodernism in Contemporary Ethics* (New York: Routledge, 1992).

into the deepest currents and concerns of human life. The moral life transpires in the ongoing give and take of duties and desires, commitments and changes. As I will suggest later in this chapter, this plurality indelibly marks contemporary moral experience and raises the basic moral question of how to be a coherent self. Here I argue that love for God, self, and neighbor are distinct though mutually entailing. The mutual entailment of love for God, self, and neighbor avoids positing a false opposition among them. But it does so without obfuscating the ongoing tension among those loves. Put differently, love for God, self, and neighbor are dialectically related to one another. Because these loves are distinct, though mutually entailing, the person's endeavor to enact them all will necessarily be a dynamic, lifelong enterprise. Because love for God, self, and neighbor are distinct, there are duties proper to each. This point is important to my argument in two respects. First, it drives my claim that although self love is actualized in love for the neighbor, it is not exhausted by it. Some argue that any good that accrues to the self in her neighbor love is to be regarded as a side effect or derivative of her basic task of love. Others suggest that any satisfaction the self experiences in her neighbor love pollutes that love; the self must love the neighbor disinterestedly. Both kinds of thinking assume a false opposition of self and neighbor and devalue the goods of reciprocity and mutuality in love. I will say more about this later. Second, the claim that love for God, self, and neighbor entail respective duties also drives the argument I make in Chapter Six about the relation between religion and morality. Briefly, I will argue that although self-relation is mediated in our relation to the divine, and that right self love is a response of love to God's self-offer, love for God demands a deliberate, self-conscious (though not necessarily explicitly theistic) self-disposal. That is, love for God requires the self to orient herself around that love, to strive to establish it as the central commitment that harmonizes her self-understanding and her acting in the world. Right self love designates a form of self-relation in which the self knows and accepts herself in the divine. In this manner, then, this book seeks to retrieve and update the classical love synthesis. Its account of the dynamic inter-relations of love for God, self, and neighbor offers a contemporary *ordo amoris*, one predicated not on a supposed competition but on dialectical tensions.

What we have, then, is a complex array of claims and counter-claims, both descriptive and evaluative, about the nature of the self, the self's relation to the divine, and the self's good or flourishing. As I noted earlier, differences between Roman Catholic and Protestant accounts of self love isolate a difficulty which contributes to the contemporary problem of self love, namely, the separation of one's religious relation to God and one's moral life. There are important theological reasons for such a separation, but the link between the religious relation to God and the moral life must be reasserted and rethought. There are two reasons why this must be done. First, the contemporary norm of self-realization is not critically assessed; because it is not assessed, we are unable to identify and argue against forms of self-relation that are destructive. Second, the separation of religious relation to God and one's moral life also fails to assess morally one's relation to God. It leaves unasked the question whether a particular form of relation to God is morally unacceptable. Granted, both the academy and popular culture offer moral criticisms of particular images of and beliefs about God, but they pay less moral attention to forms of the divine–human relation. These two reasons comprise an urgent ethical problem, both for the discipline of ethics and for human existence itself.

Within this modern milieu of the rejection and retrieval of traditional Christian theology lurks the problem of self love. Indeed, while the challenges posed to traditional links between the divine and the self's good receded in part because of a humane concern for the self, these challenges incur significant costs for the dignity and coherence of the self. Let me explore, then, several strands in the contemporary moral outlook which extend modern critiques of this traditional account and which are particularly salient to the problem of self love.

THE SELF AS PROBLEM

Modern roots

The social and intellectual changes wrought by the Reformation aided and abetted, and were aided and abetted by, the intellectual, social, and cultural changes of modernity, strands of which some argue continue and intensify in post-modernity.[12] The *nominalism* of the Reformation era asserted the priority of real, particular persons over and against universal concepts like humanity. It challenged the medieval moral emphasis (found paradigmatically in Aquinas) on living according to nature. The flourishing *mysticism* of the sixteenth century stressed the possibility of immediate experience of God, thereby qualifying the church as a mediator between the person and God and subordinating its authority to that of individual experience. This religious individualism increased given Protestant rejections of Catholic hierarchy and Protestant emphases on the individual's capacity to understand scripture and to encounter in the Word an invitation to a personal relation with God. The *humanism* of the Reformation era contributed optimism in the capacities of human beings to solve personal and social ills while *political and economic changes* dissolved the rigid socio-political hierarchies of feudalism and at least promised a more egalitarian social order.[13] These and other changes set the stage for the modern turn to the subject. The self achieved philosophical and cultural prominence thanks to the work of thinkers like Descartes, Locke, Hume, Kant, and Hegel. Their respective ways of turning to the subject initiated an epistemological revolution that placed everything else in question, while later thinkers like Nietzsche, Weber, Marx, and Freud questioned the modern subject.

A brief look at some modern conceptions of the self can surface several important themes and problems that figure prominently in contemporary approaches to the self.[14] These themes constellate in a problem that we cannot address adequately without a theological anthropology.

René Descartes (1596–1650) continued the introspective turn that St. Augustine initiated centuries earlier. Descartes insisted that mind/soul is distinct from body and from the material world.

[12] Stanley Rudman *Concepts of Persons and Christian Ethics* (Cambridge: Cambridge University Press, 1997), 81.

[13] See Steven E. Ozment, *The Reformation in the Cities* (New Haven and London: Yale University Press, 1975); Owen Chadwick, *The Reformation* (London: Penguin; Owen Chadwick, 1972); John Bossy, *Christianity in the West, 1400–1700* (Oxford: Oxford University Press; John Bossy, 1985).

[14] For an excellent historical treatment see Charles Taylor *Sources of the Self: The Making of the Modern Identity* (Cambridge, MA: Harvard University Press, 1989).

The self is essentially mind; of course Descartes then encountered difficulties accounting for sensations and feelings. The *mind/body split* with which Descartes wrestled remains today. Ironically, he wanted to replace speculative philosophy with practical philosophy, but this mind–body dualism deflects attention from the concrete and social conditions in which the self works out her self-relation. Moreover, the identification of self and mind eclipses the import of embodiment for moral knowledge and neglects the fact that the self posits her self-relation in and through her actions in the world.

The mind/body split intersects with the problem of *the self's continuity*. John Locke (1632–1704) cast the issue of identity in terms of temporal continuity. As Stanley Rudman notes, Locke's distinction between "man" and "person" proved particularly important.[15] For Locke, "man's" identity consists in the material continuity of the body, whereas he defines a "person's" identity with respect to rationality and self-consciousness.[16] What is important about Locke's approach to the self is the link he establishes between self-consciousness, moral responsibility and personal identity. Self-consciousness grounds the person's responsibility for her actions, and comprises the continuity of personal identity. Charles Taylor says of the Lockean self, "the disengagement both from the activities of thought and from our unreflecting desires and tastes allows us to see ourselves as objects of far-reaching reformation. Rational control can extend to the re-creation of our habits, and hence of ourselves."[17] This rationalist conception of the self contrasts David Hume's (1711–76) argument that the self is a "bundle of perceptions." He raises thereby the questions whether there is a *relatively stable human nature* and, with Locke, what *the conditions of human agency* might be. Hume rejected the idea of a simple, identical self, and argued instead that a human being consists in a rapid succession of perceptions. Accordingly, Hume understood ethics in aesthetic and passional terms. Reason, argued Hume, is not practical; that is, it cannot move or restrain us from acting. Morality is rooted

---

[15] Rudman *Concepts of Persons and Christian Ethics*, 81–84.
[16] John Locke, *Essay Concerning Human Understanding*, ed. with a forword by Peter H. Nidditch (Oxford: Clarendon Press; New York: Oxford University Press, 1979), II.xxvii.6.
[17] Charles Taylor, *Sources of the Self the making of Modern Identity*, 171.

in feelings that respond to useful or agreeable qualities because of our natural propensity for sympathy. A system of justice and general rules regulates this process and protects us and the moral enterprise as a whole when particular actions do not appear to be useful. Despite the differences among modern positions, such philosophical inquiry into what the self is occurs with and through ontology and epistemology and for the sake of orienting human life, disclosing the intimate and dynamic connections among ethics, anthropology and beliefs about reality.

Particularly important for the contemporary problem of self love is Immanuel Kant (1724–1804). He distinguished knowledge of things in themselves (noumena) from knowledge of things as they appear (phenomena). Kant's influence can be discerned to-day in the contemporary "abandonment of ontology as the basis for determining the nature of human personhood."[18] He stressed the *character of freedom* particularly in relation to *desire*. His account of the person centered on rationality, and his account of morality centered on the good will. Rational beings alone, said Kant, have the capacity to act according to principles (that is, have a will). Kant argued that "nothing can possibly be conceived in the world, or even out of it, which can be called good without qualification, except a *good will*."[19] As we will see, Kant's insistence that the autonomous will is inviolable and his emphasis on universalizability as a moral criterion create problems for self love. They, with his rejection of ontology, undermine our moral assessment of the choices through which we take up relation to ourselves and others. They also make for an ironic egocentrism.

Several propositions about duty underlie Kant's claim for the will's goodness. First, Kant proposed that moral worth be accorded to acts that are performed not because of inclination but because of duty. In this manner, Kant based morality not on the caprice and prejudice of human affection but the will. Kant's second proposition is simply that a universal moral law cannot have a telos as its content; put differently, the moral law cannot be defined in terms

[18] Ray S. Anderson, *On Being Human: Essays in Theological Anthropology* (Grand Rapids, MI: William B. Eerdmans, 1982), 5.
[19] Immanuel Kant, *Fundamental Principles of the Metaphysics of Morals*, trans. Thomas K. Abbott (New York: Macmillan, 1949), 11.

of some object of desire or state of affairs. Kant did grant that one's
duty can simultaneously be an object of desire, but its desirability
cannot ground its moral character. In other words, a good will is
objectively determined by law. Kant's third proposition introduces
respect into this formulation of duty. Dutiful obedience to the law
entails respect for the law, such that obedience arises solely from
this respect and excludes all inclinations and objects. A good will
is subjectively determined by respect for the law.

According to Kant, the moral law can be derived from the a
priori presuppositions of practical (pure) reason. One such sup-
position is freedom. Kant contends that a moral principle follows
from the "general concept of rational being," from the very character of rational freedom.[20] By rejecting traditional metaphysics,
Kant required the determination of moral worth independent of
any ends, because any claim about the worth of some things cannot be logically necessary. Human subjectivity alone can specify the
moral worth of an action. And since human subjectivity (i.e., practical reason) is concerned with the question of freedom, the moral
principle derived from subjectivity will express the very character
of freedom. This line of reasoning allowed Kant to argue that,
because the moral principle issues from and expresses subjectivity
and because subjectivity has universal characteristics, it must be
universalizable. Hence, Kant offered the first formulation of the
moral principle: "Never so act that thy maxim should not be willed
as a universal law."[21]

Kant's understanding of the scope of human reason bears upon
the way he conceives the human will. Kant understands the will
as self-legislative freedom. Because the moral principle issues from
subjectivity and concerns freedom as an a priori presupposition of
subjectivity, the moral principle must be rationally necessary. That
is, it must bind the will categorically. Human reasoning about possible desired ends cannot bind the will categorically because the
worth of those ends has a logically contingent, hypothetical status. This means that moral reason operates independent of desire.
Any choice, however, includes some understanding of human freedom. The first formulation of the categorical imperative suggests,
then, that the will is categorically bound by rational freedom. But

[20] Ibid., 19.   [21] Ibid., 29.

because reason gives this principle to itself, the will is self-legislative. This means that the will, though rationally bound, remains free or autonomous.

Because the moral principle must be an a priori categorical moral imperative, Kant sought to specify just what principle could bind the will irrespective of choice. As I have suggested, for Kant that principle must express the character of rational freedom. According to Kant, the structure of rational freedom is rational freedom. Thus, rational freedom is an end in itself. Kant formulated his moral principle in a second way: "So act as to treat humanity, whether in thine own person or in that of any other always as an end withal and never as a means."[22] Humanity, or rational freedom, is for Kant an idea. If freedom is only an idea, what enabled Kant to give some content to the moral law? The autonomous will (freedom) is that against which we cannot act. Kant formulated the categorical imperative in a third fashion to express this: "Act only on those maxims which have as their objects themselves as universal laws of nature."[23] Thus, the autonomous will gives negative content to the moral law.

The fact that the moral law has only negative content raises several problems for Kant's relation of reason and desire. What exactly are we not to do so as not to act against freedom? Any action seems at least to limit the choices available to others, and thereby, to constrain their freedom. But for Kant this is morally irrelevant since the choices available to anyone have no moral worth. The sheer demand that a choice be universalizable does not itself distinguish among choices as right or wrong. Kant thus arrives at the conception of a law that determines the will, the supreme principle of morality, which Kant identified as the categorical imperative: the moral project is one of making oneself worthy of happiness. While one can only accomplish this through respect for persons, the fact is that the person's responsibility is not to promote the good of others but the goodness of one's will.[24]

Hegel (1770–1831) called attention to the historical character of thinking, which prompted him to counter the Kantian account of freedom as autonomy. "The opposition of noumenal and

---

[22] Ibid., 54.   [23] Ibid., 56.
[24] William Schweiker, *Responsibility and Christian Ethics* (Cambridge: Cambridge University Press, 1995), 82.

phenomenal worlds is overcome, not by cosmic absorption or reductionism, however, but by the self-realisation of absolute reason in finite human spirits, who retain their rational individuality and existence. This emphasized the significance of self-consciousness in the concept of person."[25] Hegel recognized that freedom is shaped communally and historically. Real freedom requires us to recognize this influence and to realize our rational natures by building with others a rational community. Such a community reconciles self-interest and duty. The Hegelian and Kantian traditions differ in *the relation between the person and value*. As I noted above, Kant (and his heirs) depict the self as unencumbered, as one who constitutes her world through her choices and actions. Goodness designates a quality of the will rather than an external, objective order. Hegel and heirs depict the self as situated in history and society, which means that the self is shaped by these particulars and that value is in some measure socially constructed.

There were other important counters to Kantian thought. Some thinkers reacted against the rationalism of modernity with naturalist accounts of morality. Sigmund Freud, for instance emphasized the deception of reason and its vulnerability to natural, unconscious impulses. Versions of Marxism (in Friedrich Engels and in Lenin) have (respectively) pronounced emphases on natural laws and correspondence theories of knowledge respectively. Friedrich Nietzsche (1844–1900) offered an aesthetic existentialism in contrast to the smug rationality of modernity and in response to the wane of religious and metaphysical systems. Nietzsche joins the company of thinkers who find metaphysics untenable in religious and secular forms. Nietzsche argues that human thought is interpretive and perspectival. We cannot know things "in themselves" because there is no "true world of being." There is only the ceaseless tumult of forces arranging and re-arranging themselves in power relations. There is no order or telos to this process. Nietzsche described it as the will to power. Nietzsche's anti-ontologism, however, should not lead to nihilism. Indeed, Nietzsche's point was to affirm life without resort to fictions like God or ontological categories. The issue is how best to interpret and assess experience. Nietzsche

[25] Rudman, *Concepts of Persons and Christian Ethics*, 95.

called for a revaluation of received values in light of the will to power. It shows that most moral and religious thought reflects the "all-too-human," fosters weakness, and stunts creativity. Nietzsche contrasted such slave or herd moralities with a master morality, one that enables greater independence and creativity, the maximization of the will to power, and the emergence of a higher humanity of supermen.

It might seem that an argument for self love would find an ally in Nietzsche, and in fact there are aspects of his thought that prove helpful. Nietzsche draws our attention to the activities of interpretation and evaluation as exercises of power. And he notes rightly that moralities, as such interpretive and evaluative exercises, ought to enhance human life. In fact Nietzsche poses a two-fold challenge that shows the requirements an ethics of self love must meet. There is, first, Nietzsche's anti-ontologism, which places him in a large and generally esteemed company. The second prong of Nietzsche's challenge is the import of the will to power for an argument against slave moralities. Nietzsche seems to trap us into showing him to be right. An unadulterated argument for self love seems to exemplify the will to power (even if it proves inadequate to the task of fostering a life that maximizes the will to power). An argument against self love, or ones for it that construe it as an indirect result of or precondition for loving one's neighbor seem to be slave moralities, deployed by the masses to defend themselves against the strong. For a Christian ethics of self love to find a way out from under Nietzsche's challenge it must differ from a simple endorsement or instantiation of the will to power by directing self love to love for God and neighbor in the world. But it must do this without endorsing values that diminish human life and without naïve dependence on the fictions and constructs of religious and metaphysical thought. It must affirm with Nietzsche the interpretive and perspectival character of human thought and share his conviction that morality should enhance human life. How can it accomplish all this without exemplifying, explicitly or implicitly, the will to power?

Might the very metaphysical frameworks Nietzsche and others reject as constructs have a heuristic value? The issue is whether they help us to see what sort of person the human is. This question keeps us from dumbly re-asserting the modern self after Nietzsche's devastating critique of it. It also keeps us from concluding too quickly that this critique of the modern self is simultaneously a critique of all ontologically indebted accounts of the self.[26]

This admittedly rough identification of various modern conceptions of the self isolates some important problems that contemporary inquiry into the self confronts: *the mind–body relation, the temporal continuity of identity, the question of some relatively stable human "nature," the character of freedom and its relation to desire, the conditions of moral agency, and the relation between the person and value.* In varied ways, modern thinkers reconceive the relations among ontology, anthropology, and morality. Charles Taylor notes of modernity and its legacy that "selfhood and the good, or in another way selfhood and morality, turn out to be inextricably intertwined themes."[27]

Given the relation between anthropology and ethics, being and our thinking about it, one way we can gain some purchase on secular ethical treatments of the self is to consider how the self is related to the object of ethics. Disparate ethical appraisals constellate around the insistence that the self is *not* the object of ethics. Utilitarian ethics for instance aims not at the development of persons but some state of affairs, the maximization of utility for the greatest number of people. Marxist theories endeavor to show the economic and conflictual character of social relations. The ethics of some analytic philosophy takes the meaning and operation of moral terms as its object. This is not to say that such positions lack moral anthropologies; indeed, they entail quite important claims about human beings. The utilitarian self is a producer and consumer of utility, a rational calculator of ends but not a unique and particular center of value. Marxist theories include some accounts of truly human activity in contrast to the alienation caused by disassociation from the means of production and the ideological fog of bourgeoisie values. Analytic philosophy construes the self as an agent capable of choosing within some world of facts.

---

[26] Alasdair MacIntyre, *After Virtue*, 2nd edn (Notre Dame, IN: University of Notre Dame Press, 1984).

[27] Taylor, *Sources of the Self*, 3.

The point is that these positions do not take the self as the aim of ethics. But, in other positions the self *is* the object of ethics. Virtue and narrative ethics are clear examples of this. Virtue ethics stresses the self's flourishing and the importance of her dispositions and capacities. Narrative ethicists argue that narrative is a constitutive feature of selfhood. According to Paul Ricoeur, "the idea of gathering together one's life in the form of a narrative is destined to serve as a basis for the aim of 'good' life."[28] Some liberation ethics, various feminist ethics for example, take the self as their object as well. In different ways and for different reasons these ethics aim at the flourishing of the self. Others construe ethics as the task of showing there is no self, at least not in the sense of a sovereign, unified essentialist agent. Especially problematic for these ethics, and for many of the above, is a self defined in substantialist terms. Deconstructing and de-centering the self is an ethical task because it liberates us from the definitions imposed on us by others. Sometimes this is construed as a post-moral task, since ethics itself is considered a weapon of control. But the task of showing that there is no self given this liberatory aim also has the self's good in view. Hence, Foucault deconstructs the traditional metaphysical subject in the service of an ethics of care for the self.

Enamored by autonomy: the self as "free agent"

The modern legacy is obvious in contemporary Western culture. Autonomy ranks as a chief good and echoes in a number of central cultural values and in legal, social, and economic systems and practices. Even a brief sampling of advertising shows this: as I write the radio blares public service announcements concerning the deregulation of electricity utilities, and commercials for bank services, sport utility vehicles, and allergy medications. They all tout freedom as an unqualified good. But, the idea of freedom that contemporary Western societies inherit from modernity is largely a negative freedom, a freedom defined chiefly as the absence of constraints.

---

[28] Paul Ricoeur, *Oneself as Another*, trans. Kathleen Blamey (Chicago: University of Chicago Press, 1992), 158.

This negative freedom belongs to a complex of values like self-sufficiency, independence and self-determination. In other words, in autonomy, negative freedom meets the power of self-definition. The tension inherent to this union spawns a confusing mentality in which the power to define and determine oneself through one's choices and pursuits requires a new and, paradoxically, freedom from those very "commitments." This means that the value of autonomy confers on the self a certain sovereignty and reality prior to and independent from her choices and pursuits even as the meaning of autonomy is indexed to the capacity to define or locate oneself in her choices and pursuits. To borrow from the world of professional sports, the self is a "free agent," loosely and provisionally tied to a team, ready and willing to affiliate itself with another one should the terms be – and remain – to its liking.

There are other reasons in addition to this confusion why the contemporary exaltation of autonomy is problematic for self love. The negative freedom entailed in autonomy is an impoverished account of freedom. By treating freedom largely as the absence of external constraints, it neglects various internal conditions for and impediments to freedom. It becomes difficult to account for the ways prejudice, habit, convention, and experience can limit freedom even in the absence of external constraints. Negative freedom ignores the multiplicity and conflictual character of human motives and implies instead a relatively unified will. It misses the ways culture and consumerism circumscribe freedom – under the guise of enlarging it – by directing freedom to fairly pre-packaged identities and lifestyles. The uncritical endorsement of autonomy reinforces a sense of entitlement. This sense of entitlement is stoked by capitalism though it has more salutary roots in a modern discourse of individual rights. It insulates the autonomous self from duty to others and from criticism. An uncritical autonomy also threatens to collapse authority into authoritarianism. All of these difficulties contribute to the individualism that autonomy encourages. In sum, an uncritical exaltation of autonomy is descriptively inadequate to persons and normatively problematic.

Of course, this ongoing love affair is now curiously related to a contemporary permutation of determinism, the culture of victimization. Consider the rising number of disorders included in

psychiatric encyclopedias; they indicate a readiness to compartmentalize facets of ourselves.[29] They raise once again the question
of where the self is located. How is our identity connected to forces
that determine us? The insight of this culture is that we are profoundly relational. But the culture of victimization does not really
offer an alternative to autonomy, for it is about throwing off responsibility. By claiming to be determined by others we manage to
remove the burden of self-determination, and in that respect, we
become free by being determined.

A contemporary ethics of self love requires an appropriate emphasis on autonomy. Autonomy denotes the independent value of
the self and, among other things, the need to identify and resist
tyrannous and oppressive systems and figures. But, as I will argue,
a contemporary ethics of self love must note that human freedom is not reducible to freedom of choice. Ultimately in all the
self's disparate choices she constitutes her self; her freedom has a
unity and continuity as a condition for the possibility of her self-
relation. Further, a contemporary ethics of self love recognizes that
human freedom is more than freedom from various constraints –
it is freedom for self-commitment.

A Christian ethics of self love resists the reduction and distortion
of freedom so characteristic of our contemporary Western outlook.
When we recognize that the freedom for self-determination is only
one aspect of the freedom of and for self-relation we begin to see
that we can only know the depth and range of freedom, its power
and meaning, its promise and its frailty in relation to a source of
value that establishes freedom and a real good that beckons it.
Put theologically, we know the meaning of freedom in relation to
God. Reckoning with our status as creatures of a God who has in
Jesus Christ revealed the divine self as one who acts on our behalf
shows the limitations and illusions of autonomy. Freedom is not a
capacity for self-definition but for self-disposal or self-commitment.
And this commitment is not that of a sovereign, prior self. Rather,
the self comes to itself as such in her commitment to some other.
The meaning and value of her choices are not determined by her

---

[29] See Peter D. Kramer, *Listening to Prozac: a Psychiatrist Explores Antidepressant Drugs and the
Remaking of the Self* (New York: Viking, 1993).

having chosen them. Rather they express her free relation to or
against objective goods and ultimately to or against the source of
all value.

Deconstructing the self: the self as POW

From the 1930s through the 1960s a range of thinkers in the social
sciences and philosophy explored the concept of the self and the relations and tensions between self and society. Just as contemporary
discussions of the self both celebrate its liberation or bemoan its
endangerment, this literature happily describes the self's excision
from restrictive roles or worriedly reports the effects social changes
like urbanization had on the self.[30] In the latter half of the twentieth
century attention to the self took two (not unrelated) directions.
The self–society tension that occupied the first half of the century
spawned individualist and social/collective approaches to the self.
On the one hand, a significant array of arguments and cultural
phenomena continued to treat selfhood in more individual and interior fashions. Although social forces and institutions impinge on it,
selfhood is located interiorly (for some, given the subconscious, selfhood is not only inner but secret); even construals of selfhood which
cast it more superficially and externally still stress the individual's
self-fashioning through pursuits and acquisitions (be they material
or even more ephemeral adoptions of particular values), and often
conceive this self-fashioning as a process of discovering the "real
me." Psychologists and sociologists formulated theories of the self's
development. Some theories offer various accounts of the obstacles
or threats to selfhood, or focus on the experiences or needs constitutive of selfhood.[31] Still others describe the self's own construction

---

[30] See for instance George Herbert Mead, *Mind, Self and Society* (Chicago: University of
Chicago Press, 1934); Erving Goffman, *The Presentation of Self in Everyday Life* (New York:
Doubleday, 1959); Herbert Marcuse, *One-Dimensional Man: Studies in the Ideology of Advanced
Industrial Society* (Boston, MA: Beacon, 1964); R. D. Laing, *The Divided Self: an Existential Study
in Sanity and Madness* (Baltimore, MD: Penguin, 1965). See also Sigmund Freud, *Civilization
and its Discontents* (New York: Norton, 1930), Erich Fromm, *Man for Himself: an Inquiry into
the Psychology of Ethics* (New York: Rinehart, 1947) and Erik Erikson, *Identity: Youth and Crisis*
(New York: Norton, 1968). I am indebted to the very nice literature review by Joseph
E. Davis "Identity and Social Change: a Short Review." It belongs to the equally nice
interdisciplinary journal, *The Hedgehog Review* 1 (Fall 1999): 95–102.

[31] See Robert N. Bellah et al., *Habits of the Heart: Individualism and Commitment in American
Life* (New York: Harper and Row, 1985) and Christopher Lasch, *The Minimal Self: Psychic*

of itself.[32] And yet another strand of literature places an interesting twist on the argument that social forces impact the shape or experience of consciousness by looking at the effects of technology and psycho-pharmacology.[33] This work suggests that a distinctively postmodern self has emerged.[34] On the other hand, and in contrast to such treatments of the individual (though socially shaped) self, other thinkers have offered more resolutely social constructionist versions of the self. From communitarian thought in social/ political philosophy and Christian ethics (as found in the work of Amitai Etzioni and Michael Walzer, for instance, and, for a theological version of communitarianism, Stanley Hauerwas) to identity politics and postmodernism, selfhood is inscribed in collective, political identity.[35] Underlying both individual and collective

Survival in Troubled Times (New York: Norton, 1984). In the field of psychology, some important feminist reformulations of Freudian theory and Lawrence Kohlberg's theory of human development emerged in object-relations theorists and the work of Carol Gilligan, respectively. For an example of object-relations approaches in psychology, see Nancy Chodorow, *Feminism and Psychoanalytic Theory* (New Haven: Yale University Press, 1989). See Carol Gilligan's *In a Different Voice* (Cambridge, MA: Harvard University Press, 1982). Gilligan's feminist response to Kohlberg's cognitive theory of development arguably represents an attempt to make cognitive approaches more responsive to psycho-social factors.

[32] See Daniel Yankelovich, *New Rules: Searching for Self-Fulfillment in a World Turned Upside Down* (New York: Random House, 1981) and John P. Hewitt, *Dilemmas of the American Self* (Philadelphia, PA: Temple University Press, 1989).

[33] I will treat this in more detail next. See Joshua Meyrowitz, *No Sense of Place: The Impact of Electronic Media on Social Behavior* (New York: Oxford University Press, 1985); Kenneth J. Gergen, *The Saturated Self: Dilemmas of Identity in Contemporary Life* (New York: Basic, 1991); Peter D. Kramer, *Listening to Prozac.*

[34] The works by Lasch and Bellah and colleagues make this argument by taking up individualism. For different accounts of the sources and character of the distinctive (post)modern self see Philip Reiff, *The Triumph of the Therapeutic: Uses of Faith After Freud* (New York: Harper and Row, 1966); Nathan Adler, *The Underground Stream: New Life Styles and the Antinomian Personality* (New York: Harper and Row, 1972); Louis A. Zurcher, Jr., *The Mutable Self: a Self-Concept for Social Change* (Beverly Hills, CA: Sage, 1977); Louis A. Zurcher, Jr. and Michael R. Wood, *The Development of a Postmodern Self: a Computer-Assisted Comparative Analysis of Personal Documents* (New York: Greenwood, 1988); Robert Jay Lifton, *The Protean Self: Human Resilience in an Age of Fragmentation* (New York: Basic, 1993). For arguments which attribute this distinctive self to capitalism see Daniel Bell, *The Cultural Contradictions of Capitalism* (New York: Basic, 1976) and Richard Sennet, *The Fall of Public Man: On the Social Psychology of Capitalism* (New York: Knopf, 1977).

[35] See for example Michael Walzer, *Spheres of Justice* (New York: Basic, 1983); Stanley Hauerwas, *A Community of Character* (Notre Dame, IN: University of Notre Dame Press, 1987); Amitai Etzioni, *The Spirit of Community* (New York: Crown, 1993). For a helpful collection of essays on the recent turn to narrative, see Stanley Hauerwas and L. Gregory Jones, eds., *Why Narrative?: Readings in Narrative Theology* (Grand Rapids, MI: W. B. Eerdmans, 1989). For examples of social constructionist/identity politics see Etienne

approaches to selfhood is the problem of locating the self in the give and take between the self's location of itself and its location by others. As I noted above, among these various approaches to the self are camps which applaud these arguments and phenomena as prospects for liberation and others which bemoan them as indicators of social and moral deterioration and the endangerment of the self.

In an essay titled "The Self and its Discontents" Paul Lauritzen plots recent accounts of the self along two coordinates.[36] One axis is that of *unity/fragmentation*. Lauritzen notes that thinkers like Richard Rorty identify and celebrate the self as decentered and fragmented. Similarly, Iris Marion Young says that the subject is a "heterogeneous presence." By this she means that "the subject is not a unity, it cannot be present to itself, know itself. I do not always know what I mean, need, want, desire because these do not arise from some ego origin . . . Consequently, any individual subject is a play of differences that cannot be comprehended."[37] Young claims that the "logic of identity seeks to bring everything under control, to eliminate uncertainty and unpredictability, to spiritualize the bodily fact of sensuous immersion in a world that out-runs the subject, to eliminate otherness."[38] To do this the subject "is conceived as a pure transcendental origin: it has no foundation outside itself, it is self-generating and autonomous," yet "this project inevitably fails "because the totalizing movement always leaves a remainder" which is then schematized into dichotomous, hierarchical oppositions like good/bad, normal/deviant.[39] Others, like Paul Ricoeur and Charles Taylor insist that the self is sovereign and unified. The self is coherent and because of this we can speak meaningfully of

Balibar and Immanuel Wallerstein, *Race, Nation, Class: Ambiguous Identities* (London: Verso, 1991) and Manuel Castels, *The Power of Identity*, vol. 2, *The Information Age: Economy, Society and Culture* (Malden, MA: Blackwell, 1997), Benedict Anderson, *Imagined Communities: Reflections on the Origin and Spread of Nationalism*, 2nd edn (New York: Verso, 1991) and Mary Waters, *Ethnic Options: Choosing Identities in America* (Berkeley, CA: University of California Press, 1990).

36 Paul Lauritzen, "The Self and its Discontents," *Journal of Religious Ethics* 22:1 (1994), 189–210.

37 Iris Young, "The Ideal of Community and the Politics of Difference," *Social Theory and Practice* 12.1 (Spring 1986), 10.

38 Iris Marion Young, *Justice and the Politics of Difference* (Princeton, NJ; Princeton University Press, 1990), 98–99.

39 Ibid., 99.

the self's freedom and responsibility. Nevertheless, the self's unity does not consist in some metaphysical, substantial nature. Calvin Schrag argues that postmodern arguments for the fragmented self are decisive enough that after postmodernity we should not inquire into *what* the self is, but *who* the self is. "The presence of the who is not that of a self-identical monad, mute and self-enclosed, changeless and secured prior to the events of speaking. The presence at issue is localized neither metaphysically in a fixed, underlying substratum nor epistemologically in a prelinguistic, zero-point center of consciousness."[40] Instead, the self's unity is fundamentally a narrative unity. Schrag draws on Ricoeur's distinction between "*idem*-identity" (identity as sameness, like the kind found in substance metaphysics) and *ipse*-identity (identity as selfhood).[41] Ricoeur argues that selfhood consists in a dialectic between *ipse*-identity over the *idem*-identity; this becomes apparent when we recognize that personal identity is narrative identity.

The second axis along which we can plot recent approaches to the self is that of the *disengaged vs. engaged/sedimented self.* The disengaged self is the modern self, particularly the Lockean self. It is a self who can distance herself from the particularities of her existence, objectify and refashion her self. But growing dissatisfaction with such an account of the self and of moral reasoning leads many thinkers to focus on the particularities of the self. The Enlightenment moral thinker is disembodied and individualistic and thus an inadequate picture of the human.[42]

The modern problem of the self rests on an insight into the embeddedness of the self and arose out of a new attention to the social and historical character and of moral values.[43] Accompanying and intensifying this heightened awareness of the self's social and historical character is an analysis of the constructive mechanisms of

---

[40] Calvin O. Schrag, *The Self After Postmodernity* (Cambridge: Cambridge University Press, 1997), 33.

[41] Ricoeur, *Oneself as Another.*

[42] For helpful treatments of the emergence of postmodern critiques of modernity, see Frederick B. Burnham, ed., *Postmodern Theology: Christian Faith in a Pluralist World* (New York: Harper and Row, 1989) and David Harvey, *The Condition of Postmodernity: an Enquiry into the Origins of Cultural Change* (Oxford and Cambridge, MA: Basil Blackwell, 1989).

[43] For a recent example of such a study see Elaine Graham, *Making the Difference: Gender, Personhood and Theology* (Minneapolis, MN: Fortress, 1996).

culture. It extends insight into the fundamentally social character of the self into an assessment of the institutions, power relations, and cultural ideologies that create the arena for that sociality. For this reason, the problem of the self is tied closely to social critique; as the self came to be seen as constructed, the structures and institutions of society were deconstructed and demystified.[44] For many thinkers, the purpose of such deconstruction is reconstruction; to unravel the ways in which the self is constructed is to open a space for critique aimed at more authentic selfhood.[45] Critiques of the modern self provided opportunities to re-envision not only the self, but the self's flourishing.[46] Yet, other thinkers insist that such visions of the authentic self or an alternative society are themselves constructs and therefore arbitrary. These thinkers do social analysis with a hermeneutics of suspicion, a sense of contingency, and mindful of the brute fact of plurality. In this light self-realization ethics provide arbitrary descriptions of human flourishing; persons and groups in dominant positions promulgate them in order to control others.[47] Here the self looks less like a free agent and more like a POW.

Insight into the ways systems of power construct the self extends to an analysis of language. Language is a medium that posits

[44] See for example the work of Karl Marx, Max Horkheimer, and Max Weber. More recently, see the work of Hans-Georg Gadamer and Jurgen Habermas.

[45] The concern for authentic selfhood has been closely associated in contemporary Western culture with an individualistic ethics of self-fulfillment, and a moral relativism which protects individual subjective accounts of the kind of life in which such fulfillment consists. For criticisms of such cultural ethics, see Christopher Lasch, *The Culture of Narcissism: American Life in an Age of Diminishing Expectations* (New York: Norton, 1979). For an insightful critique of this individualism, but one which seeks to recognize and advance the moral insights which underlie it, see Charles Taylor, *The Ethics of Authenticity* (Cambridge, MA: Harvard University Press, 1992).

[46] See Juliet Mitchell, *Women's Estate* (New York: Random House, Vintage Books, 1973).

[47] See Rebecca Chopp, *The Power to Speak: Feminism, Language and God* (New York: Crossroad, 1989) and Sheila Greave Devaney, "Problems with Feminist Theory: Historicity and the Search for Sure Foundations," in *Embodied Love: Sensuality and Relationship as Feminist Values*, eds., Paula M. Cooey, Sharon A. Farmer, and Mary Ellen Ross (San Francisco, CA: Harper and Row, 1987). Both thinkers criticize other feminists for appealing to some consensus or ideal vision of women's flourishing. They claim that accounts of authentic selfhood are arbitrary and tyrannous often foster a self-realization ethics which is subjective and anti-realist. As I noted at the outset of this chapter, when the forms of self-realization are not critically assessed, the person cannot assess what attempts at self-fulfillment might actually harm herself. What is needed is an account of right self love which recognizes the self as situated but not entirely constructed or absorbed, and which also avoids the subjectivism and anti-realism which characterizes many contemporary ethics of self-realization.

and sustains evaluations and relations. Because many thinkers no longer consider particular signifiers to represent reality, linguistic realism gives way to a view of language systems as arbitrary and provisional. The assembly and interaction of words into propositions constitutes coercive, yet conventional exercises of power.[48] While such an analysis contributes to a view of the self as a meaning-maker, as one who creates value, it also contributes to a view of the self as constructed by language. Indeed, for some thinkers the self is the site of the interacting, conflicting, multiple discourses that vie for ascendancy in some description of the self:

There is no core, or essence, or nature of the human person either lying behind the structures, against which these can be measured as adequate, or transcending the structures as a free, thoughtful agent. Instead, the human person is newly understood as a network of various strands of social discourses and practices, intersecting with one another in differing patterns.[49]

Stressing the constructed character of selfhood raises the problem of agency, as Seyla Benhabib shows. Benhabib notes both a weak and a strong version of the thesis that the modern subject has died.

The weak version of this thesis would situate the subject in the context of various social, linguistic and discursive practices. This view would by no means question the desirability and theoretical necessity of articulating a more adequate, less deluded and less mystified version of subjectivity than those provided by the concepts of the Cartesian cogito, the "transcendental unity of apperception," "Geist and consciousness," or "das Man," (the they). The traditional attributes of the philosophical subject of the West, like self-reflexivity, the capacity for acting on principles, rational accountability for one's actions and the ability to project a life-plan into the future, in short, some form of autonomy and rationality, could then be reformulated by taking account of the radical situatedness of the subject.[50]

---

[48] I have in mind the work of thinkers such as Jacques Derrida and Jean-François Lyotard.
[49] Susan Frank Parsons, *Feminism and Christian Ethics* (Cambridge: Cambridge University Press, 1996), 99. See also Rosalind Coward, *Patriarchal Precedents: Sexuality and Social Relations* (London: Routledge and Kegan Paul, 1983).
[50] Benhabib, *Situating the Self*, 214.

In the strong version

> [t]he subject thus dissolves into the chain of significations of which it was supposed to be the initiator. Along with this dissolution of the subject into yet "another position in language" disappear of course concepts of intentionality, accountability, self-reflexivity and autonomy. The subject that is but another position in language can no longer master and create that distance between itself and the chain of significations in which it is immersed such that it can reflect upon them and creatively alter them.[51]

Strong versions intensify insight into the embeddedness of the self into the claim that there is no self. This claim provides a form of resistance against those hegemonic, unifying systems that constitute the self. The debate rages whether there is any subject behind the discourses that constitute its identity, some subject that precedes its construction. In order to assign any agency to the self, it appears necessary to locate some self outside of the systems and forces that construct it. Some thinkers reject the notion that such a prediscursive self exists, while others such as Benhabib argue that the processes of signification and constitution do not explain *how* the self is socialized and individualized. Benhabib notes that the self may be constituted by discourse but need not be determined by it.[52] Whether or not one posits a self, the subject is absorbed into the systems and relations that constitute it.

Some attempts to reckon with the embeddedness of the self take two pernicious forms. The first form absolutizes the situatedness of the self into an individualism run rampant. The other form is simply the inverse claim that the situatedness of the self reduces the self to systems or the intersection of determining forces. As I noted earlier, such reductionism and determinism also make it difficult to speak of the self's agency. Such positions threaten the dignity of the self insofar as they do not permit a proper self-determination and, thus, fail to address the problem of conformity, a problem which often afflicts women and minorities. Benhabib, for instance, rejects

attempts to replace the vision of an autonomous and engendered subject with that of a fractured, opaque self; the "deed without the doer" becomes the paradigm of subversive activity for selves who joyfully deny their own coherence and relish their opacity and multiplicity . . . But precisely

---

[51] Ibid.   [52] Ibid., 218.

because women's stories have so often been written for them by others, precisely because their own sense of self has been so fragile, and their ability to assert control over the conditions of their existence so rare, this vision of the self appears to me to be making a virtue out of necessity.[53]

Of course not only women are denied the conditions for proper self-determination. Indeed, theories that deny agency and fracture subjectivity ignore the obvious fact that people, regardless of gender, struggle to make sense out of their lives. In other words, they seek coherence. If the insight into the self's embeddedness denies the self that is to resist hegemonic discourses, this trajectory undermines the projects of social critique and reconstruction out of which it arose. It is true that notions of authentic selfhood which might undergird a theory of self love are themselves constructs. But to recognize this does not prohibit their potential veracity or helpfulness. The problem of the self indicates that a contemporary theory of self love requires a complex account of the self who loves herself, one which allows for the self's determination and freedom, particularity and self-transcendence.

The self is a problem beyond such scholarly debates. These debates express and reinforce an important characteristic of moral experience. Consider, for example, that our contemporary moral situation includes increased exposure to other cultures which makes us aware of our specificity; developments in disciplines like psychology and sociology make us aware of how we are determined by various forces and systems; our technological capacity to alter our environment, indeed our selves, has reached unparalleled heights; electronic communication media allow us to construct and manipulate our self-expression, even to disassociate ourselves from our own communication. All of these factors can make our own complexity morally problematic. We experience our plurality, the agency we have which allows us to fashion and communicate ourselves, as well as the constraints of our finitude and the contingency of our particularity. Our contradictory experiences of freedom and

---

53 Ibid., 15–16. See also Taylor, *Ethics of Authenticity*. Benhabib notes here the deep connection between life and thought, our being and our thinking about it. Indeed, at the crux of the contemporary problem of self love is the insight that conceptions of selfhood impact in a profound way the forms selfhood takes. In light of this deep connection, the person's capacity to reflect on her life, to engage in moral self-evaluation, is itself basic to what it means to be a person.

determination are made more acute by a daily barrage of images which depict the good life, which pander to our insecurities and center our fulfillment in certain possessions and activities.

Self-understanding, then, seems to be either a voluntaristic, non-binding election of identity or the hegemonic imposition of arbitrarily intersecting systems. Regardless, the person's self-understanding has become increasingly bifurcated from her embodied actions and relations. Right self love is an urgent contemporary problem because there is no consensus regarding what it means to be a self. Theoretical treatments of the self in contemporary ethics develop insights into the way the self is situated and constituted; when these accounts of the self meet with the plurality and complexity of our experience, the crucial moral question becomes how to be a coherent agent. Thus, the problem of the self indicates the urgency with which contemporary thinkers seek to articulate some understanding of the self's flourishing.

Yet deconstruction of the self, along with other features I note here, make it difficult to speak about the flourishing of the self except in terms of self-realization and autonomy. We can see this in popular culture and in ethical theory as the recent explosion of the language of authenticity, or, the inability to speak about the self at all. This latter reluctance is simply incoherent and, literally, self-defeating. Thinkers who celebrate the fragmentation or de-centering of the self, who deny human agency and any attempt to lend coherence to the self encounter, ironically, deep self-referential problems. Contemporary ethics of self-realization that arise out of feminist critiques and debates about the self, then, too often fail to specify criteria by which to judge whether the self harms itself in her attempts of realization. Self love constitutes a contemporary problem because the norm of self-realization, which so permeates contemporary culture and ethics, is not itself critically assessed. We can take the situatedness of the self seriously, yet avoid such reductionism and determinism by appealing to the person's capacity for self-transcendence as it is evinced in the basic activity of self-understanding. The self-transcendence that occurs through self-understanding is dialectically related to the person's relations with others and her acting in the world. So the dialectical relation between being and thinking that I noted at the outset of this chapter both requires a recognition of the embeddedness of the self as well as a rejection of positions that deny agency or the self. I will argue in Chapter Two that this recognition and rejection can be accomplished in a retrieval of ontological frameworks for selfhood, and will offer such a retrieval through my engagement of Karl Rahner and Paul Tillich.

Renewing the mind/body split in the cult of self-creation: the self as MIA

Wendell Berry notes, "novelty is a new kind of loneliness."[54] He recognizes aptly that our sense of security and fulfillment are in many respects ensured by continuity, stability, order. If loneliness, whether accompanied by actual alone-ness or experienced in the company of others, is a kind of disconnect which sets us at sea, leaves us feeling bereft, and activates our longing for communion (with others or of the kind that solitude provides), Berry has captured only one way of experiencing disconnect. Above I hinted at another kind of disconnect, one called by self-described and closet postmodernists alike as liberating, joyful, a relief. Both of these experiences of disconnect feed and are fed by contemporary technology, economic consumption, and hosts of social, economic, scientific practices like cosmetic surgery, mood-control through drugs and herbal cocktails, and the like. These increasing capacities for self-creation also contribute to the contemporary problem of self love, raising in very practical ways questions of where or in what the self resides. Advertisements tell me that a new hair color is "me," or that a particular refrigerator suits my lifestyle. My true or best self is something elusive, but in reach. Indeed, she resides at the shopping mall. Or at the spa/retreat center. Or at the gym, or the new workplace. More radically, though still quite commonly, I can undergo surgery to mold and shape my body into a "new me" (though my novel self is one had through conformity to cultural standards of beauty). Herbs and drugs can make me "feel more like myself." Paradoxically, then, authenticity is available through self-alteration.

---

54 Wendell Berry, "Healing," *What Are People For?* (New York: North Point Press, 1990), 9. The piece includes a refrain of "Order is the only possibility of rest."

Sherry Turkle's study of identity and Internet technology illustrates this facet of the problem of self love. Turkle perceives the connections between postmodern theory and Internet technology. "As players participate, they become authors not only of the text but of themselves, constructing new selves through social interaction. One player says, 'You are the character and you are not the character, both at the same time.' Another says, 'You are who you pretend to be.'"[55] One college junior Turkle interviewed spoke about using multiple windows to inhabit multiple MUDs (multi-user domains, like chat rooms and games). He touted his increasing capacity to compartmentalize these roles/activities:

I split my mind. I'm getting better at it. I can see myself as being two or three or more. And I just turn on one part of my mind and then another when I go from window to window. I'm in some kind of argument in one window and trying to come on to a girl in a MUD in another, and another window might be running a spreadsheet program or some other technical thing for school . . . And then I'll get a real-time message [a message that flashes on the screen as soon as it is sent from another system user], and I guess that's RL [real life]. It's just one more window.

"RL is just one more window," he goes on to say, "and it's not usually my best one."[56]

I noted above that postmodern theory debunks the unitary self and views of language as referring to some reality; according to Turkle computer technology closes the gap between lived experiences and just those "illusions" postmodern theory debunks. "Traditional ideas about identity have been tied to a notion of authenticity that such virtual experiences actively subvert. When each player can create many characters and participate in many games, the self is not only decentered but multiplied without limit."[57] Turkle notes that we have become accustomed to opaque technology, which in turn prompts us to take things at interface value; we are moving into a culture of simulation and are comfortable with representations of reality. The rise of psycho-pharmacology and the mapping of the human genome are other examples of our embrace of the opaque, because they encourage the view that we are

---

[55] Sherry Turkle, *Life on the Screen: Identity in the Age of the Internet* (New York: Simon and Schuster, Turkle 1995) 12.
[56] Ibid., 13.   [57] Ibid., 185.

programmable, that new and improved selves can be assembled genetically, chemically, cosmetically and surgically, and textually. Turkle is receptive to the positive possibilities that computer technology in general and the Internet in particular offer. But she is wary of "cycling through" so many personas. The "slippage" between real life and our Internet relationships, personae, communities, and roles can have destructive psychological and interpersonal effects.

One way Turkle indicates the positive psychological value of such identity experimentation is by appealing to Erik Erikson's description of adolescence as a moratorium, a period during which society grants tacit permission for adolescents to experiment. "Computers don't just do things for us, they do things to us, including our ways of thinking about ourselves and other people."[58] So technology can provide a moratorium still needed in adulthood, a space for refreshment, self-repair, release, self-mastery.[59] "The computer can be . . . experienced as an object on the border between self and notself. Or, in a new variant on the story of Narcissus, people are able to fall in love with the artificial worlds that they have created or that have been built for them by others. People are able to see themselves in the computer."[60]

The opportunity to adopt new identities in cyberspace renews the mind/body split. The more time one spends in virtual spaces the more real those spaces seem to be. ' "After all,' says one dedicated MUD player . . . , 'why grant such superior status to the self that has the body when the selves that don't have bodies are able to have different kinds of experiences?' When people can play at having different genders and different lives, it isn't surprising that for some this play has become as real as what we conventionally think of as their real lives, although for them this is no longer a valid distinction."[61] Certainly the Internet allows people to define themselves through their self-presentation, in contrast to a self-definition that reacts to others' projections onto them. One MUD player reported to Turkle, "You can be whoever you want to be. You can completely redefine yourself if you want. You can be the opposite sex. You can be more talkative. You can be less talkative. Whatever. You can just be whoever you want, really, whoever you

---

[58] Ibid., 26.   [59] Ibid., 204.   [60] Ibid., 30.   [61] Ibid., 14.

have the capacity to be. You don't have to worry about the slots other people put you in as much. It's easier to change the way people perceive you, because all they've got is what you show them. They don't look at your body and make assumptions. They don't hear your accent and make assumptions. All they see is your words."[62] The virtuality of cyberspace permits all of this freedom and exper- imentation because it seems to insure anonymity and, importantly, because it is possible to log off. The capacity to disengage one- self from virtual reality, to exit cyberspace, makes that space seem consequence-free. One's agency can fracture in such a way that her activities in cyberspace and her transactions with others seem confined to that space, or trivial. They are not means by which one constitutes oneself. Indeed, these activities have no lasting effect at all. For example, Turkle reports the volatile and confusing matter of a cyber-rape. In an Internet game room, or MUD, one player seized control of another player's character and raped it. He de- fended his action by claiming that it was within a game, that the rape was not real because it was done only with words. Similarly confusing and painful issues arise when one spouse learns another is having cyber-sex with someone else: do such exchanges amount to "real" infidelity? Do they allow some release that helps to pre- vent infidelity in "real life"? Or do they make "real life" infidelity seem more appealing and more possible?

Confusion about what and who the self is arises via attempts to discern and fashion where the self is; it is not limited to cyberspace. And the temptation to regard one's concrete actions as of little consequence for one's identity is reinforced in other contexts. One of my students remarked perceptively that his Spring Break trip to Mexico was presented in just this fashion; the prevailing slogan among business proprietors and students alike was, "What goes on in Cancun stays in Cancun." Despite the fact that the de-centering of the self captures our experiences of multiplicity and provides a way to resist others' attempts to inscribe and circumscribe our identities, it renews the mind–body split in troubling ways. The cult of self-creation disregards and devalues the body or alternatively exalts it. It indexes authenticity to our agency, in particular our

---

[62] Ibid., 184.

agency as consumers or personas. Yet it also severs identity from our acting insofar as in our self-fashioning we remain ever free to create ourselves anew, to locate our "true selves" in some other facet or role of our lives. Thus, it becomes difficult to evaluate morally the means by which we try to realize ourselves.

Given Christian theological ambivalence about the body, a Christian ethics of self love seems ill-equipped for addressing contemporary versions of the mind-body split. And some Christian ethics monger guilt and judgment, and insist on static norms freighted with distortions like sexism and wielded in social and ecclesial self-interest, so that a Christian ethics of self love seems restrictive and demoralizing in contrast to the freedom of the marketplace and of cyberspace. The novel yet "true" self that we pursue, or craft, or find in these places is not a prisoner of war but missing in action. She remains one purchase or Botox-injection ahead of us, or ever in need of an upgrade, never improved so much that we can be "finished." She dodges our introspective grasps and wanders the space "between" mind and body, between the versions of ourselves we fashion or that are imputed to us by others and the concrete acts and relations we forge and undergo. She seems, quite falsely, to be free from any and all of the "old selves" that are not to our liking, and free from the standards and preferences of others. She seems to be free, finally, to love herself. But this freedom is predicated on a kind of self-loathing from which there is no rest, because it centers on "improving" or "fixing" oneself. So, not only is it difficult to evaluate morally the means by which we try to realize ourselves, our very attempts at self-realization trap us in an ironic self-relation that simultaneously yokes our identity to our agency and severs the two.

A Christian ethics of self love can locate the self in a personal history that connects agency and identity in a way that overcomes this irony. In Christ the self becomes a "new creation." As a new creation the newness is not utterly novel. The self is already a creature, part of a creation God sees as good. This means that the "new self" is not of one's own making. It means that the newness consists not in an obliteration of the old, but its perfection. One encounters one's true self not via self-alteration, but a forgiving and sanctifying revelation. Self-loathing gives way to self-acceptance. To be a new creation means that the self's authenticity is not indexed to one's own activity or to the determinations of other creatures, but to one's creatureliness as established, sustained, and redeemed by God. That creatureliness does not consist in a static nature. The self becomes a new creation *in Christ*. This means her identity is dynamic and relational. Though it is not a matter of her own making, it unfolds responsively. Newness in Christ vivifies and reorients her agency. Freedom is set free for commitment, knowledge is illuminated in the light of faith, desire is redirected to the good. Her agency becomes less a matter of consuming or grasping and more participatory. She constitutes herself in her acting, but the meaning of those acts and the identity of the agent are shown and kept in play as she grows in a personal relation with Christ. Christ's own self-disposal in love shows the meaning of being human, and offers us the possibility to be more truly and particularly so. This is because Christ shows that human beings are creatures who are called to love. This point brings us to the problem of desire.

The problem of desire

Here I define desire broadly as a response to value. Human beings have desires, in positive forms of attraction and negative forms of aversion. Human beings also are desire, creatures who live by devotion or faith (St. Paul), or servitude or love (St. Augustine) or concern (Paul Tillich), whose identity is conferred in relation to some dominant care, cause, or commitment. These various ways of putting the matter highlight important experiential and theoretical differences, but the basic point is that the human condition of desiring (which has psychic and physical dimensions), manifests itself for better or worse in particular desires. Desire includes more than lack and vulnerability; it also includes ecstasy or self-communication and therefore power. Desire is a mode of separation and connection. To inquire into the problem of desire, then, is to investigate moral problems of acting, feeling, and choosing in the service of transforming our way of being in the world.

Desire is problematic for self love in a number of ways. Here are three of them. Desire is problematic, first, insofar as moral condemnations of self love tend to reduce self love morally to vices of selfishness and acquisitiveness. The next chapter will consider this difficulty especially as it is handled among Christian moral thinkers. Desire is problematic, second, with respect to moral flourishing. This is apparent in eudaimonistic ethics and the perennial philosophical problem of how virtue and happiness are (not) related.[63] Can we sustain the claim that all persons seek happiness (whether or not this is a synonym for human flourishing)? How then do we make sense of self-destructive courses of behavior? Is it satisfactory to resort to the claim that these are irrational? And does this move cripple us in the face of a growing culture of victimization? Can we identify some actions and relations as incompatible with flourishing even when those engaged in them testify that those actions and relations fulfill and satisfy them? If we emphasize human flourishing as the moral project, or at least as the inevitable side-effect of some other conception of the moral project, can we answer adequately the post-moral question: why be moral? And if we try to answer this question by appealing to the claim that our fulfillment (here the language of flourishing seems contrived at best) lies in self-sacrifice can we do so without valorizing patently self-destructive or even indirectly self-aggrandizing lifestyles? Can we do so in a way that avoids wielding this claim to justify and sustain the oppression and misery of others?

This question leads ineluctably to the third respect in which desire is problematic, namely, with regard to moral justification. Specifically, desire in secular academic arguments and in Western culture has become increasingly privatized and immunized. It is important to spend some time with this difficulty because it helps us to make sense of and respond to the previous two. For a variety of reasons, contemporary thinkers generally hold that no consensus about the good can be achieved. Desire in turn becomes privatized and rendered idiosyncratic in a "to each his own" mentality. It is increasingly exempt from moral and social criticism. The heart wants what it wants, and the best we can do is adopt a norm of nonmaleficence to govern its exercise and a procedure of tolerance to adjudicate our respective pursuits. It becomes difficult to order

---

[63] See Ilham Dilman, *Raskolnikov's Rebirth: Psychology and the Understanding of Good and Evil* (Chicago and La Salle: Open Court, 2000).

love except on its own grounds, i.e., according to its own capricious-ness. This in turn makes it difficult to determine whether desire's objects and pursuits are worthy ones, as well as why that which is unworthy or undesirable can still attract while what is worthy can repel.[64] The privatization and immunization of desire has its roots in modernity's separation of fact and value. Sometimes, as in Kant, value is squired away from the realm of morality, not per-mitted to pollute the good will. Sometimes, as in poststructuralist theory, value is said to be produced by socio-linguistic systems. In either case, "one desired effect of the distinction between fact and value is the segregation or liberation of the will. The will as the carrier of value is detached from the ordinary factual world."[65] The separation of fact and value contributes to the disenchant-ment of the world; comprehensive teleologies (theistic and secular) fall away and the world appears, as in existentialist thought, as a neutral space into which individuals are thrown and left with the burden of making meaning, of creating value where there is none. In other words, the privatization of desire is fed by and feeds moral relativism and subjectivism. Moral relativism refers to the belief that moral values are matters of personal preference. Of course, a moral relativist might feel very strongly about her own (or her community's) moral code. But she cannot provide reasons for it on grounds other than preference or custom or expediency. In moral subjectivism the maxim that "the heart wants what it wants" meets the injunction to "love and do what you will." Thus, implicit in sub-jectivist attitudes toward desire is a schizophrenia in which desire's rule denies our agency (we cannot alter what we desire or bring our-selves to desire) and in which desire functions as a hallmark for our sovereign and unfettered will (we are malleable enough to adopt and exchange pursuits, loyalties, and goods according to fancy and expediency).

The dilemmas of desire indicate once again that the self-realization which contemporary culture urges entails dual tasks of self-determination and self-definition. Yet the grounds on which we might morally evaluate particular forms of self-relation are eroding.

---

[64] William Ian Miller considers briefly the way that desire depends on disgust. See his provocative book *The Anatomy of Disgust* (Cambridge, MA, and London: Harvard University Press, 1997) especially 112–19.
[65] Murdoch, *Metaphysics as a Guide to Morals*, 52.

A Christian ethics of self love speaks to the problem of desire because it affirms God as the source of value. This point is important for the problems of moral justification that desire raises. Our experiences of conferring value and of being confronted by it become intelligible in light of the affirmations that God endows creation with goodness and that we are co-creators with God. A Christian ethics of self love also affirms God as the highest good. This does not mean that God sits at the top of a worldly scale of goods; this claim denies God's transcendence, which is precisely what we mean to affirm when we say that God is the highest good. An ethics of self love that centers on God as the self's highest good aims at enhancing the self. Because it views the self as a creature, this enhancement is indexed not to the will's creation of value in acts of power but to goods encountered in creaturely life, and to a source of value that transcends and establishes these goods. Also, the enhancement of the self is not over and against others. The goods discovered in creaturely life comprise objective reference points and situate the self in a world and in relation to others. This is not a neutral space but one the self encounters and in which she moves through interpretive and evaluative activities. Nor is it a space of value that is somehow contained or domestic. God and not the will to power effects the revaluation of values that directs human constructs and projects. And this in turn indicates that the problem of self love is more basic than one of selfishness. It concerns proper self-relation. We only identify pride as problematic because we recognize it as a distorted or false form of self-relation. This is why the cluster of problems explored above pose the contemporary problem of self love; each makes it more difficult for us to evaluate morally the concrete acts and relations through which the self takes up her self-relation in the world, with others, and before God.

THE NORM OF SELF-REALIZATION

I want to characterize our moral situation, with all its promise, tensions, and contradictions, as one which gives rise to the norm of self-realization. The norm of self-realization captures the constellation of problems I note above. It obliges us in the absence of consensus about what the self is that is to be realized. In this manner, it expresses subjectivism and risks voluntarism on the one hand

and collectivism on the other. By subjectivism I mean the tendency to treat appeals to desires, wants, and personal experience as unassailable and morally sufficient grounds to legitimate a course of action or a relationship. This subjectivism neglects or absolutizes the communal shaping of desire (which is especially problematic in a consumerist culture), finds expression in voluntarism, intuitionism, uncritical appeals to projects of self-realization and ideals of authenticity, and it risks complacency and self-indulgence in the moral life. It also enervates practical moral decision-making insofar as competing and conflicting desires are not adjudicated as possible motives for acting, and the collective wisdom embodied in authoritative resources is subordinated to the primacy of an agent's subjective preferences. Voluntarism suggests that the human capacity for self-determination is essentially unfettered and, further, that we are who we decide ourselves to be. Voluntarism isolates the agent from any significant determination by others and the world and from our bodies. It prizes human autonomy to the exclusion of other values and privileges the will over reason. It suggests the world is a neutral place, a canvas onto which we project our valuations and the meaning of which we determine for ourselves and can alter at will. Voluntarism implies a theory of value, then, that is reductive, and is at odds with some aspects of our experience. It cannot account for the way we are confronted by value or for the experience of moral obligation. The experience of moral obligation suggests that something or someone worthy elicits and/or places constraints on our acting. It testifies thereby to value's independence from the self. The norm of self-realization also threatens collectivism to the extent that it erodes the grounds for moral and social criticism and insofar as arguments against substance-metaphysics versions of the self subsume the self into linguistic or socio-economic systems.

Secular approaches to the self in the academy and culture at large re-cast rather than resolve the problem of self love. It is not simply a matter of enervating confusion about the self. Rather, many available secular approaches to the self are reluctant to develop normative anthropologies and lack the resources with which to do so adequately. This book seeks to develop an account of self love that can incorporate and extend modern criticisms of traditional

Christian ethical accounts of the divine–human relation, yet can also offset their difficulties by retrieving certain insights and claims from the tradition.

THE NEED FOR THEOLOGICAL MORAL ANTHROPOLOGY

It should be clear by now that even though I think the postmodern deconstruction of the self rests on legitimate concerns and offers indispensable insights, I join thinkers like Iris Murdoch and Charles Taylor in recognizing the deep connections between moral ontologies, moral anthropologies, and theories of value, or axiologies. I also join thinkers like Stanley Rudman and Calvin Schrag in recognizing the importance of identifying the self in its praxis. Says Rudman, "the Christian faith need not be tied to a substance metaphysic. In fact, it is important that the Christian faith should be free to pursue the search for truth in this area as in any other. Aristotelian or Thomist ideas of substance are not an essential part of Christian truth, and there may be better ways of expressing this truth."[66] Schrag thinks postmodernists have decisively jettisoned classical substantialist and modern foundationalist views of the self, but he argues that a meaningful sense of self can emerge after these devastating critiques, a praxis-oriented self, understanding, representing and fashioning herself in discourse, action, community, and in transcendence.[67]

While I share with these largely secular (though religiously sympathetic) arguments an approach to the self that stresses self-understanding and praxis, I depart from them by arguing that theological anthropologies that are indebted to conceptual frameworks of being yield important insights into self-relation, especially given the contemporary problem of self love. A theological account of self-relation makes more sense of our moral experience because it has the linguistic and symbolic resources to articulate it and because it is an exercise of practical reason. In other words, a theological account of self-relation does more than speculate on or describe our being in the world; it orients our acting and relations with others and in the world. As Schrag and Rudman note, Christian theology

[66] Rudman, *Concepts of Persons and Christian Ethics*, 173–74.
[67] Schrag, *Self After Postmodernity*.

need not employ arguments indebted to substance metaphysics. Conceptual frameworks of being, or ontological accounts of the self encounter problems, as trenchant critics of them rightly note. But they also offer insights, and given the inescapably historical character of our thinking, attempts to rework and redeem them are exercises in self-understanding. Ontology helps us attend to our creatureliness, while a hermeneutical approach to that creatureliness keeps us mindful of this attention as an interpretive and evaluative activity. A theological approach brings out the best of these two and offsets their difficulties. A hermeneutical theological method prevents us from reifying ontological categories, something that would entail losing sight of the truth of hermeneutics and losing sight of God's relationality and sovereignty. God sets the hermeneutical criteria, or transvalues our values, by placing before us the question whether our constructs impel us in love for others.

So I judge that a theological account of self-relation will be more adequate a response to the contemporary problem of self love than the foregoing options are. But, the validity of the theological account I offer must be established dialectically through engagement with alternative positions. We can note why this is so by appealing to the very idea of right self love. Why ought I to understand my good as something different than, not reducible to, my preferences, cares, etc.? The idea of right self love cannot make sense apart from some source of value that is independent of us. It designates one form of self-relation over and against alternative forms and thereby testifies to something that is beyond our individual and communal flourishing, something that demands our respect and devotion. In Chapter Three I will develop this argument in conversation with recent work in philosophical hermeneutics. Briefly, I will argue that contemporary inquiry into the problem of self love ought to explore the character of self-relation, particularly its reflexive, interpretive, evaluative, and embodied features. Theological accounts fare better than secular accounts because they provide a way to transcend our own desires and constructs in moral self-criticism but do so in a way that does not valorize autonomy, subsume the self into the systems or communities that situate her, or, importantly, exempt her religious relation with God from moral criticism.

CONCLUSION

In this chapter I sketched a broad but inter-related set of changes in theology, ethics and philosophy, cultural phenomena, and insights from the social sciences. I suggested that these changes express and reinforce a distinctive contemporary moral experience. Put simply, the complexity and fragmentation of our moral situation requires a contemporary account of right self love. Moreover, a contemporary account of right self love must be developed out of a moral anthropology. In the following chapter I argue this point by noting difficulties in available theories of self love and by calling for a retrieval of ontological frameworks for the self.

I also argued here that the contemporary problem of self love requires a theological response because of the theoretically faulty and practically enervating norm of self-realization. Nevertheless, a theological ethics ought to be warranted on theological grounds. Moreover, a turn to Christian ethics for this theological account cannot be easy or direct given Christian tradition's ambivalence about self love and various challenges philosophy has posed for Christian ethics, especially to Christian moral anthropology. Let us consider Christian ethical resources for a contemporary account of right self love.

CHAPTER 2

Self love in Christian ethics

As historians of ethics have noted, since the eighteenth century theological ethical attention has shifted away from the divine–human relation to interpersonal human relations.[1] As the classical coordination of self love with love for God receded, so, too, did many resources for thinking about the self's relation to the divine as the central sphere of moral activity. Rather, concern for the neighbor became the province of ethics. The person's interior life and religious status before God were disentangled from the person's relation to others, and were distinguished more sharply from public activity and relations. While an historical and causal account of this shift lies beyond the scope of this project, we should note several important aspects of this shift. First, it signaled that the self's relation with God should not instrumentalize the neighbor. Second, it testifies to divine intentions that do not concern and may even thwart individual human flourishing. Third, and somewhat ironically, it re-cast the self's relation with God in terms of an existential decision or posture. This reconception of faith is part of a larger apologetic project which shifted attention away from revealed religion toward forms of natural religion which tended to emphasize the moral dimensions of Christianity and render faith as an aid to living well. While positions which exemplify this shift vary considerably, the self's relation to the divine often was re-thought either in terms of dependence (Schleiermacher) or freedom (Ritschl). That

---

[1] Stephen Post, *A Theory of Agape: On the Meaning of Christian Love* (Lewisburg, PA: Bucknell University Press, 1990). In part, this shift constitutes a response to the development of philosophical ethics and to an increasing distinction between dogmatic and moral theology. See also Gérard Gilleman, *The Primacy of Charity in Moral Theology* (Westminster, MD: Newman, 1959).

is, in classical positions the transcendental conditions of the divine–human relation were understood in terms of love, while in modern thought dependence or freedom have been taken to be the most basic transcendental mode of being before God. Moreover, the self's existential stance often was correlated to service toward the neighbor, either as its origin or its fruit.

Thus, for several centuries when Western theological ethics treated self love it generally did so with respect to love for neighbor. Granted, in most theological ethical inquiries into love, whether their center of gravity is love for God, neighbor, or self, at least fleeting attention is given to each of the three. But my point is that this historical shift of emphasis indicates a distinctively modern perspective or consciousness. For this reason, recent interest in the flourishing of the self, in the form of virtue ethics, spirituality, etc., represents a (post) modern re-appropriation of classical concepts and tools for thinking about the self's good.[2]

Meritorious insights underlie this shift from God to neighbor. And, in any event, modern consciousness does not allow a naïve return to pre-modern classical accounts of the divine–human relation. Still, the shift incurs certain philosophical and theological costs. The relative silence in contemporary Christian ethics about love for God yields an anemic theological anthropology. Too often, the person's self-transcendence is truncated and the religious dimension of human life is neglected. Perhaps we do not appreciate the costs of this mistake because Christian ethics directs our attention too quickly past them to the neighbor. By correlating self love to neighbor love, we forego the opportunity to morally evaluate religious accounts of self love and the divine–human relation. We also make self love beholden to neighbor love. Self love becomes, at best, neighbor love's poor sibling. This move denies any positive content to self love, or it makes self love a precondition for or remainder of neighbor love. Here again, we relinquish an

---

[2] See, for example, Martha Nussbaum, *The Therapy of Desire: Theory and Practice in Hellenistic Ethics* (Princeton, NJ: Princeton University Press, 1994); Pierre Hadot, *Philosophy as a Way of Life: Spiritual Exercises from Socrates to Foucault*, ed. and intro., Arnold I. Davidson (Oxford and Cambridge, MA: Blackwell Publishers, 1995); Diana Fritz Cates, *Choosing to Feel: Virtue, Friendship and Compassion for Friends* (Notre Dame, IN: University of Notre Dame Press, 1997).

opportunity to enrich our theological anthropologies. And, ironically, we forego an opportunity for a subtle moral evaluation of self
love. How so? We reduce accounts of the nature of self love to moral
evaluations of it (e.g., self love is always selfish, or self love is simply
the instinct for self-preservation). Moreover, contemporary discussions not only correlate it with neighbor love and neglect love for
God, they tend to begin and proceed according to some account of
love rather than some account of the self who is to love. This adds
to our list of costs by two: (1) either self love becomes divorced from
the concrete relations and bodily specificity of the person, or (2) it is
completely identified with sacrificial action on behalf of the other
and thereby potentially mutilates the moral identity of the person.
Cognizance of the former danger is the insight of many postmodern theories; the latter danger has been forcefully and compellingly
protested by many feminist ethicists.[3] Nonetheless, feminist challenges to traditional Christian love ethics also tend to explore self
love with respect to love for neighbor and to engage the tradition
with respect to debates about the nature of love.

This chapter will consider available theories of self love and
feminist criticisms of sacrificial love ethics. The attitudes toward
and theories of self love presented here are by no means exhaustive,
though they are largely representative. In this chapter I argue that
this prevailing tendency to conceptually correlate self love with
neighbor love and to locate debates about the ethical propriety of
self love around disputes about the nature of love (typically types of
love and their moral status) encounters problems. These problems
mean that although a theological account of self love is required,
there can be no easy or direct turn to Christian ethics to supply one.
A survey of Christian ethical arguments about self love will illustrate
this by showing Christian tradition's ambivalence about self love as
well as the way recent arguments for self love are susceptible to the
subjectivism and other difficulties that attend secular approaches
to the self.

---

[3] I have in mind thinkers such as Seyla Benhabib, Beverly Harrison, and Judith Plaskow.
Notwithstanding the considerable differences among them, each critiques the way in
which the traditional Christian denigration of self love has been used against women and
minorities to perpetuate oppression.

A TYPOLOGY OF SELF LOVE

In recent literature on love among Christian thinkers, self love is typically regarded in one of four ways.[4] First, and most often, self love is pernicious. Indeed, for thinkers such as Anders Nygren, self love designates the basic human moral problem. This position comprises the background over and against which other positions have developed and thus, re-appears in modified versions in some of the other options. Second, others take self love to be morally neutral; neither evil nor good, self love is a natural, reasonable attitude of the self towards itself. Here self love may refer to a basic instinct for self-preservation, or to a self-affirmation that is sine qua non for neighbor love. And, to complete the spectrum, there are those theologians who insist that self love is a moral duty. Among these latter thinkers, self love is, third, either a derivative duty, necessary in order to fulfill other, higher moral duties, or, fourth, an independent duty. As a derivative duty, self love is permitted so as to enable the agent for agape (Christian love). Paul Ramsey, for example, as rigorous as his agapic ethics may be, concedes that the agent must exercise sufficient care for the self so as to free and fortify the self for works of neighbor love. Others, however, understand self love as an independent moral duty, for example Gene Outka, who grounds self love on the same dignity that demands love for others. Not everyone who represents this fourth option insists that self love is a positive duty for the same reasons as Outka, but whether self love is understood in terms of the rewards of neighbor love or is taken to be good on the basis of the person as the *imago Dei*, a common thread seems to be that self love is a duty because it coincides with or is subsumed under neighbor love. For this reason, positions on behalf of self love tend to collapse its nature and their moral evaluation of it. Still others argue on behalf of self love as a positive duty; feminists counter the sacrificial agape tradition with a redemption of eros or argument for mutuality, while

---

[4] Although I depart from his own position in significant ways, I am indebted to Gene Outka for his insightful typology of the literature available on self love. See his *Agape: an Ethical Analysis* (New Haven: Yale University Press, 1972), especially 55–74 and 285–91. See also Edward Vacek S. J., *Love, Human and Divine: the Heart of Christian Ethics* (Washington DC: Georgetown University Press, 1994), 205–08.

Edward Vacek coordinates self love with love for God in what he calls an ethics of cooperation. This book's argument for self love seeks to incorporate and amend feminist defenses of self love, and is one that has much in common with Vacek's position.

While the above typology indicates that Christian ethical attitudes towards self love are not as monolithic as they are often suggested to be, the overwhelming emphasis, in theory and in tenor, is negative. Let me turn, then, to the so-called sacrificial agape tradition. It encompasses a range of attitudes toward self love. I will begin with Nygren, who regards self love as entirely pernicious. In doing so, some important considerations will come to light which will help us gain some purchase on the other available approaches.

Self love and sacrificial agape

Self love as pernicious

Anders Nygren regards self love as entirely pernicious. He differentiates self-interested, erotic love from other-regarding, agapic love, correlating agape with neighbor love and eros with self love. Quite simply, this means that agape designates *the* Christian form of love while eros refers to the basic religious and moral problem to be overcome. Nygren contrasts the two loves with characteristic force:

Eros is acquisitive desire and longing.	Agape is sacrificial giving.
Eros is an upward movement.	Agape comes down.
Eros is man's way to God.	Agape is God's way to man.
Eros is man's effort: it assumes that man's salvation is his own work.	Agape is God's grace: salvation is the work of Divine love.
Eros is egocentric love, a form of self-assertion of the highest, noblest, sublimest kind.	Agape is unselfish love, it "seeketh not its own", it gives itself away.
Eros seeks to gain its life, a life divine, immortalised.	Agape lives the life of God, therefore dares to "lose it."
Eros is the will to get and possess which depends on want and need.	Agape is freedom in giving, which depends on wealth and plenty.

Eros is primarily *man's* love; God is the *object* of Eros. Even when it is attributed to God, Eros is patterned on human love.

Eros is determined by the quality, the beauty and worth, of its object; it is not spontaneous, but "evoked," "motivated."

Eros *recognises value* in its object – and loves it.

Agape is primarily *God's* love; God *is* Agape. Even when it is attributed to man, Agape is patterned on Divine love.

Agape is sovereign in relation to its object, and is directed to both "the evil and the good"; it is spontaneous, "overflowing," "unmotivated."

Agape loves – and *creates value in its* object.[5]

Agape designates love for the neighbor as such; it is both universal in scope and independent of any merit or change in the neighbor. Agape loves the neighbor in her particularity; but it is at the same time ignorant of distinctions between neighbors insofar as they might be *conditions* for agape. Every neighbor, as neighbor, is to be loved equally, though the way particular neighbors are treated might not be identical. Any love based on preference or partiality is for Nygren only self love. The person loves that other because of whatever goods the neighbor adduces to the self.

Nygren's position may presuppose psychological egoism. Psychological egoism is a descriptive theory about human motivation. It is not simply the claim that self-interested, acquisitive self love can be discerned throughout human history, but rather that self-interest comprises the sole motive or spring of human behavior in every person throughout history. While psychological egoism has several variations,

the underlying thesis is that acquisitive self-love constitutes de facto the sole spring of behavior, identical for every man. Men pursue their own individual and private satisfaction and they cannot help pursuing it. If their behavior at times seems ostensibly altruistic, this is only disguised acquisitiveness. Their conscious aims, if other-regarding, are never their real and determinative ones. At the deepest level, all aims are genetically derived from one and may be reductively analyzed into one and only one.[6]

5 Anders Nygren, *Agape and Eros*, trans. Philip S. Watson (London: S.P.C.K., 1957), 210.
6 Outka, *Agape*, 60.

Nygren, for example, writes,

> does there indeed exist any other love than that which builds on the foundation of self-love? Is it conceivable or possible in human life as human life is at present constituted? . . . The fact is that the resources of natural human life are exhausted in and with egocentric love. There is nothing in the life and activity of the natural man which does not bear the marks of . . . seeking its own. It is therefore wholly under the dominion of sin, and on that basis there is no possibility of manifesting love in the Christian sense of the word, a love that seeketh not its own, but loves God with all its heart and its neighbor as itself.[7]

Nygren paints such a grim picture that the only hope of Christian love rests on God as the primary agent in agape. For Nygren, agape is invasive; the Christian is "merely the tube, the channel through which God's love flows."[8] Thus, the person exercises no agency whatsoever in either love for neighbor or love for God. Because the pursuit of the self's good is by definition sinful, and because the person cannot possibly do anything to be properly related to God or neighbor, Nygren's position does not admit any notion of right self love. His account of the nature of self love and his moral evaluation of it are identical.

Notwithstanding its difficulties, Nygren's position bequeaths several insights important to a contemporary theory of right self love. First, Nygren articulated forcefully the basic claim that improper self-relation presents an obstacle to proper God-relation and proper neighbor-relation. Second, his insight into the wily character of improper self love suggests that a theory of right self love must entail some element of renunciation or discipline. This point is important given the privatization and immunization of desire that I noted in the last chapter. Sacrifice belongs as part of self love not simply to insure that one prefers others to oneself in cases of conflict; sacrifice requires us to transcend desire sufficiently to gauge the correspondence (or lack thereof) between desire and one's basic moral commitments, to reform desire (to the extent one can do so) through such reflection, attention and prayer. This point will prove important later, when I assess feminist criticisms of Nygrenesque agape. Whatever difficulties such a negative appraisal of self love

---

[7] Nygren, *Agape and Eros*, 722–23.   [8] Ibid., 735.

might present, Nygren shows that improper self love cannot simply be given a corrective ethics of self-realization. Rather, third, an adequate account of proper self-relation must be advanced under the criteria of proper God-relation and proper neighbor-relation. In Nygren the weight of these criteria disallowed a fuller analysis of proper self-relation. But by constructing an account of self love on the basis of the self, we can develop Nygren's insight into the dependency of proper self-relation on proper God- and neighbor-relation in a way that maintains the controlling criteria of love for God and for neighbor.

Nygren's argument displays important features of any position on self love. To note these will lend some comparative clarity to the remaining positions on self love. I find three particular features. First, each account of self love includes some claims about the springs of human action, that is, descriptive judgments about what attitudes, wants, intentions, etc., normally enter into moral action, as well as normative judgments about how those ought to be configured. The general consensus is that self love comes rather naturally to the person.[9] We will see that some thinkers, such as Paul Ramsey, admit that one can be morally culpable for failing to exercise basic responsibility for the self even if only because this impairs one from serving the neighbor; but by and large even those for whom self love is a positive moral obligation are more concerned with the danger of inordinate self love. As we will see, it is a testament to the feminist critique of Christian accounts of self love that in more recent literature the failure to establish oneself as a self has come to be regarded as a "roughly equivalent danger."

Second, each option also includes some sense of how the three loves of self, neighbor, and God are related or ought to be related. For example, questions arise such as whether there is substantive overlap among any or all of the loves, or whether any of them are always or potentially in conflict. Because Nygren defines self love in opposition to love for the neighbor, the two inevitably conflict. A recurrent question in the literature is how to interpret the "as yourself" of the love command, that is, to ask whether and how

---

[9] Self love can be attributed either to the person's created nature, or to his fallen state.

self love is paradigmatic for neighbor love and if self love has some positive moral status independent of neighbor love. I specify the relation of love for God, self, and neighbor in a different way than the available positions do by arguing that right self love consists in a response to God (love for God) that is actualized and assessed in love for the neighbor.

Third, and finally, each assessment of self love includes some basic understanding of love in general. That is, the available theories of self love tend to be determined by an analysis of love rather than the lover. This more fundamental understanding of love is often differentiated into types of love (e.g., agape, eros, philia, among others), and one of these types is often taken to be the form of Christian love (usually, agape). Sometimes the nature of love is understood as some complex of them wherein basic experiences of bestowing or apprehending value, of (re)unification, or of participation comprise the central character of love.[10] The differentiation of love into types helps to render the complex variants and modulations of love relations, and for this reason these types remain helpful, though insufficient for the contemporary problem of self love.

Self love as natural and morally neutral

Some thinkers regard self love as natural, and, moreover, morally neutral in character. This may be because they confine the moral life to interpersonal actions and relations; that is, the self's relation to itself is for thinkers like Timothy O'Connell outside the scope of morality.[11] Presumably, self love belongs to the province of other disciplines like spirituality or psychology. This moral indifference to self love begs the question of loving oneself rightly when people obviously encounter grave difficulties in doing so. For others, self love, while itself morally neutral, may bear upon specifically moral loves. It may be that self love, as the person's quest for happiness, or as a more or less conscious pursuit of self-interest, is prior to love for others. For example, Margaret Farley suggests that one must

---

[10] For an account of love as bestowal and appraisal, see Irving Singer, *The Nature of Love*, 3 vols. (Chicago: University of Chicago Press, 1987). For an account of love as reunification, see Paul Tillich, *Love, Power and Justice* (Oxford: Oxford University Press, 1954). For an account of love as participation, see Vacek, *Love, Human and Divine*.

[11] See Timothy O'Connell, *Principles for a Catholic Morality*, rev. edn (San Francisco, CA: HarperSanFrancisco), 111.

love oneself in order to love others insofar as love for others entails some affirmation of the self as worthy of giving to another.[12] The psychological egoism found in Nygren's account can reappear here as a morally neutral factor. Self love is then an ineradicable, but not morally culpable, feature of all human activity.[13] Or self love may be a fruit of neighbor love. In loving the neighbor rightly, some goods (e.g., satisfaction, moral habituation, discipline) may accrue to the self organically or indirectly. Or self love is paradigmatic for neighbor love; the "as yourself" of the golden rule implies as much.

The upshot of all this is that we need not worry over self love. But the argument that self love is natural and morally neutral is not really a stable or independent position. If its moral neutrality is really one of moral indifference, we ignore the serious problem of self love or relocate it to areas that are insufficiently equipped to address it. If the moral neutrality of self love rests on claims that self love is a pre-condition for, by-product of, or paradigm for neighbor love, we gloss conflicts between self love and neighbor love in a way that evacuates self love of its independent positive content.

The argument that self love is natural and morally neutral is also unstable because it can pitch toward an endorsement of positive self love, but in a way that keeps it beholden to neighbor love. Gene Outka's *Agape: an Ethical Analysis* illustrates this. In a more recent

---

[12] See Margaret Farley, *Personal Commitments: Beginning, Keeping, Changing* (San Francisco, CA: HarperSanFrancisco, 1986).

[13] There were also a number of thinkers who began to argue that self love was natural and is morally permissible or even a foundation of morality. Joseph Butler argued that self love, as the general desire for our happiness, entails an intrinsic positive regard for various particular objects of desire. Self love is an intermediate principle between desire and conscience, as is benevolence. Self love and benevolence organize desires and are ordered by conscience. Butler, then, refutes egoism on the grounds that desire is intrinsically other-regarding, that benevolence (and not only self love) can motivate us, and because conscience is a faculty that can examine actions and motives disinterestedly. And yet, Butler argued that conscience and self love are ultimately in harmony; virtue and rectitude are not contrary to happiness. See his *Five Sermons Preached at the Rolls Chapel: and a Dissertation upon the Nature of Virtue*, Introduction by Stuart M. Brown (New York: Liberal Arts, 1950). In contrast to Butler's rationalism, Jonathan Edwards offered a moral sense theory; the springs of human action lie in our affections, directed toward perceived goods. He distinguishes two forms of morality. The lower form, restricted benevolence, is a natural human morality grounded in self love. The higher form, what Edwards identified as true virtue, embraces more than these partial objects. It is a consent to and love for being in general. This true benevolence does not conflict with natural morality because it is love for God and all things in God. See his *On the Nature of True Virtue*, foreward by William K. Frankena (Ann Arbor, MI: University of Michigan, 1960).

essay, Outka argues more directly and fully that self love is a positive obligation, and I will consider this position later. But *Agape* helps us to see the difficulties of natural and neutral self love.

In *Agape* Outka rejects psychological egoism, and, thereby, Nygren's agape–eros dichotomy. In doing so, he transforms the link between self love and human nature from a nefarious acquisitiveness to a reasonable vitality. Outka describes self love as a natural energy or vitality, as *epithymia*. He qualifies the positive assessment which *epithymia* designates for some:

> The unavoidable element of self-love I now have in mind ... has minimally to do with a certain unreflective and vital energy which the agent brings ... One might formally regard it as part of the spontaneous self-love which is not blameworthy but not particularly praiseworthy ... Natural vitality easily becomes inordinate and destructive. Agape ought to remain the controlling criterion for epithymia, so as to guard the integrity of the other person against violation and abuse.[14]

Outka further acknowledges that some thinkers for whom self love is reasonable and prudent understand self love not as the unreflective attachment of *epithymia*, but as a more conscious self-affirmation. For them, self love coincides with neighbor love either because it must be sequentially prior to or at least must accompany agape. Outka does not adopt any one of these options, but simply notes that, unlike psychological egoism, the agapist may hold them without inconsistency.

Of course, claiming that some account of self love in relation to neighbor love can be consistent with agape is not the same thing as claiming that self love is reasonable and prudent. To be fair, Outka's task in *Agape* is not to forward a constructive account of agape, but, rather, to analyze the uses and theories of agape in contemporary Christian thought. The text, however, *may* indicate that Outka prefers an account of self love as natural and morally neutral.[15] Outka appears to endorse self love as a basic, natural self-regard for two reasons. First, the self may be loved for the

[14] Outka, *Agape*, 287–88.
[15] Barbara Hilkert Andolsen notes this. See her "Agape in Feminist Ethics," in *Feminist Theological Ethics: a Reader*, ed., Lois K. Daly (Louisville, KY: Westminster/John Knox, 1994).

same reasons that the neighbor is loved. "The agent's basic self-regard, then, ought not to be simply dependent on the number of his achievements or the extent to which he is found likable, but on his being as well a man of flesh and blood and a creature of God, a person who is more than a means to some other end."[16] This "basic self-regard" is warranted by one's creatureliness. It does not mean that self love has an independent, positive content; rather, the contrast Outka draws between self-interest and other-regard ought not to require the self to be exploited by the neighbor. He calls this the question of whether to issue to the neighbor a blank check.[17] For Outka, the *principal* reason for refusing the blank check is because it is inconsistent with agape. Outka contends that agape is universal in scope and has equal regard for neighbors at its center. He, too, distinguishes equal regard from identical treatment. Note that concern for the neighbor rather than concern for the self prohibits the self from allowing herself to be exploited (e.g., sometimes the neighbor's good must be achieved by working against the neighbor's weakness). For Outka the blank check can *also* be refused out of some basic self-regard. "Just as the neighbor must be regarded as a human being prior to a particular human being, so even the self must value itself in the same way."[18] Here, too, self love (basic self-regard) lacks independent positive content. At the very moment that self love is being said to set some limit on love for the neighbor, love for neighbor is made the paradigm and warrant for doing so. And, not allowing oneself to be exploited begs the question whether self love entails particular duties and goods in its own right.

Second, Outka seems to endorse self love as natural and morally neutral when he claims that, structurally speaking, only the self can take responsibility for itself. Another cannot realize its projects, develop its capacities, or exercise its freedom.[19] We can consider this responsibility as a reasonable, prudent exercise of self love. Here again the position slides towards an endorsement of positive self love. But because Outka is wary of the ease with which natural

---

[16] Ibid., 291.
[17] Outka's position displays some affinities with Kierkegaard on this point. See *Agape*, 21–24.
[18] Here Outka exhibits the influence of Kant. See *Agape*, 23.
[19] Ibid., 305.

self-assertion may become inordinate and destructive, he subjects self love to the criterion of agape. Indeed, for Outka self love, as this responsibility for the self, leads him to an account of "agent-stringency." The evaluative principle of agent-stringency requires the agent to hold herself to a higher standard of other-regarding accountability than that to which she holds others. In sum, Outka grounds self love on the same basis as love for neighbor and assesses self love with respect to neighbor love as its criterion, and perhaps even as its end. His description seems to subsume self love under neighbor love (the self as neighbor to herself) and to suggest that self love, while distinct, is ordered to neighbor love rather than independently allowed.

While I want to argue that self love constitutes an independent, positive moral obligation, I share two convictions with Outka's position here, two convictions which come to play a larger part in Outka's recent thinking, wherein he commends self love directly. First, when Outka seems to ground self love on the same basis as love for neighbor, he argues that this basic self-regard depends on one's being a creature of God. While I would not warrant self love on the basis of the self as neighbor to oneself, I do contend that self love constitutes an obligation for the self because the self, like the neighbor, has been created to love God. Second, the structural reasons for self love also factor into the theory of self love which I forward. They help to explain the categorical self-relation of the person and can perhaps provide a way to think about the person's transcendental self-relation (e.g., a person is ultimately responsible for her response to God). Moreover, the structural necessity of self love offers a way to develop the feminist insight into the sin of failing to establish oneself as a self. I will return to this later.

Self love as a derivative obligation

For some thinkers self love is a secondary moral obligation when it is derived from the primary obligation of neighbor love. Paul Ramsey argues this. His position shows affinities with the first two even as he makes a distinctive argument for self love. On the one hand, for Ramsey the "as yourself" found in the golden rule does not constitute a command to love oneself, but rather suggests that self love is paradigmatic for neighbor love. Self love is paradigmatic because it endures apart from merit; its constancy toward its object provides a model for how the Christian ought to love the neighbor.[20] On the other hand, Ramsey understands self love as acquisitive. Indeed, he claims that the love command presupposes self love in order to wrench one away from it.[21] Christian love is always disinterested and diffusive, while self love is acquisitive and selfish. As acquisitive, self love is compatible with various objects.[22] In other words, both neighbor and God can be loved acquisitively. Thus, for Ramsey, the nature of self love is not determined by its object, but rather by the type of love it instantiates – erotic selfishness. For this reason, Ramsey opposes self love to obedient love, the former being a teleological pursuit of the self's good (whether that good is conceived to lie in some base object or even beatitude itself), the latter being a deontological love for the neighbor as such. Any good that might accrue to the self thereby would be a completely unintended consequence. Thus, the Christian must be converted from self love.[23] Indeed, Christian love is self love inverted.[24]

Because the very nature of self love is opposed to Christian or obedient love, Ramsey considers two traditions in ethics which commend self love, one in terms of an enlightened selfishness, the other through a mutual love between self and neighbor. Enlightened selfishness designates the pursuit of "superior values" for the self's sake (such as beatitude) or even the simple hope that one's love be requited. Because Christian love is not a matter of its object but rather its quality or type, enlightened selfishness is reducible to self love. The intentional pursuit of self-realization, which Ramsey calls philosophical idealism, is also self love. In fact, according to Ramsey, philosophical idealism is the chief rival to Christian love, "because what idealism calls 'the good' Christian ethics calls sin or idolatry."[25] Idolatry has "two moods" to which the modern person

[20] Paul Ramsey, *Basic Christian Ethics* (Louisville, KY: Westminster/John Knox, 1950), 233.
[21] Ibid., 102. Ramsey agrees with Kierkegaard on this point.
[22] Ibid., 148.
[23] Ibid., 189. It is important to note that for Ramsey derivative self love is not a precondition for loving the neighbor in the sense that one must love herself before she can love another. See 105.
[24] Ibid., 100.
[25] Ibid., 301–02. Philosophical idealism includes the pursuit of self-realization through self-giving. Ramsey does not deny that some good might accrue to the self through Christian love; the point is that the Christian can never intend any good for herself. What is loved

is susceptible: "he first despairs over man's littleness, his limitation by physical necessity and death, and in despair he is unwilling to be himself the creature of dust he knows he is. At the same time he despairingly and defiantly wills to be himself in the guise of some god, some deified program or institution whose creatureliness he refuses to acknowledge."[26] Ramsey is unclear as to whether the person is equally susceptible to each mood, but the point to be taken is that the failure of the self to be itself is an instance of idolatrous self love.[27] Unwillingness to be oneself is not corrected by positive self love, but, rather, by a simple willingness to be oneself, by a self-acceptance which is divested of any self love, a self-acceptance that frees the self *from* concern for itself and *for* love for the neighbor.[28]

This same subconscious egoism prevails in accounts that extol mutual love relations. For Ramsey, when the self identifies itself with some other, or with some common good, the self only relates itself to itself. This not only instrumentalizes the proximate object of love, for example the neighbor, but also constitutes an absolutization of the finite. Even the common pursuit of superior values such as beatitude is an idolatrous instantiation of self love.

Given Ramsey's contrast between enlightened selfishness and obedient love, or philosophical idealism and Christian love, "no more disastrous mistake can be made than to admit self-love onto the ground floor of Christian ethics as a basic part of Christian obligation, however much concern for self-improvement, for example, may later come to be a secondary, though entirely essential aspect of Christian vocation."[29] Neighbor love, however, requires

is not as morally salient for Ramsey as how it is loved; since one is clearly obligated to love the neighbor, the moral issue is the kind of love in which neighbor love consists.
[26] Ibid., 297–98.
[27] Such a point offers an interesting response to feminist critiques of the traditional Christian emphasis on pride as the basic sin. Judith Plaskow, for instance, argues that pride does not adequately convey the sin of many women, which, rather than self-assertion, is the failure to establish oneself as a self. But on Ramsey's account, self love is so pervasive that this failure ought to be understood as the self's attempt to escape being for another. Here he agrees with Kierkegaard. See ibid., 297–98, and Judith Plaskow, *Sex, Sin and Grace: Women's Experience and the Theologies of Reinhold Niebuhr and Paul Tillich* (Lanham, MD: University Press of America, 1980).
[28] Ramsey, *Basic Christian Ethics*, 104–05.
[29] Ibid., 101. Given the universal scope of neighbor love, some theologians used the idea of vocation to make sense out of how one might actually serve their neighbor. See for

the self to be itself, to accept itself and to develop itself as the vocation of neighbor love requires.[30] In enlightened selfishness and mutual love, duties which might appear to be duties to the other are really performed for the self; but, in Christian vocation, duties toward the self are really duties of neighbor love, "duties to the neighbor performed first upon the self."[31]

Self love has no independent legitimacy. It is justified only as a secondary dimension of neighbor love. This means that Ramsey is unable to make sense of any duties to the self that might arise out of love for God and/or traditional Christian claims about God as the good of the human as such. Ramsey misses a profound theological anthropological insight on this count; he seems to understand the capacity for human self-transcendence as an overwhelming proclivity to idolatry.[32] While, empirically speaking, we might find some evidence for this, Ramsey is so wary that he may suggest a version of psychological egoism reminiscent of Nygren: "At all times and places men worship idols, i.e., themselves, and not just under certain variable conditions."[33] According to Ramsey, to live outside this idolatrous self love is an ideal possibility, actualized through Christ's love. Ramsey is correct, but he understands the nature of self love too narrowly. Insofar as the nature of self love rests on this descriptive anthropological claim, Ramsey fails to take seriously the way in which the human is created to love God.[34] It is unclear why a purely responsive love for God cannot include, in fact ought not to include this claim about the human – for it is not at odds with the insistence that God loves first, nor does it require a synergism in which our answer of love secures God's continuing love.

Despite these difficulties in Ramsey's account of self love, there are several insights in his position that are important to a contemporary theory of right self love. First, his critique of enlightened selfishness and philosophical idealism provide helpful and incisive checks to amorphous self-realization ethics. An adequate account of right self love must remain cognizant of the dangers entailed in self-realization. These dangers include more than a

example Gilbert Meilaender, *Friendship* (Notre Dame, IN: University of Notre Dame Press, 1981).
[30] Ramsey, *Basic Christian Ethics*, 161–62.
[31] Ibid., 163.   [32] Ibid., 297.   [33] Ibid.
[34] Ramsey places greater emphasis on the fall than on creation.

propensity to instrumentalize others in the pursuit of one's own interest. As he shows, even the earnest pursuit of religious and moral flourishing can be the locus of self-deception and idolatry. I adopt this insight in order to argue that the person's religious relation to God, then, is subject to moral evaluation. Second, he understands the "roughly equivalent danger" of failing to establish oneself as a self in terms of selfishness. Rather than explain such a failing as the result of being victimized by forces and relations, Ramsey's assessment of this failure makes sense of the person's responsibility for such a failure and indicates that proper self-relation has the character of a task or demand. While some feminists would maintain that some persons exhibit this failure precisely because they are victims (say of abuse), Ramsey's assessment can help a theory of right self love do justice to the complex ways in which the person's capacities for proper self-relation are both shaped by relations, institutions, and systems, and yet remain a matter of personal responsibility. Finally, Ramsey understands proper self-relation to consist in an acceptance of one's creaturehood, a willingness to be oneself before God in gratitude and faith. The way in which he identifies proper self love with an acceptance of one's status as a creature of God complements my own attempt to analyze self love on the basis of the lover.

Self love as an independent moral obligation

There are at least four reasons why some thinkers argue that self love is a definite, independent moral obligation.[35] First, thinkers who represent this option seem to find that the descriptive claim that the human has an unreflective self-attachment or even a basic acquisitiveness is not complex enough. It recognizes dangers such as pride and selfishness, but neglects the roughly equivalent dangers of excessive self-sacrifice or the failure to establish oneself as a self.[36] Second, a self love that is derived from and devoted to neighbor love excludes a number of duties the self has toward itself. That is, self love encompasses some attitudes and actions, particularly a kind of stewardship that the self exercises with respect to itself, which is not

---

[35] Here I follow the analysis provided in Outka, *Agape*, 70–74, and 289–91.
[36] See footnote 27 of this chapter regarding Ramsey and Plaskow.

reducible to other-regard. Moreover, these duties towards the self might on occasion trump duties towards others. Third, self love is not an alternative to neighbor love, but, rather, is correlative with it. Self love and neighbor love are *temporally* coincident (and not only eschatologically commensurable), such that conflicts between them are either only apparent, or are ordered to the self's good. This argument takes on different variations: sometimes thinkers stress that the self is realized in regard for the other, or that self-sacrifice is its own reward. Finally, self love is deemed a definite obligation because the self ought to be valued for the same reasons as one ought to value others.

Let me consider defenses of self love that run along two different, though not incompatible lines. My own defense of self love borrows from both and endeavors to address their respective difficulties. Like the previous arguments about self love, these defenses are driven largely by accounts of love rather than accounts of the self.

The feminist critique of traditional Christian accounts of self love
Modern theological ethical thinkers note that the idea that self-sacrifice begets some goods to the self, at least spiritual, eschatological goods, is often employed to console or manipulate individuals and groups into accepting their station in life. Many feminist thinkers advance this criticism forcefully and compellingly. Feminists take issue not only with the emphasis on sacrifice found in much agapic love ethics, but also with the denigration of the self, creation, and mutuality they find in traditional accounts of the divine–human relation. Let me detail some of the features of this challenge.

To begin, some feminists criticize the understanding of agape in terms of sacrifice and the denigration of self love (eros) that typically accompanies it. Eros is prideful self-assertion, the quintessence of self love. Feminists charge, however, that such an account is dangerous. Their reasons are two-fold. First, while sinful self-assertion, the primary obstacle to agape, may represent the experience many men have had throughout the Christian tradition, it fails to account for women's experience. Often the tradition collapses self love with the sin of pride, thereby making self love the primary human sin. From the nineteenth century on, feminists began to note that the claim that self love designates the basic moral problem excludes the experience of women, whose failing can be characterized not as prideful self-assertion, but as excessive self-abnegation. Second, feminists noted that the traditional Christian injunction against self love and the sacrificial ethics that served as its corrective have been used to oppress and control women. Let me consider each of these criticisms in turn.

The sacrificial agapic ethics presupposes an account of sin which is inadequate to women's experience. A number of feminists raise this charge, and their arguments have proved so compelling that many recent writers on agape at least acknowledge that prideful self-assertion is accompanied by a "roughly equivalent danger" of excessive self-abnegation. This sin, argue feminists, has been largely the sin of women. Some characterize it as sloth, others as the "lack of an organizing center."[37] "Women have a tendency to give themselves over to others to such an extent that they lose themselves. Thus they squander their distinctive personal abilities. The virtues which theologians should be urging upon women are autonomy and self-realization. What many male theologians are offering instead is a one-sided call to a self-sacrifice which may ironically reinforce women's sins."[38]

Judith Plaskow elaborates this sin of self-abnegation in a study of Reinhold Niebuhr and Paul Tillich. She understands women's sin as the "failure to take responsibility for self-actualization."[39] Plaskow's study focuses on the inter-relation of cultural (male) definitions of femininity and expectations for women, and their internalization by women. Plaskow points out that the traditional understanding of sin as prideful self-absorption ignores the fact that "'Women's sin' is precisely the failure to turn toward the self. The sin which involves God-forgetfulness and self-forgetfulness is not properly called 'pride,' even where the word is used in its religious sense."[40] Moreover, when sin is so understood, virtue, by

[37] Valerie Saiving Goldstein, "The Human Situation: a Feminine View," in *Womanspirit Rising: a Feminist Reader in Religion*, eds., Carol P. Christ and Judith Plaskow (San Francisco, CA: HarperSanFrancisco; Christ and Plaskow, 1979), 25–42. See 37.
[38] Andolsen, "Agape in Feminist Ethics," 151.
[39] Plaskow, *Sex, Sin and Grace*, 3.   [40] Ibid., 151.

contrast, becomes self-sacrifice and self-denial. Plaskow argues that the virtue of sacrifice became linked closely to cultural definitions of femininity which women have internalized to such an extent that self-abnegation has become basic to women's experience. This association and internalization can be explained in terms of the division between public and private spheres; the fact that women are associated with the private, domestic sphere, where sacrifice is deemed more appropriate and necessary, means that women are socialized to practice this Christian virtue to their detriment. Plaskow maintains that the link between women's nature and the virtue of sacrifice has been supported by the myth of the "eternal feminine" nature of women, their passivity and closeness to nature. Thus, the feminist critique of a sacrificial agapic ethics is closely inter-related to criticism of the denigration of nature and the body found in some Christian thinkers (which I will address next) and criticisms of any claims about what is essential to the nature of women.

The argument that an agapic ethics is theoretically inadequate given women's experience is typically accompanied by the claim that it is dangerous and that its practice can mutilate the identity of and oppress women. Historically, femininity was identified with nature whereas masculinity was identified with spirit or culture. Ironically, this means both that women are deemed naturally more virtuous (because they are more passive and nurturing) and that women are devalued, even associated with evil. Thus women's sexuality, when linked to motherhood, is understood to make women more inclined to self-giving and care, while women's sexuality, when divorced from reproduction, is often rendered as seductive, manipulative, and, therefore, evil. This dualism need not be rehearsed here, but it is valuable to note the deep ambivalence within the Christian tradition regarding the essential nature of women.[41] Plaskow points out that women's sin is "in large measure a product of social, cultural forces. While each woman has to define her own relation to her culture's expectations and in this sense may be said

---

[41] Rosemary Radford Reuther's, *Sexism and God-Talk: Toward a Feminist Theology* (Boston, MA: Beacon, 1983) remains a good resource for this point. See especially chapter 7. See also Karl Stern, *The Flight from Woman* (New York: Farrar, Straus, and Giroux, 1965).

to freely affirm her cultural destiny, the horizon of her struggle with social expectations is set by her society; it provides a fixed range of choices."[42] For women within the Christian tradition, this horizon includes negative valuations of the self, the body, and nature. Moreover, when sin is understood as prideful self-assertion and virtue as self-sacrifice, and when such thinking has been the reasoning of male theologians, the sacrificial ethics which follows allows those in positions of power to oppress women and minorities.

Similarly, Beverly Wildung Harrison critiques the dualisms that have permeated the Christian tradition because they pose exclusive alternatives for moral behavior.[43] The opposition of self love and love for others, or pride and self-sacrifice, extends beyond a particular norm applicable to particular moral cases; as Harrison notes, the opposition correlates to the whole of Christian existence. While some feminists criticize the denigration of the self which lies at the heart of such a synecdoche but still allow an appropriate place for sacrifice in the moral life, others reject the virtue of sacrifice altogether. Harrison writes, for instance, in a critique of divine command ethics, "it is time to insist that the notion of 'obedience' itself is simply antithetical to what we mean by 'ethics' or 'the moral point of view.'"[44] Thus, she lodges the criticism of sacrificial agape within an overarching criticism of attitudes toward and valuations of the self.

Too many Christians, even of the progressive sort, still believe, in accord with male-stream Christian teaching, that an irresolvable theological and moral tension exists between self-assertive or self-interested acts (that is, those involved in the struggle for our/my liberation) and "loving" and "good" Christian acts. Nevertheless, we feminists maintain that radical Christian theology should be predicated on the assumption that there is no ontological split between self/other; there is no monolithic polarity of self-interested action versus other-regardingness. All people – each of us-in-relation-to-all – have a mandate, rooted in God, to the sort of self-assertion that grounds and confirms our dignity in relationship.

---

[42] Plaskow, *Sex, Sin and Grace*, 167. Plaskow is careful to note that sinful self-denial is not a flaw inherent in women by treating it as an aspect of women's experience as social experience, one constituted by the internalization of and reaction to and against definitions of femininity.

[43] Beverly Wildung Harrison, "Sexism and the Language of Christian Ethics," in *Making the Connections: Essays in Feminist Social Ethics*, ed., Carol S. Robb (Boston, MA: Beacon, 1985), 28.

[44] Ibid., 38.

Self-assertion is basic to our moral well-being. The human struggle for liberation is precisely the struggle to create material, spatial, and temporal conditions for all to enjoy centered, self-determined social existence.[45]

Harrison notes that Christian theological esteem for sacrifice is grounded on Christological formulations that she regards as masochistic; Jesus' self-immolation to please the Father set the paradigm for the Christian's response to Jesus.[46] She offers an alternative Christology wherein Jesus accepted sacrifice for the sake of radical love. The crucifixion of Jesus demonstrates that Jesus intended to make and sustain right relationships, even if the price for such reciprocity was his own life. Such radical love sets an example of solidarity and mutuality that requires a giving and receiving that masculinist Christianity does not teach. Harrison is emphatic:

Mark the point well: We are not called to practice the virtue of sacrifice. We are called to express, embody, share and celebrate the gift of life, and to pass it on! We are called to reach out, to deepen relationship, or to right wrong relations – those that deny, distort, or prevent human dignity from arising – as we recall each other into the power of personhood.[47]

Harrison notes, for example, that both otherworldly and world-denying spiritualities ought to be rejected as incompatible with women's experience. Women, she claims, are less cut off from the real than many in the Christian tradition would claim or wish. This connection indicates that women have been and are those who hold the power to build up persons and community. This power is rooted in embodiment. Harrison opposes the disinterested, detached, disembodied love ethics found in much of Christianity with a body-mediated, sensual, mutual understanding of love. A self-sacrificial understanding of agape has been understood as the pinnacle of Christian love, but such a reading of Christianity ignores a parallel emphasis in the tradition on mutuality and solidarity.

Rather than the passive, self-effacing love many Christian ethicists have urged, Harrison enjoins us to understand love as a mode of action. "We do not yet have a moral theology that teaches us the

45 Beverly Wildung Harrison, "Theological Reflection in the Struggle for Liberation," in *Making the Connections*, 241.
46 Ibid., 262.
47 Beverly Wildung Harrison, "The Power of Anger in the Work of Love," in *Making the Connections*, 19–20.

awe-full, awe-some truth that we have the power through acts of love or lovelessness literally to create one another."[48] For Harrison love is the "power to act-each-other-into-well-being."[49] In this regard, Harrison offers a representative feminist understanding of love as mutuality. Such an account is more compatible with the relationality and contextuality of the self and provides a vision of human flourishing which does not threaten to mutilate the self's identity. Harrison and Plaskow are both sensitive to the way a love ethics can commend a lifestyle in which the self dissipates itself into relations, roles, and commitments.

Difficulties in feminist approaches to self love

Theological ethical approaches to love have shifted in keeping with larger changes in Christian ethics, away from the divine–human relation and toward interpersonal relations. Along with this shift, Christian love ethics focus more on the nature of love than on theological moral anthropology. Feminist criticisms of the tradition replicate this focus; typically they offer either a redemption of eros or an alternative account of love, generally as mutuality. As a result, such feminist positions in fact reinforce the dichotomy established by the tradition between a self-sacrificing, disinterested love and a love that seeks reciprocity and the self's fulfillment thereby. Like other literature on self love, feminist treatments encounter problems because of their methodological focus on the nature of love and their conceptual correlation of self love with neighbor love rather than love for God. Moreover, these problems subsequently account for much of the literature's substance. Here I argue that the very concerns and features that mark feminist love ethics are undermined by this substantive and methodological focus on love rather than the lover. Specifically, this debate's methodological and substantive focus on love eclipses matters of moral anthropological import, and when coupled with false modesty about normative anthropologies, severs the question of how the self can love itself from the question of whether her acts and relations appropriately embody (or not) her desires, motives, and commitments. Let me

---

[48] Ibid., 11.   [49] Ibid.

note briefly several of those concerns and the way each stands in tension with the focus on love.

As we have seen, feminist love ethics reject the denigration of selves found in much of the tradition. It is the source of much self-loathing and of estrangement between human beings and creation, and those individuals who have been associated with creation (persons of color and women). Because this estrangement is often coupled with and warranted by accounts of human nature and ontological and moral dualisms, feminists countered it with versions of self-realization ethics that seek to liberate women (and for some, men as well) from such relations of domination and subjugation. Some feminists do so by emphasizing distinctly feminine virtues, such as care. Radical versions of this counter call women toward gender separatism, the formation of women-only communities and the creation of non-sexist customs, relations, and practices. Others argue that this amounts to a reversal (and therefore replication) of patterns of domination and subjugation. Regardless, feminist ethics share an appreciation for autonomous self-determination. Although some conservative feminists continue to look toward rather traditional understandings of women's nature, these "essentialist" ethics are outnumbered by, and themselves give some heed to, principled suspicion of such accounts. The result is that feminist emphases on self-determination are generally accompanied and furthered by the argument that no universal account of selfhood can be forwarded.

Thus, it seems that the liberation of women requires a certain moral subjectivism. This charge is important and merits some consideration. Susan Frank Parsons helpfully maps feminist ethics according to three paradigms, a liberal paradigm that takes its bearings from the Enlightenment, a social constructionist paradigm that includes both Marxist and postmodern varieties, and a naturalist paradigm. Parsons identifies a set of concerns that cut across all three paradigms, specifically, the problem of universalism in ethics, an emphasis on community as the site for redemptive relationships, and the question whether a gender-sensitive natural law ethics is possible. These concerns provide points of contact between secular and Christian feminists and, Parsons argues, can be furthered by work in Christian ethics. Parsons recognizes the special import of the universalism problem, especially as it is raised in debate over the relationship between feminism and postmodernism. Parsons notes that postmodernity's iconoclasm and its emphasis on the sheer diversity and particularity of persons simultaneously relativize ethical categories and initiate a properly moral prohibition of idolatry. Does an ethics of deconstruction leave us without any frameworks, categories, and theories? What then becomes of ethics? Is it reduced to moral triage? Parsons asks "whether women may do without some generalisations about themselves and their situations, and a framework in which these may be discussed, distinguished from one another, and evaluated. Without some theoretical perspective, and indeed some meta-narrative of justice, it is difficult to understand how conflicting interests can be balanced and alternative possibilities considered."[50] It is precisely because feminists set for themselves critical and reconstructive tasks that they must defend the possibility of ethics. And yet their hermeneutics of suspicion subordinates ethics to the sort of post-moral freedom to which Christ calls persons.

For this reason Parsons seems to favor a "nonfoundational realism" that consists in ongoing participation in political and moral debate.[51] The conversation itself becomes redemptive and its continued development helps to debunk potentially coercive pictures of community while (indeed *by*) allowing different voices to express themselves. Since the feminist quest for an appropriate universalism means that feminists are unwilling to abandon altogether the possibility of ethics, feminists remain committed to reflection on human flourishing. Yet, "there lie within feminist writings deep-seated suspicions about descriptions of human nature, of the meaning of the human body, and of the fulfillment for which humanity is intended."[52] This is because, as Nieztsche and Foucault argue, attempts to identify some origin or basis for identity fail to see that identity is created by institutions, discourses, and relations. On this count, the project of feminism seems to be the radical

[50] Susan Frank Parsons, *Feminism and Christian Ethics* (Cambridge: Cambridge University Press, 1996), 195.
[51] Ibid., 215.   [52] Ibid., 225.

deconstruction of normative accounts of human nature. As Lisa Cahill puts it, "in brief, we must liberate without saying what counts as liberation."[53] Cahill goes on to say that "the rhetoric of difference, when elevated to the level of a philosophical principle, can devitalize the cause of justice on behalf of those whom it was initially aimed to serve. It threatens to place the 'different' beyond the scope of one's own moral comprehension, concern and responsibility."[54] Given this risk, this deconstructive project may reintroduce a mind–body dualism by rooting resistance in some basic desire.[55] To be sure, feminist ethics appeal, often, to experience as a source and criterion for ethics. But increasing recognition of the particularity of experience across class, racial, and ethnic backgrounds makes experience less a substantive norm than a regulative one. That is, it is precisely because experiences are so particular that their normative weight demands cognizance of and respect for experiences that differ. Appeals to authenticity, to one's "true identity" become ever more immune from criticism when we eschew supposedly untenable and potentially tyrannous accounts of selfhood and celebrate the self's desire, often quite apart from asking whether certain forms, objects, or expressions of desire must be subject to ethical criticism. In this way, we undermine the concern to liberate selves. Desire is formed and shaped culturally, and particularly in a consumerist society is not always (or even often) an infallible compass for "finding oneself" or a surefire means for self-realization.

Indeed, as Nygren's rigorous agapic ethics shows, and as Outka remains aware, persons have an inexhaustible capacity for self-deception. So we cannot correct the tradition's denigration of the self and of eros with a norm of self-realization, be it under the banner of a celebrated eros or of mutuality. Granted, the feminist critique of sacrificial agape contributes the crucial insight that one can sin by failing to establish oneself as a self. But it does not follow that all efforts at self-realization are morally equal. Put differently, in their wariness of normative accounts of the self, feminist love ethics do not develop adequately criteria by which to evaluate morally

---

[53] Lisa Sowle Cahill, *Sex, Gender and Christian Ethics* (Cambridge: Cambridge University Press, 1996), 28.
[54] Ibid. [55] Parsons, *Feminism and Christian Ethics*, 232.

forms of self-realization, nor do they call into question the norm of self-realization itself.

In addition to affirming the self and advocating autonomous self-determination, many feminist ethicists seek to redefine love as reciprocal or mutual. Rather than require persons to love disinterestedly, feminist love ethics claim that a shared love promotes the good of both persons and realizes thereby the fullness of love. In fact the celebration of disinterested love is predicated on a false opposition between the self and other. Persons really are so inter-related that the good of one includes that of others. And yet, this properly anthropological claim stands in tension with the feminist focus on providing an alternative account of love. The opposition of agape and mutuality continues to posit false oppositions between God, self, and neighbor. In part, this is because love for God is left out of the self–neighbor equation. But it is also true that continued attention to the nature of love obscures the need for more anthropologically based analysis of the inter-relation of God, self, and neighbor. Moreover, both the redemption of eros and the replacement of sacrificial agape with mutuality reductively analyze love. Recall Beverly Harrison's emphatic opposition of mutuality and sacrifice. Just as a norm of sacrificial agape erroneously disregards the good of reciprocity as part of the fullness of love, mutuality likewise threatens to eclipse the role sacrifice plays. This becomes particularly risky, given the subjectivism of much feminist love ethics; if the norm of self-realization is to be replaced by a norm of right self love, the projects, pursuits, loves, and relations through which the self seeks to realize itself must be subject to moral evaluation.

I judge that feminist critiques often reductively analyze Christian love into either the sacrificial ethics which they reject, or into an ethics of mutuality which is itself problematic. When an ethics of mutuality is commended as a corrective to a sacrificial love ethics, and self-determination as a corrective to self-abnegation, several possible dangers ensue: (1) such an ethics might exclude anything that smacks of self-denial, sacrifice, or obedience even though these may be legitimate, even essential, elements of proper self-relation; (2) such an ethics might fail to grapple with the risk of idolatry, the wily character of self-deception, and the potential for efforts of self-realization actually to harm the self; and (3) such ethics err if they confine relation with God to a moment within or fruit of proper self-relation. That is, in the rightful concern to celebrate the concreteness of human embodiment, in their suspicion of eschato-logical escape-clauses or consolations, such ethics might neglect or reject the divine–human relation altogether, or confine it to some fruit of the struggle for justice or some resource for a this-worldly self-realization. In doing so they truncate the self by ignoring or diminishing the human capacity for self-transcendence.

This brings me to the final feature of feminist love ethics that I want to note, embodiment. Here again, the substantive and methodological focus on the nature of love thwarts or stands in tension with this feature. Feminist ethics typically criticize modern emphases on the rational subject for being disembodied. When subjectivity is disembodied it is divorced from the particularities of historical and cultural existence. It also devalues connative forms of knowledge and can result in or warrant dualisms of mind over body, male over female, among others. By contrast, an ethics that stresses embodiment values sensual and emotional forms of knowledge. Moreover, the feminist emphasis on embodiment calls attention to the fact that, as it is often put, "our bodies are ourselves."

And yet, because of the feminist suspicion of accounts of human nature, the concern for an embodied ethics is done a disservice. Fear of falling into physicalism or essentialist ethics has led many fem-inists towards voluntaristic ethics in which one's intention deter-mines the moral status of an act. The more reticent thinkers become to morally evaluate specific acts, the more disembodied their ethics threaten to become. Granted, embodiment ought not to be re-duced to distinct biological processes, nor an embodied ethics re-duced to the consideration of physical acts. Instead, moral reflection on our embodiment ought to attend to the sources of moral knowl-edge it yields and the daily practices and activities which comprise the bulk of our moral lives. But these legitimate concerns should not obstruct thinking about the relation between intention and the act itself (classically what is termed the object or matter of the act). Without due cognizance of this relation, it becomes impossible to assess if the actions and relations one undertakes really are ordered to the end one intends. Put differently, the person's identity becomes separated from her acting in the world and with others – her moral identity becomes fundamentally a matter of intentions that may or may not be embodied suitably in her actual conduct.

Self love and self-relation

In his earlier work, *Agape*, Gene Outka offers two reasons why self love might be reasonable and prudent. In doing so he helps to show the instability of arguments that self love is morally neutral and he lays the groundwork for a later essay in which he commends self love directly.[56] For Outka, love for God, the primary moral obligation, demands that we love as God loves, universally. This universal scope includes the self.[57]

While one can love oneself rightly, Outka tempers this optimism with a suspicion of the self, an "ineradicable unease."[58] Outka writes, "I am tempted incurably to make myself the center of existence, presuming to ignore or flout God, and doing injustice to my neighbors. This temptation is more than a weakness, susceptible to correction by human effort and learning. It is rather always potentially pernicious, giving no final peace in this life."[59] He adds, "inordinate self-assertion does pose the preeminent threat to the law of love."[60] While Outka contends that universal love is not a matter of calculation among duties, he nonetheless claims it allows a "practical swerve" away from concern for what the self owes itself and toward what the self owes the neighbor.[61]

Outka's suspicion of the self, however, is a more complex matter. In fact, he recognizes two equivalent dangers to which the self is susceptible; the self is given not only to the inordinate self-assertion of pride, but also to what Outka designates as sloth. Sloth refers to

---

[56] Gene Outka, "Universal Love and Impartiality," in *The Love Commandments: Essays in Christian Ethics and Moral Philosophy*, eds., Edmund N. Santurri and William Werpehowski (Washington DC: Georgetown University Press, 1992).

[57] This does not mean that the self ought to include itself in impartial calculations that seek to balance neighbor love with self love. Outka explores two sets of reasons why universal love is not coextensive with impartiality. Although one of the main tasks of the essay is to distinguish universal love from impartiality, that discussion lies outside the enterprise of this chapter except for the reason that, structurally speaking, there are some things which the self can only do for itself; this fact seems to carry some normative weight. I will take it up more closely in what follows.

[58] See Outka, "Universal Love and Impartiality," 82–84.

[59] Ibid., 82–83.   [60] Ibid., 83.   [61] Ibid., 82.

a range of activities and attitudes, such as torpor, passivity, directionless activity, all of which leave the self as indeterminate.[62] Pride and sloth are both forms of faithlessness to God:

> It is faithless for me to suppose in my pride that I objectively matter more than other persons. . . . It is likewise faithless for me to suppose in my sloth that God-relatedness obtains only for my neighbors and that I am to regard my particular life of obedient willing as of no account or to neglect the manner of existence given distinctly to me.[63]

In opposition to pride and sloth, to faithlessness, Outka understands proper self love in terms of obedient willing.[64] On Outka's account, the idea of obedient willing provides an argument on behalf of positive self love with a theocentric control. Obedient willing entails the surrender of natural self-assertion; the self is thereby transformed, "regained as created and addressed by God."[65]

Outka commends self love in part because of the basic likeness the self shares with the neighbor, in part because the self is included in the scope of universal love, and in part because of what he calls structural differences between the self and the neighbor. It simply is the case that, with respect to sheer capabilities, the self must perform certain duties toward itself. Structural differences

> point to an element of subjectivity we cannot eradicate. . . . I must do justice not only to the temptation to inordinate self-assertion, but also to the greater control I normally retain over my actions and refusals than I do over others'. To acknowledge that regions of responsibility accordingly differ is anything but an exercise in self-assertion. Rather, it supports the exhortation to look first at the evil within oneself.[66]

Outka looks to structural differences in order to affirm self love directly and links these structural differences to love for God. That is, an analysis of love governed his earlier work; but in this more recent position he expands and develops his attention to the lover.

---

[62] While Outka recognizes that both pride and sloth are sins, and that one is not a victim in sloth, but is rather complicit in one's "self-evacuation," he nevertheless resists reducing sloth to a form of pride (as Ramsey may be said to do). For Outka sloth includes distinct activities and attitudes which deserve attention in their own right. See ibid., 54.

[63] Ibid., 56.   [64] Here Outka echoes Ramsey.

[65] Outka, "University Love and Impartiality," 52.   [66] Ibid., 85.

Still, if the human exists in relation to and is created to respond to God, the nature of self love cannot depend only on structural self-responsibility, but must factor in theological anthropological claims. Let us turn, then, to another argument on behalf of positive self love, found in Edward Vacek, who develops his account of self love as part of a larger project which stresses the primacy of love for God.[67]

Vacek defines self love formally as a "matter of how we relate to ourselves."[68] As such, self love is an instance of what Vacek takes to be the "participative" character of all love. Self love denotes intra-individual participation. Right self love, as intra-individual participation, is a matter of rightly integrating the various dimensions of one's personality, both prepersonal dynamisms such as biological and psychological processes, and personal acts, which belong to the self's intellectual and religious dimensions. "Self love is not a matter of importing some external standard of goodness to hold over against our actual self, but rather the affirmation of the real self in its movement toward what it is not yet. In our love for ourselves, we become ever more aware not only of our own present goodness, but also of our incompleteness – we are not yet what we shall be."[69] Thus, even when specified as integration, Vacek's understanding of self love remains rather formal. While Vacek does indicate that this task of integration requires the person to engage her freedom, it is important to note that Vacek confines self-relation to categorical, or historical, activity. He explores various ways in which the self is related to itself in order to argue that acts are not selfish simply by virtue of being self-relating acts, and that the fullness of Christian life thus includes some consideration of the self. Vacek thereby avoids the earlier problems of collapsing the nature and moral evaluation of self love because he does not understand it as pernicious or acquisitive (or good) per definition. Vacek indicates that there are various forms of self love, each of which needs to be evaluated in its own right and balanced against other forms.

Vacek, in fact, identifies two basic types of self love: direct and indirect, or, respectively, agapic and erotic love for the self. In direct,

[67] Vacek, *Love, Human and Divine.*   [68] Ibid., 74.   [69] Ibid., 38.

agapic self love, the self loves itself for its own sake. In indirect, erotic self love, the self loves others for the sake of the self. Under these two basic types of self love fall various forms of self love, both proper and improper. Erotic self love can be an improper form of self love, or it can be a proper form. Moreover, agapic self love is not per definition morally legitimate, but can also be morally culpable. Thus, the categories of agapic and erotic self love remain rather formal in character. According to Vacek, the moral value of any particular instance of self love depends upon the conscious intention of the self. This is because that intention constitutes the meaning of a self-enacting action. According to Vacek,

consciousness is always "intentional," that is (1) someone's (2) consciousness of (3) something. Subject and object, or, in personal relations, subject and subject, are essentially related in and through the conscious act.... Subject, object, and conscious act require one another.[70]

In other words, the same objective act that the self performs toward itself can be differentiated morally according to the intention of the agent: a self-interested act could be selfish, or it could be self-affirming.

Having given a formal account of self love, Vacek seeks to provide right self love with a religious defense based on the basic phenomenological-theological argument which undergirds his project. According to Vacek, God first loves us and wants our good. We respond to God by accepting this love, and this acceptance includes acceptance of ourselves. This participative relation with God requires our cooperation. We should love ourselves as one way of cooperating with God's love for us. Hence, love for God may warrant self love, but self love does not coincide with love for God, i.e., Vacek does not say that we love ourselves when we love God.[71]

This is because for Vacek love consists in existential participation, whereby the lovers achieve a unity-in-difference: their union in love actually serves to differentiate them. Moreover, love refers to intentional movement; thus, Vacek rejects understandings of

---

[70] Ibid., 43. Vacek is correct to note that the agent's intention does impact the meaning of an act, but we need to remember that the intention does not exhaust the moral character of an act.

[71] I take it that this is the logic entailed in the classical commensuration of self love and love for God.

love which expand, say, love for a spouse into an affirmation of being in general. Rather, according to Vacek, love is directed to some particular object and is affected by it; one's conscious intention shapes the meaning of the love. This means that love for God and for neighbor cannot be collapsed. Although they are related to and lead to one another, when one loves a neighbor one is not necessarily intending to love God thereby. Moreover, it means that there is a distinctive form of Christian love, since the Christian stands within a tradition and intends something quite different than an atheist intends in loving. "The religious relation not only helps us to resee the world; it also adds a new dimension to what our acts mean. If . . . our acts are ways that we cooperate with God, then that cooperation is part of the very meaning of our acts."[72]

For Vacek love is an emotion, a cognitive act whereby one becomes conscious of value, is affected by it, and responds to it. Thus, to varying degrees, emotion engages human freedom and subjectivity, and the person can determine herself. Who one is shapes what one can love, but these loves also constitute who one is, particularly by liberating and expanding one's capacities to love.[73] In order to be conscious of value, affected by it and responsive to it, one must be open to value or goodness. This openness varies from one person to another, and one can foster openness or resist it. Vacek links this openness to value with moving closer to or away from God.[74] The Christian life, Christian love, is a matter of allowing one's relationship with God to become determinative of one's person.

Given his theory of love as participation, Vacek argues that the divine–human relationship has a history wherein both God and the human are affected; that is, the relationship brings something new

---

[72] Ibid., 3. Because I construe the structure of understanding differently than Vacek, I modify the role intention plays in self love. In my account the person's intention does not constitute love but mediates it. Love for one's spouse for instance can be a categorical mediation of a more unthematic love for God. Similarly, the intention to cooperate with God when we act mediates our self-understanding.

[73] Ibid., 63–65.

[74] Vacek writes, "In this expansion or contraction, people draw near to or they separate themselves from God." See ibid., 42.

into existence. It depends upon both God's freedom and human freedom. Though human freedom depends on God, Vacek nevertheless argues that human freedom codetermines God's involvement in the world.[75] Indeed, Vacek is at pains to show that the individual makes a distinctive, irreplaceable contribution to God's scheme of salvation.[76] While I do not share the process metaphysics which underlies Vacek's account, I take it that his position offers an insight which is crucial to a theory of right self love: if one takes seriously God's love for the person, one cannot denigrate the self in love for God, even though love for God stands as the primary love command. Put differently, the person's religious relation to God must be evaluated morally.

Vacek's position helps us to see the merit of turning to the self for an account of self love. But there are several ways in which his account fails to meet the needs of the contemporary problem of self love. Vacek's stress on intention as morally determinative of love cannot respond adequately to the problem of subjectivism, nor is it adequate in light of the person's self-relation. Vacek claims that the person's intention determines the moral character of self love in order to show that self-relation is not sinful per se, because he wants to understand love as both emotional and cognitive, and because he wants a divine–human relation in which both God and the human are affected. He makes conscious intentions determinative of the self's moral relation to itself and, thus, determinative of whether it is a proper or improper self love. Vacek seems to confine the nature of self love to those conscious intentions; even though his account of love rests on anthropological claims about love as participative, for Vacek self love consists in self-referential actions, some of which engage prepersonal dynamisms. That is why he breaks self love down into direct and indirect forms that are, strictly speaking, both forms of self-relation. This invites subjectivism and voluntarism and implies that concrete actions and relations are malleable enough to take their moral meaning from intention alone. Thus, and ironically, self love floats strangely free from the concrete actions and relations in which the self takes up its relation to itself.

[75] Ibid., 26.   [76] See ibid., 104–05.

TOWARD AN ACCOUNT OF RIGHT SELF LOVE

In Chapter One I detailed the complex inter-relations of various trends and claims in philosophy, theology, ethics, and contemporary culture which comprise challenges to normative accounts of selfhood. Here I sought to show that the available theories of self love, for and against, yield many important insights, but finally pose the contemporary problem of self love as much as speak to it. An adequate account of self love must begin with the self, that is, with a moral anthropology. This is best accomplished by reformulating the very ontological frameworks that our contemporary moral outlook rejects. To be certain, such reformulations must incorporate and extend the insights that drive challenges to those conceptual frameworks. These frameworks offer means with which to combat the subjectivism that attends the norm of self-realization and resources for developing more sophisticated moral anthropologies; indeed, they yield anthropologies that are truer. Why? Because morality is rooted in being and because the parameters of moral choice are found in the structures of being. This relation is not direct or ahistorical. Rather, the dialectical relation between being and thinking, which I noted at the outset of this book, means that critical reflection on experience can orient thinking by disclosing basic human needs and aspirations, and goods that correspond to them. Lisa Sowle Cahill notes that feminist and postmodern deconstructions allow values like autonomy "to slide in as tacit universals, operative without intercultural nuancing or explicit defense."[77] While these values are important to the experience of being a self, they certainly do not exhaust the experience and value of agency. Cahill argues for the relative invariance of the body through history and across cultures and identifies a number of shared bodily experiences that offer reliable yet revisable grounds for moral dialogue and critique. She places herself among other scholars (religious and philosophical) who appreciate the Aristotelian–Thomistic tradition and share the conviction that "all cultural differentiations have at their core a shared human way of being in the world, one closely linked to our bodily nature; to our abilities to reflect, to choose, and

---

[77] Cahill, *Sex, Gender and Christian Ethics*, 2.

to love; and to our intrinsic dependence on a community of other human beings, not only for survival, but also for meaning."[78] I join Cahill and these others but seek to develop the relation between bodiliness and consciousness at greater length and in the service of the contemporary need for an account of right self love.

One way to recoup the language of being while avoiding the difficulties of classical and scholastic metaphysical frameworks is to construe subjectivity hermeneutically. The activity of understanding is central to what it means to be human, and to what it means to be a moral creature. In light of this insight, the elaborate ontological frameworks crafted by some thinkers are heuristic devices that fund reflection on the relation between being and our thinking about it. With this in mind, I develop in this book a hermeneutical account of self-relation by developing the interpretive character of the conceptual language of being.

It is my basic thesis that right self love designates a mode of being in which the self determines itself in a response to God that is actualized in but not exhausted by neighbor love. Right self love is the person's self-determining response to God. This claim retrieves insights from classical accounts of the divine–human relation, particularly the claim that God is the highest good and the good of the human as such. It corrects contemporary ethics which neglect or deny the religious character of the human and the religious dimension of the moral life, and provides one of two controlling criteria for self love: love for God. Because self-relation can take proper or pernicious forms, love for God provides a way to assess morally the person's self-relation. The person's flourishing resides in a way of being which is evaluated with reference to something that transcends the self in power, meaning, and worth. In other words, as a controlling criterion for self love, love for God identifies false and destructive forms of self-relation and lends coherence to the person who loves. However, this response can only be actualized and assessed in the achievement of identity, that is, in the person's concrete actions and relations. This claim incorporates and extends feminist and (post) modern critiques of traditional accounts and provides a second criterion for self love: neighbor love. Self love, as

[78] Ibid., 51.

a mode of being in relation with God, must be made concrete in the categorical or historical actions and relations of the person. And the self can only establish and determine herself as a self in history and in relations with others. But, self love is not exhausted by neighbor love. Thus, while self-sacrifice has an appropriate place within an account of both self love and neighbor love, it is not some middle term which makes the two co-extensive. Self love entails love for God, but love for God is only assessed in neighbor love; thus the person's religious relation to God is subject to moral evaluation.

CONCLUSION

This chapter builds on the previous one to show that a contemporary account of self love requires a return to the classical love synthesis and a retrieval of conceptual frameworks of being. Various secular, postmodern, and feminist challenges to that synthesis and those frameworks help to set parameters for a contemporary account of self love, and the available theories of self love help to identify the needs and concerns a contemporary account of self love must address. Let us turn, in the following chapter of this book, to crafting a moral anthropology centered on the dynamic structure of self-awareness. Such an account does not begin soteriologically or even theologically, but rather, existentially. This existential starting point will allow me to argue that the person's self-understanding provides the mediating structure for the divine–human relation. By shifting the center of gravity from love, or from God as the lover, to the person who loves, it will be possible to retrieve classical insights, extend modern critiques, and amend contemporary self-realization ethics.

CHAPTER 3

A hermeneutical account of self-relation

Self love is not first and foremost about the self's interests vis-à-vis her neighbor's. It is a more fundamental problem of proper self-relation. An ethics of right self love, then, requires rich normative anthropologies. Yet as the first two chapters showed, such anthropologies face important challenges. This chapter begins to argue for a particular approach to moral anthropology, a hermeneutical account of self-relation. It insists that the basic activity of self-understanding or interpretation is central to self-relation. In this way the approach accommodates and fruitfully relates key insights of theological and contemporary secular approaches to the self. Theologically it is faithful to the claim that God is closer to us than we are to ourselves. Self-relation reverberates within the self's relation to God. Yet a hermeneutical approach also recognizes that human beings construct systems of meaning to orient themselves in the world. These systems include claims about God. For this reason, I begin with some comments about self-understanding and self-relation and then develop them in a constructive theological manner by engaging the work of Karl Rahner and Paul Tillich. Specifically, this chapter argues: (1) that the person is created in relation with God, (2) that the person's self-determination constitutes a response to God, and (3) that this relation and response are best characterized in terms of love. In doing so this chapter initiates an interpretive or hermeneutical account of self-relation and argues that self-relation is reflexive, embodied, and interpretive.

By proceeding in this way I do not mean to imply that philosophical anthropology provides the foundation for Christian ethics. This would deny or compromise the sovereignty of God and the unique role of Jesus Christ. It also risks the integrity of theological discourse, as though theology plays handmaiden to other ways of describing and explaining reality and has, at best, a utilitarian value.[1] Rather, this way of proceeding honors the Christian claim that God's self-disclosure (in Jesus Christ) is not alien to what and how human beings come to know anything that is true. Put in classical theological language: grace perfects nature. Moreover, the turn to self-understanding does not make the reality of God something to be shown or established (although there is no shortage of proofs that proceed this way). My concern is to take up Augustine's insight that God is "more inward than my most inward part and higher than the highest element within me."[2] More intimate than my self-presence is the presence of God. Hence, as Augustine confessed to God, "what I know of myself I know because you grant me light."[3]

Still, Charles Taylor notes that for Augustine "to focus on my own thinking activity is to bring to attention not only the order of things in the cosmos which I seek to *find* but also the order which I *make* as I struggle to plumb the depths of memory and discern my true being."[4] In this spirit this chapter recasts the problem of self love more broadly than Christian ethics has been wont to do and retrieves and reworks ontologically grounded accounts of the self that philosophical and Christian ethicists alike avoid. The chapter gives theological and moral content to its hermeneutical account of self-relation by stressing (in Augustinian and Thomistic style) that the self is created to love God, to know the truth and to live in communion with others, and by arguing for embodied integrity as the good that characterizes right self love.

SELF LOVE AND SELF-UNDERSTANDING

If, as I argued in the previous chapter, a contemporary account of self love should begin not with love but with the self, this account

---

[1] Alistair McFadyen offers an intriguing argument about the integrity of theology as an explanatory discourse. See his *Bound to Sin: Abuse, Holocaust and the Christian Doctrine of Sin* (Cambridge: Cambridge University Press, 2000).

[2] St. Augustine, *Confessions*, trans. Henry Chadwick (Oxford: Oxford University Press, 1991), 43.

[3] Ibid., 182.

[4] Charles Taylor, *Sources of the Self: the Making of the Modern Identity* (Cambridge, MA: Harvard University Press, 1989), 141.

begins with the fact that human beings ask about the meaning of their lives and seek to orient and guide them. Self love is more than an object of ethical inquiry. It captures the breadth and depth of the moral life. What ought I do? What should I seek? Who am I? Who do others say that I am? Who do I want to be? These questions ramify throughout our lives. They cannot be separated from one another (as much as proceduralist ethicists might wish) nor can they be confined to spheres of our lives (like our interpersonal, domestic relations) or to aspects of our selves (e.g., religious beliefs, nicely segregated from our professional personas). They are variations on the fundamental question "How should I live?" This question presupposes that there are myriad ways of being in the world; some are more worthy than others; to some extent I am free and responsible for deciding how to live; how I live at present is in some respects not right or good. Further, the question "How should I live?" is asked (sometimes in despair, sometimes in hope) in light of a personal history, one given and dictated, also chosen and made, ever arising in and ever eluding our attempts to make sense of, deny, or embrace it. The question "How should I live?" is also asked in a particular social and historical space, in a web of relations. We are presented with various ways of being in the world, schooled in them by parents, teachers, peers, communities, and institutions, by the arts, popular culture, advertising media. This schooling sends conflicting messages, that some ways of being are better than others ("better" meaning anything from more worthy, to more satisfying, to more fun) and that these various ways are more or less equally valid and so are matters of personal preference, means, and abilities (and so "better" here means "better *if you so choose.*")

Our moral being in the world and our moral thinking are dialectically related. As I argued in the first chapter, various features of the contemporary moral outlook prompt the question of how morally to construe self-relation and how to understand the self who is to be realized. Significant contemporary secular accounts threaten to truncate the self by denying its transcendence or reducing the self into that which determines her. Ethics arises out of the experience of moral conflict, our sense that neither we nor the world is exactly as it should be. Our lives are marked by plurality and tension, joy and disappointment; we experience our own agency yet experience ourselves as determined and limited by other people and systems. Indeed, we can experience our own freedom in the form of self-limitation as we make choices which close off other possibilities, and do things which, for better or worse, we cannot undo. In the midst of this we ask about the meaning of our lives, and struggle to integrate this plurality of goods and ills, of freedom and determination. Since the aspiration for coherence entails at least an implicit affirmation of oneself the pressing moral question is not, as existentialists suggest, how to affirm the value of life under the threat of its negation but how to be a coherent self. An adequate account of self love must take seriously the person's aspirations for coherence, integrity, and identity by constructing a framework for understanding the self. To recognize these two needs is to inquire into the relation between moral being and our thinking about it.[5]

We can identify the dynamic relations between moral being and moral thinking and the way self-relation unfolds and is wrought in relation to something other than the self by turning to recent work in philosophical hermeneutics and Christian ethics.

Moral being and moral consciousness

Recent work in philosophical hermeneutics provides means with which to appropriate conceptual frameworks of being (like those found in Rahner and Tillich) and to respond to the difficulties these

---

[5] The structure and method of my argument delve into this relation between moral being and moral thinking. By beginning an account of self love with an analysis of moral being, I mean to proceed via a method which the problem itself warrants. At the same time, however, this book implies a Christian ethical method that applies beyond the problem of self love. It implies a position about what kind of thinking Christian ethics entails, and, thereby, suggests in what the discipline of Christian ethics consists. I divide the book into an examination of self love as a moral problem and as a moral principle. This division suggests that Christian ethics requires, on the one hand, that we generate normative accounts of the moral life which are adequate to and build off of an interpretation of our moral situation and of our selves as moral agents, and, on the other hand, that such interpretive and normative enterprises must serve and be tested by practical needs and meta-ethical demands. The division is not meant to suggest that such activities may be demarcated sharply from one another. Rather, it indicates the circular shape of Christian ethical thinking: human thinking about our way of being in the world involves us in thinking about ourselves as beings who can and do engage in such thinking.

often entail. Ancient forms of hermeneutics focused on interpretation, especially of written texts, but at least since Schleiermacher hermeneutics has broadened its scope; contemporary hermeneutics addresses the question of meaning and the shape of historical and linguistic consciousness. As William Schweiker notes, hermeneutics "connects insights from classical practical philosophy with those of reflexive thinking found in ancient and modern thought. As a form of reflexive thinking, hermeneutics explicates the truth of consciousness becoming aware of itself; we are *self-interpreting animals*. As a type of practical philosophy, hermeneutics insists that understanding and meaning are bound to action and practice."[6] In contemporary hermeneutics, then, meaning designates an event of connection – ideas and experiences interact and present, as Paul Ricoeur puts it, a "world." Against the claims of some postmodernists, meaning is not reducible to signs or empirical perceptions, though of course these are constitutive features of meaning. Meaning designates a domain or space, one we inhabit, into which (by virtue of our socio-historical location) we are thrown, but also one we fashion and furnish. We exercise our agency *within* such spaces and *on* them. Hans-Georg Gadamer notes the practical import of this account of meaning; meaning involves the interaction of self and other in the creation of a space of significance for the sake of orienting action. This space of significance is not neutral; rather, as Charles Taylor and Iris Murdoch argue, it is a space in which we make distinctions of worth. Contemporary hermeneutics, then, links moral anthropology to a theory of value (axiology). Because hermeneutics connects reflexive thinking to practical philosophy it is necessary to specify the anthropological-axiological link in an account of the moral good and an imperative for action (Chapter Four), to explore the exercise of agency in the choice(s) of particular goods and vis-à-vis moral norms (Chapter Five), and to validate these claims (Chapter Six).

Two particular points should be noted. First, we should note the important hermeneutical insight that the relation of self and other is inscribed in, indeed, is constitutive of, consciousness. Acts of

[6] William Schweiker, "Understanding Moral Meanings," in *Power, Value and Conviction: Theological Ethics in the Postmodern Age* (Cleveland, OH: Pilgrim, 1998), 76.

meaning-making testify to an other that is irreducible and therefore presents some claim upon the self. Contemporary thinkers identify this other and this encounter in a variety of ways. My point is that this hermeneutical claim helps us respond to and offset the individualism and subjectivism that dog conceptual frameworks that are indebted to substance metaphysics. It thereby allows us to appropriate and improve on classical and modern theological and moral anthropologies.

Second, and related to the inscription of self/other in consciousness, the practical import of a hermeneutical approach suggests that love for God and neighbor serve as controlling criteria for self-realization. This chapter will argue that the person's response to God is best understood as love for God or its opposite. Love for God is a criterion for self love because the person's flourishing as such is keyed to right relation to God. The self truly loves herself when she loves God. Thus, love for God can shed light on what proper self-relation entails. A second criterion for self-realization is love for neighbor. As the next chapter will explore, because the person is fundamentally social and insofar as freedom is correlated with responsibility, the person's flourishing requires right relation to other persons.

William Schweiker points at the connection between reflexive thinking and practical philosophy in his ethics of responsibility. A brief look at his argument will illustrate the contributions philosophical hermeneutics can make to theological anthropology and suggest the contribution a theological perspective makes to secular ethics. Schweiker's use of philosophical hermeneutics prompts him to describe the moral life in terms of the practice of radical interpretation. "Radical interpretation is reflective, critical inquiry aimed at the question of what has constituted our lives in terms of what we care about and what ought to guide our lives under the demand of respect for others. It is the form conscience takes in the lives of social, linguistic, self-interpreting agents."[7] According to Schweiker, goodness is not perceived in the same way that things in the world are perceived; rather, we perceive goodness in light of

---

[7] William Schweiker, *Responsibility and Christian Ethics* (Cambridge: Cambridge University Press, 1995), 176.

what endows existence with worth. Further, linguistic and symbolic resources mediate our sense of the non-instrumental value of the world, others, and ourselves; they transform our understanding, confer our identity, and orient our acting.

Schweiker defines radical interpretation as "the testing and transformation of the values and norms a person or community endorses as important to its life by some event, idea, or symbol which deepens the sense of responsibility, that is, the sense that the integrity of life ought to be respected and enhanced."[8] Schweiker's theory of radical interpretation involves a modification of Charles Taylor's claim that strong evaluation is constitutive of being a moral agent. He supplements Taylor's emphasis on evaluation by insisting on the importance of interpretation, that is, the need to explicate the relation between self and other. This expands the moral life beyond private decisions about what to care about because moral self-criticism is demanded of us and empowered by something other than us. Interpretation binds our cares to respect for others as such. Moreover, radical interpretation ought to employ theological claims, because the name of God symbolizes the transvaluation of ultimate power in an affirmation of the worth of finite reality. "Understanding ourselves through the name of God has the effect ... of binding our power as self-understanding agents to specific norms that concern the recognition, respect, and well-being of finite life."[9] So, "the knowledge of the worth and dignity of others and ourselves is grasped through an interpretive act of understanding life from a theological perspective."[10] Schweiker argues that radical interpretation binds us towards acting in ways that respect others and the world. He may seem a bit too sanguine on this point. Why such a sure link between understanding and action? Radical interpretation identifies the springs of moral action not in terms of our interests or evaluations, but understanding. Radical interpretation is an act of self-criticism that transforms a condition for acting (what we care about) through recognizing "a good that grounds the moral life and ought to be respected in all our actions."[11] The identification of non-instrumental value issues in an imperative for acting.

[8] Ibid., 159.   [9] Schweiker, "Understanding Moral Meanings," 96.
[10] Ibid.   [11] Ibid., 101.

A contemporary ethics of self love requires some amendments of Schweiker's theory of radical interpretation, in large part because an ethics of self love amplifies certain aspects of moral anthropology and certain questions in moral theory beyond Schweiker's consideration of them. Thus, for a contemporary ethics of self love, one difficulty with radical interpretation is its relatively disembodied character. To be fair, Schweiker builds the theory out of an anthropological-axiological argument that identifies bodily, social and reflective dimensions of human existence. Human needs and goods that correspond to them are basic to our apprehension of value. Yet radical interpretation seems to be a rather cerebral praxis issuing in an affective transformation and orienting future action. The practice of radical interpretation could be described in more embodied and social forms. Schweiker argues that care and respect are both morally basic, but the account of radical interpretation at least makes reflection prior to affection. His theory could provide further for the cognitive import of our emotions. Further, the practical character of radical interpretation could be specified not only in terms of orienting future action, but reckoning with the empirical, historical, and moral significance of past action. Christian ethics has construed conscience as antecedent and consequent to acting. Admittedly, a misdeed or event could prompt the practice of radical interpretation, but what is missing from Schweiker's theory is fuller recognition that this practice is undertaken by embodied agents. This would mean that radical interpretation affects not only one's present identity and orients future action but that it reworks the meaning of one's personal history as well. For example, radical interpretation can illuminate the truth of our past; we may come to see that our account of a failed relationship was self-serving, or that we have been in denial about an addiction, or blind to our own talents and aspirations. This is why right self love is characterized by embodied integrity. We take up our self-relation in our concrete acts and relations. These can spark the practice of radical interpretation, can be objects of it, and can provide insight that informs it. I will return to this argument in the following chapters but some of these points can be noted now with a look at how some Christian ethicists explore the dialectical relation of being and thinking under the rubric of practical reason.

Self love and practical reason

Various theories of practical reason indicate the profound inter-relation of moral anthropology, axiologies, and concepts of morality or ethics. Lisa Cahill seeks to renew the Aristotelian–Thomistic account of practical reason along more embodied, social, and historically sensitive lines. She argues that practice yields knowledge, knowledge that can bridge moral concepts/claims and concrete experiences, needs, and goods. Practical reason "can facilitate the move from *theoretical* equality or universality to the concrete, effective means necessary to equalize social *participation*."[12] Jean Porter argues that like most empirical concepts, morality can only be understood in terms of a formal element that is revealed by reflecting on paradigmatic examples of morality. Basic moral notions emerge and exemplify morality as a general concept. Yet, our understanding of such concepts is not exclusively verbal – it is also manifest in appropriate action with respect to that which a given concept designates. For instance, Porter notes that she may be unable to define a tree in precise scientific terms, but her knowledge of what a tree is is nonetheless evident in the fact that she waters and fertilizes them. Hence, for Porter, practical reason provides a way beyond moral skepticism and anti-realism, but also a way to recover the place of human flourishing in ethics against ongoing moral attempts to excise it. Drawing on Thomas Aquinas, Porter identifies the proper functioning of practical reason as the virtue of prudence, which is part of a set of virtues that offer a "program for action for all those who want to grow in personal goodness. It offers a criterion for truly virtuous action, and it suggests a way of reflecting on our acts in the light of the context set by the ordered ideals of the cardinal virtues. This process, in turn, sets up its own dialectic of action and reflection, which is self-corrective and expansive . . . the person of prudence is someone whose life displays this pattern of self-corrective reflection."[13] Porter notes rightly that this implies a

---

[12] Lisa Sowle Cahill, *Sex, Gender and Christian Ethics* (Cambridge: Cambridge University Press, 1996), 39.

[13] Jean Porter, *Moral Action and Christian Ethics* (Cambridge: Cambridge University Press, 1995), 165. See also Jean Porter, *The Recovery of Virtue* (Louisville, KY: Westminster/John Knox, 1990).

theory of action whereby good human actions perfect the agent's powers and capacities and are performed in accordance with right reason.

John Finnis offers a different account of practical reason. Finnis wants to clarify the way(s) in which ethics is practical. In an obvious, pedestrian sense ethics is practical because it concerns human actions. But the primary and crucial way that ethics is practical is "because my choosing and acting and living in a certain sort of way (and thus my becoming a certain sort of person . . .) is not a secondary (albeit inseparable and welcome) objective and side-effect of success in the intellectual enterprise; rather it is *the very objective primarily envisaged* as well as the subject-matter about which I hope to be able to affirm true propositions."[14] Finnis's thesis is that "one's primary understanding of human good, and of what it is worthwhile for human beings to seek to do, to get, to have and to be, is attained when one is considering what it would be good, worthwhile to do, to get, to have and to be – i.e., by definition, when one is thinking practically."[15] Practical reason is practical because it identifies actions or objects as good, as desirable to get, have, do, or be. It does so as a prelude to pursuing these actions or objects. The point of practical reason is to pursue them intelligently. Thus, says Finnis, if one is asked to provide reasons for a particular action, implicitly or explicitly an intelligible answer to the question "What for?" displays one's action as a participation in, a way of realizing, one of the basic goods of human existence.[16]

All three accounts of practical reason respond to skepticism about human flourishing – attempts to remove it from the domain of ethics (i.e., to demarcate the domain of ethics more narrowly), to denials of any historical and cultural stability that grounds a picture of human flourishing in any foundational sense. Finnis's argument moves in the reverse direction of Cahill's and Porter's. Cahill begins with critical reflection on bodily experiences, needs and corresponding goods. This provides a relatively stable basis from which we can form judgments about human flourishing and on which we can ground moral arguments. Porter begins with the social praxis of practical reason; the use of moral concepts in discourse and in

---

[14] John Finnis, *Fundamentals of Ethics* (Washington DC: Georgetown University Press, 1983), 3.
[15] Ibid., 12.   [16] Ibid., 36.

action depends on some consensus about them, which can help to guide us through disagreements and in making moral decisions. This dialectic of action and reflection ought to be self-corrective and ought to characterize our lives. Finnis, however, begins with an account of practical reason and from this identifies the goods of human existence, an idea of human nature that accords with them and with the good of practical reasonableness.

I am not interested in adjudicating these theories of practical reason. They are offered in the service of argumentative agendas to which I cannot here attend.[17] But they do contribute insights into the dialectical relation of being and thinking that are important for a contemporary ethics of self love. Porter and Schweiker point to the social, linguistic and historical mediation of self-relation and of the self's encounter with others in the world. Cahill stresses the embodied character of these encounters and relations. Finnis emphasizes the participative character of thinking about and making moral choices. And Porter notes the analogical character of moral concepts given the dialectical relation of action and reflection. These insights echo in an account of self-relation as reflexive, embodied, and interpretive.

THE SELF

My thesis is that right self love designates a morally proper form of self-relation characterized by the moral good of embodied integrity and governed by the moral norms of love for God and neighbor. Integrity consists in a true self-understanding embodied in one's acts and relations with others and in the world. Right self love will look different in particular lives because of the particularity of persons. We can say, however, that this true self-understanding will include honesty about one's strengths and talents, one's vices and faults, one's needs and wounds and cares. Right self love includes a strong sense of oneself that in its very strength is vulnerable; it is a self-acceptance which is not exculpatory or conditioned on becoming better, which takes the courageous risk of being oneself without recourse to self-justification or self-congratulation, a willingness to

---

[17] For example Finnis argues against the so-called proportionalists among Roman Catholic ethicists.

venture oneself knowing that one will "get it wrong," hoping and trusting that the venture itself is an act of love. One embodies this true self-understanding in acts and relations that do not evade the risk, dull the pain, or underestimate the joy of being oneself, acts and relations that are ordered to and expressive of the self's inherent, non-instrumental goodness as a creature loved by and made to love God, acts and relations undertaken and characterized by care and respect for others, justice and honesty, mercy and peace-ableness. Since the moral good is *embodied* integrity, accounts of self love in particular and moral anthropology in general must provide for the moral evaluation of particular acts and relations. This does not deny the appropriate place and status of the affections or emo-tions; it affirms their cognitive import but also links them to concrete actions and relations. Unless we can identify whether particular acts and relations are incompatible with our authentic good, right self love is impossible. Moreover, love for God and neighbor are likewise threatened. To speak of an authentic human good no doubt sets off various alarms. Who is to determine in what the human good consists? How will such accounts be used? What power relations will they effect? These are legitimate and indispensable questions. Any account of the human good must reckon with its cultural and historical character and its uses must be subject to criticism. But, false modesty in this regard can do more harm than good.[18] This in turn allows us to explore a set of questions that center on the status of explicit faith in self love and in (Christian) ethics more generally.

The very fact that self love is an object of moral and ethical reflection provides direction for an account of the self who is to love herself. To begin, ethical inquiry into self love indicates the basic fact that human beings are self-interpreting creatures. What we undertake and undergo affects our self-understanding. In turn, how we understand ourselves in the world orients our acting in it. Human beings ask about the meaning of their lives and seek to orient them around various needs and goods, obligations, and commitments. So an account of right self love can take direction from the fact that we are creatures capable of thinking about our

---

[18] Given my sympathies with natural law, I judge that critical reflection on basic human needs and the goods that correspond to them can fund an account of the human good.

selves and about what we care about. Indeed, such thinking points to the deep connections between our cognitive and connative dimensions. From the beginning, then, before we need concern ourselves with selfishness or selflessness, the very fact that we can think about self love brings to the fore the possibility of various forms of self-relation and the central role our self-interpretation plays with respect to them.[19]

Self-interpretation, then, provides a key to self-relation. To be sure, there are more and less elaborate forms of self-interpretation, activities of "navel-gazing" as might be found in the practices of journal-keeping, therapy, even new year's resolutions. These all involve some deliberate reflection on the life the self wishes to live, the self she wishes to be, in contrast with what is. In less explicit ways, we interpret the events around us, even the minutiae of our lives and world, in simple decision-making. By claiming, however, that self-relation is understood helpfully in terms of self-interpretation, I do not mean to suggest that our self-relation (whether praise- or blame-worthy) is reducible to how we feel about ourselves, though of course self-relation has affective dimensions. Admittedly, an emphasis on self-interpretation seems to invite dreadful "I gotta be me" forms of self-rationalization. But the connection between self-relation and relation to God means that a realist ethics of self love is necessary, and the self's inter-subjectivity means that ethics cannot allow for such privatized appeals. Given all this, I want to consider

---

[19] My point is not only that we can be related to ourselves in better and worse forms but that we have a certain versatility in this regard. In other words, if we are to speak of self love not simply as a moral problem to be overcome (and overcome only by grace) but as a moral ideal to be lived (and lived only by grace) we must allow the possibility of moral change and development. We reflect morally on self love because we are capable of understanding ourselves, of revising our self-understanding, and of being in the world differently thereby. Put differently, in our self-interpretation we can transcend our selves and our environment and consider alternative ways of being in the world. Indeed, the very fact of self-relation hinges on the human capacity for self-transcendence – we can transcend ourselves morally to the extent that we can subject ourselves, subject even our self-awareness, to our own critical reflection. Thinkers differ wildly over the possibility and potential degree of moral change, as well as the role human effort can or cannot play in effecting such change. To some extent, differences can be characterized along Roman Catholic and Protestant lines. My argument in Chapter Five bears on the problem of moral change because it couples an appreciation for human agency with an emphasis on self-acceptance in the divine. This self-acceptance is, to use Paul Tillich's words, the acceptance that we have been accepted though we are unacceptable. See Tillich's *Morality and Beyond* (Louisville, KY: Westminster/John Knox, 1995).

the import of three modest claims about self-relation – that it is reflexive, embodied, and interpretive.

Many thinkers have noted that our self-awareness discloses an awareness of what is other than us. Some thinkers explore the connections between knowledge of self and knowledge of God by means of transcendental reflection or ontological analysis. Karl Rahner claims that the person is a question to herself; in asking about herself she already knows something of the answer. Indeed, in our acts of knowledge and especially in our experiences of freedom and love, we affirm more than the object of our knowledge or love – we affirm the horizon that encompasses both knower and known, lover and beloved. We call this horizon God. Because God is the condition for the possibility of our freedom and love, and is the horizon that gives intelligibility to everything that is, we know ourselves – and everything else – in the divine. Paul Tillich also claimed that our self-awareness points to that which exceeds it in power and meaning. "Man is the question he asks about himself, before any question has been formulated. . . . Being human means asking the questions of one's own being and living under the impact of the answers given to this question. And, conversely, being human means receiving answers to the question of one's own being and asking questions under the impact of the answers."[20] The human participates in the structure of being, like everything else that is, but unlike other beings he is immediately aware of the structure. Tillich designates this structure as self and world – the person's self-relation is mediated through his world, and yet, as a self, he can transcend environment and have a world.

Other thinkers explore the connections between knowledge of self and knowledge of God not by considering the conditions for the possibility of reason, but the centrality of value to our experience of ourselves.[21] As we have seen, several contemporary philosophers do this. Iris Murdoch insists that ethics requires empiricism in addition to metaphysics because our immediate moral instincts cannot be altogether encapsulated in abstract formulations.[22] For

---

[20] Paul Tillich, *Systematic Theology* 3 vols. (Chicago: University of Chicago, 1951–63), vol. 1, 62.

[21] It would be interesting to revisit classical and medieval debates about the priority of being or good in light of these options.

[22] See Iris Murdoch, *Metaphysics as a Guide to Morals* (New York: Allen Lane/Penguin Press, 1993).

Murdoch consciousness is a moral domain and as such is central
to what it means to be human; consciousness perceives and makes
discriminations among value according to the principle/reality of
Good. Harry Frankfurt argues that "second-order" desires and volitions constitute the self; they are the desires and volitions that
we *want* to define us.[23] Similarly, Charles Taylor argues that such a
"radical evaluation" shows that we are valuing and self-interpreting
creatures.[24] Schweiker offers a theological response to and refor-
mulation of these positions in his approach to conscience as "radical
interpretation."

Because these thinkers note the dynamic relation between knowledge of ourselves and knowledge of an other – the ground of
being, the source of value – they join thinkers throughout the
Christian tradition, including Augustine, Calvin, Kierkegaard and
Schleiermacher, who recognize that subjectivity is reflexive. Put
theologically, to endeavor to understand ourselves is to grasp ourselves in relation to the divine. Therefore, to inquire into the problem of proper self-relation is simultaneously to inquire into the
problem of proper relation to God. This point is important because it means that self-realization is not reducible to the self's
subjective preferences. Of course, thinkers like Freud, Nietzsche,
Marx, and Derrida express suspicion of this reflexive turn, and
rightly so. The connection between self-awareness and awareness
of God is neither immediate nor free of distortions. For this reason,
I will argue that right self love encompasses both truthfulness in
self-understanding and the coherence of our actions and relations
with this truth (i.e., embodied integrity). To make this argument
brings me to the embodied character of self-relation.

Recognizing the embodied character of self-relation brings two
important points to the fore. Embodiment captures both the bodily location of the self and the social-historical-cultural-discursive
location and formation of the self. These points may seem fairly
obvious, though they have been and are contested by some. Recall the comments of those who claim the personas and lives they
assume in cyberspace are more real than "real life." Consider the

[23] Harry Frankfurt, *The Importance of what We Care About* (Cambridge: Cambridge University Press, 1988).
[24] See Taylor, *Sources of the Self: the Making of the Modern Identity*.

uniform, interchangeable self that is implied in some versions of liberalism and utilitarianism. It is worth reflecting, then, on the import of embodiment. Let me consider first the bodily location of selves.

Mark Johnson notes that we encounter others and the world only through embodied structures of understanding.[25] This point provides an important qualification to the foregoing stress on consciousness, one that counters temptations toward voluntarism, intuitionism, or singularly rational approaches in ethics. Of course, what embodiment designates and what role it should play in ethics is debated. For my purposes, it may prove helpful to distinguish (though not separate) having a body and being a body. Having a body means, among other things, that the self is "more" than the body she has. This "more" allows and requires a critical approach to the ways bodies are defined and evaluated, the moral status of biological features and bodily experiences, the social construction of gender, and social institutions like marriage and kinship. A variety of positions and schools of thought are available on such matters. Forms of biological determinism and essentialism continue, for example, in the field of sociobiology, in emerging work in and attitudes about genetics, and in varieties of feminism (sometimes called "new" or "post" feminism) that tout women's liberation and fulfillment through an embrace of traditional virtues, values, and social venues. These attempts to ground social differences in biology compete with social constructionist positions. Tamer versions of social constructionism may treat the body as elementary material onto which social constructions like gender are added. Other social constructionist theories reject the notion that the body, biologically understood, is somehow prior to social construction. Indeed, stronger versions of social constructionism assert that the body has a history, that it is "so enmeshed in other aspects of culture that only by thoroughly contextualizing examinations of bodily representations and practices can it be possible to grasp its full significance."[26] Michel Foucault argues that bodies are texts, inscribed and proscribed

---

[25] Mark Johnson, *The Body in the Mind: the Bodily Basis of Meaning, Imagination and Reason* (Chicago: University of Chicago Press, 1988).

[26] Elaine Graham, *Making the Difference: Gender, Personhood and Theology* (Minneapolis, MN: Fortress, 1996), 126.

by hegemonic systems and discourses.[27] Recent work by French feminists and psychoanalysts construe the body as a site of resistance; by "writing the feminine body," they assert their specific experiences in contrast to the prevailing masculine discourse of the body.[28] These rival attempts to elide, recover, and rewrite the body fail to satisfy insofar as they make the body irrelevant or all-determining. Elaine Graham makes this point, suggesting that "bodies might be conceived as being both 'artifacts' or fabrications of culture; but also genuine 'vantage points' for renewed creative agency and transformative practice."[29] These issues are profoundly important for other moral questions, like the relations among the body, personhood, and human nature. Stanley Rudman notes that persons have been variously defined in terms of material criteria (e.g., body, brain), mental criteria (e.g., self-consciousness, rationality, intentionality), moral criteria (e.g., rights), and religious criteria (e.g., soul).[30] The term person is often associated with (sometimes made synonymous with) human being, though the two are at least logically distinct. There is much at stake, then, in specifying the criteria for personhood. Rudman notes that part of the confusion that ensues arises from a failure to see that the designation "human being" often functions as more than a biological category; it, like person, has evaluative and moral content.

Being a body means, among other things, that our bodies locate our way of being in the world. Being a body grounds my experience and sense of value, identity, and power. Sensory experiences of pleasure and pain provide initial encounters with value. My experience of physical wants and needs and their fulfillment fund and sometimes accompany my experience and sense of other, for example emotional, needs. Being a body provides an initial and ongoing sense of my identity through my capacities to relate to others, to find myself related ("You don't choose your family"), to isolate myself from the material world and social relations. Being

---

[27] See, for instance, Michel Foucault, *The History of Sexuality: an Introduction*, trans. Robert Hurley (New York: Random House, 1978) and *Discipline and Punish: the Birth of the Prison*, trans. Alan Sheridan (New York: Pantheon Books, 1977).

[28] See for instance the work of Julia Kristeva and Luce Irigaray.

[29] Graham, *Making the Difference*, 145.

[30] Stanley Rudman, *Concepts of Persons and Christian Ethics* (Cambridge: Cambridge University Press, 1997), 3.

a body initiates my experience of power as well, given my bodily vulnerability and control. My vulnerability is apparent in infancy and early childhood, of course, but continues in my need for protective clothing, in the fragile susceptibility of my plans, my mood, my sense of myself and the world to the simple onset of a cold or an irritable bowel. My control, my capacity to exert power is apparent in my physical mobility, my physical action upon or manipulation of the material world or others, in the physiological benefits I reap through exercise and a healthy diet.

My body marks the boundary between aspects of my identity that seem inward – my thoughts and feelings, for example – and those that seem external – my physical actions, those characteristics and roles attributed to me by others and those I attempt to project. The boundary character of the body asserts itself in involuntary and unconscious physical manifestations. I may blush or speak in a slightly higher register when I lie, experience feelings of arousal at inopportune moments or in response to a person who in every other respect I find unattractive, or develop physiological manifestations of emotions or stress, e.g., fatigue.

Cahill identifies the following transcultural bodily experiences: "being 'one in many,' as mind or spirit and body, as bodily parts in a whole, and as qualified by identity and change over time; sexual differentiation (male–female); sexuality, kinship, both vertical and lateral; birth; infancy; aging; eating; need for shelter; need for protective clothing; autonomous mobility; physical action upon the environment, physical skill; sensuality (five senses); pleasure and pain; communication (expressiveness and receptivity); emotions; mind-altering states of the body and bodily states caused by the mind; sleep and dreams; health and illness; inflicted injury, up to and including killing; death, being a corpse, decay."[31] These experiences are had only within cultural systems that elaborate their meanings, socially differentiate their forms and significance, and ritualize them. But bodily transactions with the world and others matter and last. They ground moral conversation, contribute to our common humanity, constitute our relations, and set some parameters for moral deliberation.

[31] Cahill, *Sex, Gender and Christian Ethics*, 78.

My specific concern here is not to allow the social and cultural mediation of and reflection on having a body to displace from normative consideration (and quite ironically so) what being a body means. Margaret Farley notes that being a body means that women can reclaim their bodies from male control.[32] Her point deserves attention, but it captures only part of the normative significance of being a body. Another (certainly not the last) normative implication of being a body is that ethics must assess the moral goodness and rightness of concrete acts and relations. This may seem an odd claim; after all, ethics grapples with topics like capital punishment, economic relations, hosts of problems in bioethics and so forth. What I mean might be clarified by the problem some, especially Roman Catholic, ethicists consider under the rubric of "intrinsically evil acts." Are there some acts which, notwithstanding a good intention and apart from at least some of the relevant circumstances, are always wrong? An affirmative answer typically requires some claim about the fundamental disorder between certain acts and the authentic human good. What intention or circumstances, for instance, could possibly morally redeem rape? This question entails theories of action and identity that cannot be offered here. Moreover, due attention to human historicity might make an account of embodied freedom a more promising tool than the concept of intrinsically evil acts. But the basic point is that our actions and relations both *express* and *determine* our relation to our selves, others and the divine. Insofar as the beliefs, values and commitments we have serve as conditions for the possibility of interacting with the world and with others, our actions and relations will disclose or express them. Yet self-relation and relation to God and to neighbor are also activated and shaped in our concrete endeavors. We do indeed fashion our selves and to some extent can elect to "be" differently; we cannot separate who we are from what we do, or from the relations these actions effect and affect. We may be more than the sum total of our actions and relations but we are not finally other than them. In them we approximate or betray our good and therefore take up some relation to ourselves, to the divine

---

[32] Margaret Farley, "Feminist Theology and Bioethics," in *Feminist Theological Ethics*, ed., Lois K. Daly (Louisville, KY: Westminster/John Knox, 1994), 200.

and to others. This is a crucial point if one's moral identity is to be anchored in anything other than subjective intention. Embodiment, then, requires a moral *lectio* of the body as a "text" produced by others and as a symbol, a medium of my self-enactment.

Given all of the above, to do justice to the reflexive and embodied character of self-relation, it is important to recognize that our self-relation and our relation to God are mediated in two respects, via linguistic and symbolic systems and via our cares and commitments. Put differently, a third feature of self-relation is that it is interpretive, both in its cognitive and connative dimensions. As Schweiker notes, "In understanding, knowing and valuing interact for the sake of orienting human life; exploring the act of understanding is then the crucial clue for grasping our distinctively human way of existing in the world."[33] The practical character and import of understanding is important for the claim that self-relation is embodied and for my call for more attention in ethics to particular acts and relations. But for the moment let me remain with this two-fold mediation of self-relation. It suggests several things.

First, the mediation of our self-relation and our relation to God through linguistic, cultural, and symbolic systems raises the problem of truthfulness in self-understanding. The linguistic, cultural, and symbolic systems that mediate consciousness are not utterly self-referential in meaning. The claim that subjectivity is reflexive implies that "'meaning' is the self-transcendence of the linguistic code. To understand something as meaningful is to grasp how some medium of communication (paradigmatically, language) intends what is other than itself and to understand oneself *in* that space of otherness."[34] This means that the linguistic, cultural, and symbolic resources that mediate consciousness must be subject to criticism and revision. This point bears on current debates in ethics over realism and anti-realism.[35] It also bears on moral psychological problems of identity, self-deception and the extent to which high degrees of reflectiveness are or are not necessary for a morally good

[33] Schweiker, "Understanding Moral Meanings," in *Power, Value and Conviction*, 79.
[34] Ibid., 81.
[35] See Geoffrey Sayre-McCord, ed., *Essays on Moral Realism* (Ithaca, NY and London: Cornell University Press, 1988).

life.[36] By claiming that truthfulness in self-understanding is part of the moral good of integrity I mean to combat subjectivism in ethics, capture the theological perspective that the meaning of life is found in relation to God and suggest that right self love requires ongoing self-criticism as well as criticism of others' representations and evaluations of our selves. Notwithstanding the provisional character of these representations and evaluations, their socio-historical contingency and their inexhaustible and largely impenetrable psychosocial depths, right self love demands that in some measure we know and accept the truth about ourselves. Second, the mediation of self-relation via our cares and commitments requires us to affirm the importance of intuitions, desires, aspirations and emotions as they inform us about and configure our relations to others and the world. It suggests that agency is grounded more deeply than choice – indeed it suggests that our self-relation (in both its praise- and blame-worthy respects) is in large measure constituted by the relations, commitments and communities that situate and shape us.

While I cannot offer a theory of emotions here, some clarification of the status of emotions is in order.[37] Emotions involve cognitive, motivational, and evaluative states. It is important not to neglect any of these aspects in order to render the complexity of emotions well. For example, too heavy an emphasis on the cognitive character of emotions could ignore the fact that the same perceived state of affairs can elicit different emotional reactions in different people. In addition to cognitive, motivational, and evaluative states, emotions sometimes include physiological changes. There is no necessary relation between a given emotion and a particular physiological change – my pulse quickens when I am gripped by fear or by desire. Emotions are private and social experiences. Emotions seem to be inward experiences. A person can sometimes conceal them, can sift through them, attend to one emotion and repress

---

[36] See Owen Flanagan, *Varieties of Moral Personality: Ethics and Psychological Realism* (Cambridge, MA: Harvard University Press, 1991), especially chapters 6 and 15, and Owen Flanagan and Amélie Oksenberg Rorty, eds., *Identity, Character and Morality: Essays in Moral Psychology* (Cambridge, MA: MIT Press, 1990), especially chapter 2 which treats Frankfurt and Taylor.

[37] See the entry "Emotions and feelings" by Jane O'Grady in the *Oxford Companion to Philosophy*, ed., Ted Honderich (Oxford and New York: Oxford University Press, 1995) for a succinct survey of theories of emotions and a number of the issues I raise here.

or deny another one. Yet emotions arise in our transactions with others in the world. As inward as they seem, one can sometimes detect the emotions of another even when he cannot. The very fact that persons and groups share words that designate emotions suggests the social character of emotions – not only access to those of others, but the exegesis of our own inner lives with an emotional concordance.

Emotions illuminate our agency as well and disclose our relation to values. Emotions are states we undergo, reactions to others, events, states of affairs. The responsive character of emotions affirms the reality and priority of value. We find it in the world. It confronts us. But emotions are also part of our experience of being agents. They can be springs of action. We invest emotionally in a person, object, place, or idea. We confer value, for better or worse. Beverly Harrison suggests these two points. Harrison says that without feelings "our power to image the world and act into it is destroyed and our rationality is impaired. But it is not merely the power to conceive the world that is lost. Our power to value the world gives way as well."[38] And yet she also says "There are no 'right' and 'wrong' feelings. Moral quality is a property of acts, not feelings, and our feelings arise in action. The moral question is not 'what do I feel?' but rather 'what do I do with what I feel?'"[39] Here Harrison exempts emotions from moral criticism. Instead, she accords them a role in moral criticism. The matter at hand is epistemological and axiological. Emotions can open reason to value, to perceptions, to what is true and real and good. But emotions can also distort reason and blind it. Emotions can act as a moral compass, but they can also be random, and they are almost surely deeply psychologically seated. So emotions are ambiguous. They need to be educated and ordered. Yet this askesis should be undertaken with a hermeneutics of charity as much as one of suspicion, with reverence for and acceptance of emotions, remembering that we and our relations are more than our emotions.

The two-fold mediation of subjectivity points to the profound connections between the cognitive and connative dimensions of

[38] Beverly Wildung Harrison, "The Power of Anger in the Work of Love," in *Making the Connections*, ed., Carol S. Robb (Boston, MA: Beacon, 1985), 13.
[39] Ibid., 14.

self-relation and the moral life. To note these connections is, I judge, to accept in qualified ways both feminist accounts of embodied selves and the epistemologies that often accompany them as well as the rational accounts which feminists and others (e.g., communitarians) have criticized. By moving self-relation to the methodological and substantive center of moral anthropology and casting the problem of self love in terms of identity, meaning, and action we tap into and speak to debates in ethics over questions of the right versus questions of the good, public versus communally specific moral arguments, and the relative moral importance of acts versus feelings/intentions. More immediately we avoid reductionistic accounts of the self and the moral life.

Let me note some basic concepts I employ to capture these features of self-relation.

Person, identity, and integrity

There are three concepts that are basic to my argument. First, *person* refers to the double reflexive dynamic of the self, wherein one's self-awareness unfolds in an awareness of the divine. Second, *identity* refers to the socio-historical specificity of the person, as well as the relations, commitments and roles that constitute the texture and shape of the particular person's moral life. I do not confine moral goodness to some quality, faculty, or activity of the person, but, rather, coordinate it to the flourishing or perfection of the person. Thus, identity encompasses both particular facts and characteristics about a given person, but also has reference to God's will for that person. Because all persons are created to respond to God, there will be some substantial, universal aspects of identity which belong to all persons, but the term, per definition, also suggests that identity is a highly individual matter. This leads me, third, to the concept of *integrity*, a moral ideal for all persons; integrity provides a way to retrieve traditional concepts of moral failing and perfection, for example, concupiscence. Because self-relation can take various forms, some of which are morally legitimate and some of which are pernicious, it is necessary to distinguish the unity of person and identity in self love per se (be it proper or pernicious self love) and the unity of person and identity in right self love. The concept identity, then, is a descriptive concept that encompasses the person's particularity; in order to designate the particular form of self-relation entailed in the idea of right self love, I will use the term integrity. Integrity, it will be seen, denotes a distinctive way of being in which the dignity and coherence of the person's life are known in relation to the divine and embodied in her actions and relations.

Chapter One suggested that (post) modern rejections of ontological frameworks for the self contribute to the various features of our contemporary moral outlook that pose the problem of self love. Can we recoup these frameworks? Why should we want to rework them? They counter the subjectivism and relativism of contemporary moral arguments with moral realism. Further, they can help us to take seriously our embodiment and the integrity of the natural world, though they need to be critically appropriated for this task. What follows provides theological content to the hermeneutical account of self-relation I just initiated and begins to show that this account is a tool for reworking ontological frameworks for the self. Most generally, it can activate some good will toward such positions without sacrificing critical rigor by divesting us of a suspicion that may blind us to their insights. Hermeneutical approaches spark a dialectical process of reasoning in which arguments are read against each other as a way to think through aporias, and they place this process in the service of critical, inductive reflection on experience. Despite the fact that thinkers reject ontologies as static and ahistorical, they can be rendered more dynamically and historically and in this way help us to make sense of experience and agency.

Both Rahner and Tillich react against old-style metaphysics and physicalism, yet appropriate the conceptual language of being in different ways. Rahner understands being in terms of an Aristotelian–Thomistic model of causality that he transforms transcendentally. In doing so he applies classical conceptual language of causality to epistemic acts. Tillich understands being in terms of the basic ontological structure of subject and object, or self and world. Tillich sought to avoid the reduction of philosophy to the epistemic; he offers an ontology of freedom. While there are considerable points of substantive similarity, Rahner offers a causal and Tillich a bi-polar account of being. Tillich's bi-polar framework stresses the power of being over non-being. According to Tillich, the human struggles against the threat of non-being to establish herself as a person. Self-relation is characterized by centeredness; it is the actualization of the structures of self-relatedness in obedience to the will of God. Tillich does understand the self as a multi-dimensional unity; to interpret being in static terms would do a disservice to his thought. Unbalance among the dimensions of the self begets disruption, destruction, nonbeing. Being before God, then, is a matter of actualization and integration, of centered participation in the power of being. Rahner appropriates and transforms Thomistic causality so that his analysis of being, like that of Aquinas, delves into the act of being, what it means to be coming into and remaining in existence. For Rahner the person's transcendental exercise of freedom, her self-engagement, is a dialogical capacity for love. To become before God is to grow asymptotically in self-acceptance in a definitive stance before the horizon of absolute mystery. Each account brings something distinctive and valuable to the idea of right self love. Actually, their similarities (the influence of existentialism and German idealism, their contemporary lifespans and German heritage) help us to appreciate what different frameworks, metaphors and methods can contribute to the task of moral anthropology. What is lost in starkness is compensated for with nuance. For instance, Tillich contributes the importance of integration, and thereby speaks to the fragmentation and compartmentalization which can afflict the self, while Rahner's appeal to mystery can offset tendencies towards systematization and the glorification of our power for its own sake.

Neither Rahner nor Tillich developed an account of self love; Tillich even states in several places that the concept of self love is problematic. Moreover, neither Tillich nor Rahner are typically labeled ethicists, which is odd, considering the number of works in ethics each produced; both understood that Christian theology pushes organically to ethics, to the question of how we ought to live before the divine. Each has been variously described as a systematic and dogmatic theologian, as a pastoral thinker and philosopher of religion. Both thinkers amassed many admirers and critics. Some criticisms are vehement, others simply regard Rahner and Tillich, important in their own time, as tired and passé. There are several important criticisms which have been advanced against both of them, and which suggest that Rahner and Tillich do not serve my project well.

The first set of objections center on the relation between human nature and the divine. I cast this set broadly so as to include charges of anthropocentrism, monism, and equivocation on the relation of nature and grace. These various critiques can be grouped together because each concerns the issue of difference between God and the person. For various reasons and under various labels, both Rahner and Tillich are said to undermine the difference between Creator and creature. For instance, some critics contend that Rahner's anthropocentrism constricts the divine reality within human limits and ignores the import of revelation for an adequate understanding of the human. Some thinkers charge that Tillich's ontological analysis of being effects a monism whereby the person's essential nature is identical with God's.[40] Second, both Rahner and Tillich are said to neglect the inter-personal character of the person, to isolate self-relation from the embodied and social conditions of the person. This charge of individualism appears to place Rahner and Tillich at odds with my claim that self love is only actualized and assessed in neighbor love. Third, the ethical writings of both are criticized for courting subjectivism. Rahner's transcendental Thomism emphasizes the person's self-determination through a fundamental choice; it risks a *voluntarism* in which the self's moral identity is chiefly a matter of her will. Her concrete acts and relations have a subordinate role, and their value is determined by her. Tillich's ontology prompts him to describe conscience as the "silent call" of being; it risks an *intuitionism* in which subjective wants and experiences provide sufficient moral warrants and the moral

---

[40] See Glenn Graber, "The Metaethics of Paul Tillich," *The Journal of Religious Ethics* 1 (1973), 113–33. See 125–26. Graber goes so far as to say "One's essential nature = the essential nature of other persons = God," 125. Graber has misread Tillich on this score.

emphasis falls on an authenticity that is determined individually rather than indexed to concrete, objective acts and relations. Thus, both threaten a subjectivism that reduces values to matters of personal choice and renders moral obligations as situation-specific. If this charge is correct, then, their positions would not promise much that could be used to critique the norm of self-realization. Finally, readers of Rahner and Tillich struggle with how to adjudicate the normativity of their Christian commitments and their foundational, universal claims about the person.

These particular criticisms are important to the problem of right self love. To stress the self's difference from God, for instance, is to argue that self-relation finds its source and power in the divine other; the self cannot aim directly at her flourishing, but achieves it by going out of herself. To stress the social character of the self is to offset the solipsism that might attend an account of self love. The risk of subjectivism raises the issue of how to evaluate morally the self's relation to God. Put differently, what form of moral thinking arises from the self's relation to the divine? Finally, the tension between normative Christian commitments and a general account of moral existence indicates the need to specify the role between faith and self-relation, or the connection between particular forms of discourse and the self's understanding of itself.

In sum, Rahner's and Tillich's respective metaphysics make for bloated anthropologies that constrict revelation and drag our attention away from our social and historical location, construction and concerns. Moreover, Rahner's voluntarism and Tillich's intuitionism invite a moral subjectivism that contributes to rather than addresses the contemporary norm of self-realization. Reading their arguments with a hermeneutical account of self-relation can offset these difficulties while retaining the theological and moral insights of their respective metaphysics. Doing so also provides a way to develop a positive theological anthropology and a (Christian) account of right self love.

THE SELF AS CREATED IN AND FOR RELATION WITH GOD

God made us to love him. In his creative love, God establishes and sustains our being at every moment. In the intimacy of self-presence we experience a dependence in freedom vis-à-vis some other who both transcends it and whose very proximity makes possible a mutual in-dwelling of creator and creature. We can parse the reflexive character of self-relation in good theological fashion, then, by reflecting on the self as question, as creature, and as free.

The self as question

Rahner and Tillich provide two models of understanding. Both emerge from human questioning the meaning of existence. Rahner may not employ the language of self-interpretation but he clearly finds asking about the meaning of existence to be more than one activity alongside others. Such questions tap into and disclose something about the human as questioner – they indicate and constitute an openness to an (the) answer. Rahner hits on the so-called hermeneutical circle: the question posed by the human "creates the condition for really hearing, and only the answer brings the question to its reflexive self-presence."[41] The person not only asks about the meaning of her existence, she experiences herself as that question. This question may be ignored or repressed or neglected, but it cannot be escaped, "for it exists and has nothing outside itself which could be the answer. It is the question which is its own answer when it is accepted in love." Rahner goes on to say, "Man is moved by this absolute question. If he enters into this movement, which is the movement of the world and of the spirit, he really comes to himself for the first time, and comes to God and to his goal, the goal in which the absolute beginning itself in its immediacy is

---

[41] Karl Rahner, *Foundations of Christian Faith: an Introduction to the Idea of Christianity*, trans. William Dych, (New York: Crossroad, 1993), 11. Rahner's endeavor to give an introduction to the "Idea of Christianity" is simultaneously an inquiry into the totality of Christian existence. The fact that Rahner specifies his anthropological starting points in human knowing and freedom fits the dialectic of being and thinking, or anthropology and epistemology which runs throughout this book. Not all scholars of Rahner recognize the importance of his analysis of freedom, but instead confine his starting point to his metaphysics of knowledge. Such approaches inflate the importance of Rahner's early works, *Spirit in the World* and *Hearers of the Word*. I draw upon Rahner's later work. See *Spirit in the World*, trans. William Dych (New York: Herder and Herder, 1968) and *Hearers of the Word*, trans. Michael Richards (New York: Herder and Herder, 1969). For a helpful introductory treatment of Rahner's thought which is structured according to *Foundations*, see Leo J. O'Donovan, ed., *A World of Grace: an Introduction to the Themes and Foundations of Karl Rahner's Theology* (New York: Seabury, 1980).

our goal."[42] Because one cannot ask about something about which
one does not already know something, Rahner argues that the answer to human questioning is entailed in the question itself. Thus,
if the human is that question, the answer is something in which
the human already participates. Rahner speaks of the dynamism
of knowledge as having a *Vorgriff*, a pre-apprehension of meaning.
The *Vorgriff* means that human knowing occurs within a horizon
which encompasses the knowing subject and the object of knowledge and which directs this knowing beyond the finite, particular
object. This means that when we ask about ourselves we (1) experience our transcendence; (2) disclose our openness to its horizon
(what Rahner terms absolute mystery); and (3) affirm this horizon
as the condition for its possibility.

Rahner explores this connection between the person's questioning and her orientation towards mystery by analyzing human
knowledge and experience. He designates the reflexive character
of subjectivity as transcendental experience.[43] Human knowledge
manifests this experience because the object of knowledge is always
co-known with the subject's awareness of its knowledge.[44] This
awareness of one's own subjectivity, this transcendence, constitutes
an unthematic openness to being as such. It is a necessary, though
not always self-conscious affirmation of being.[45] In this openness,
this orientation to mystery, the person possesses an unthematic
knowledge of God.[46] The reflexive character of self-awareness has
a doubleness, because it unfolds in an awareness of God. Still, the
person's transcendental relation to God is not an unambiguous object of reflection. Because God is both the power of transcendental
movement and the goal, reflection on transcendence will be an interpretation of the human vis-à-vis this horizon. As Rahner puts it,
the unthematic awareness of God becomes thematized though not

[42] Rahner, *Foundations*, 192.
[43] See ibid., 31–35 and 57–71. See also James J. Bacik, *Apologetics and the Eclipse of Mystery: Mystagogy According to Karl Rahner* (Notre Dame, IN: University of Notre Dame Press, 1980).
[44] Rahner, *Foundations*, 18.
[45] Ibid., 69. Hence, he can say that anthropology is theology and vice versa. Rahner goes so far as to say that anthropology is Christology.
[46] This transcendental knowledge of God is a posteriori insofar as subjectivity is always situated in an encounter with the world and with other people (see ibid., 51–52). Thus, speaking and thinking about God points to the transcendental experience and knowledge of God, but does not exhaust or completely objectify this experience and knowledge.

necessarily in explicitly theistic terms. This transcendental method is a valuable resource for crafting an account of self-relation and is amenable to a hermeneutical account in particular because the claims Rahner makes remind us that our self-interpretation and our acts of meaning-making are responsive and responsible to something we have not created.

While Rahner describes understanding with what we can call a model of thematization, Tillich employs a correlational model of question and answer.[47] According to Tillich, "reason in both its objective and subjective structures points to something which appears in these structures but which transcends them in power and meaning."[48] Reason has the dimension of depth, such that it points to truth, beauty, justice, and love, but this depth is hidden under the conditions of existence. Under the conditions of existence the depth of reason expresses itself in myth and cults. These myths and cults formulate the question which the human is and suggest the interpretive character of self-relation.[49] Because the answer to the questions implied in existence cannot be derived from existence, but must be given, they are answered by revelation. The ecstatic reception of revelation does not destroy reason, but opens it to a new dimension, thereby disclosing something valid about the relation between the human and the ground of reason and the mysterious

---

[47] As with Rahner, the very character of Tillich's systematic project discloses its suitability. Tillich's *Systematic Theology* is structured by creation and salvation. "Insofar as man's existence has the character of self-contradiction or estrangement, a double consideration is demanded, one side dealing with what he essentially is (and ought to be) and the other dealing with what he is in his self-estranged existence (and should not be)." Tillich, *Systematic Theology*, vol. 1, 66. The various parts of Tillich's *Systematic Theology* move from essential being to estranged existence to ambiguous life, each of which Tillich speaks of in terms of different symbols and concepts and according to a Trinitarian structure. Being raises the question of God, existence quests for the Christ, and life quests for the Spirit; the chief symbols are respectively God, New Being, and Spiritual Presence. For methodological reasons, the system is framed by a treatment of reason and its quest for revelation, and history and the Kingdom of God. For a discussion of Tillich's theological method see Uwe C. Scharf, "Dogmatics between the Poles of the Sacred and the Profane: an Essay in Theological Methodology," *Encounter* 55 (1994), 269–86, especially 269–77. For a discussion of the relation between religious symbols and interpretation, see Donald F. Dreisbach, "Paul Tillich's Hermeneutic," *Journal of the American Academy of Religion* 43 (1975), 84–94, especially 91–93, which takes up Tillich's method of correlation.

[48] Tillich, *Systematic Theology*, vol. 1, 79. See Robert C. Coburn, "The Idea of Transcendence," *Philosophical Investigations* 13 (1990), 322–37.

[49] Tillich, *Systematic Theology*, vol. 1, 62.

abyss to which reason is driven.[50] In other words, the basic question of being and nonbeing, the question which the human is, is answered when reason is grasped ecstatically by the ground of reason, by God. In this way, Tillich makes the double reflexive move which Rahner made, showing thereby that in the very structure of subjectivity the self experiences itself (however non-theistically) as related to the divine. Thus, Tillich's ontological analysis offers a different account of and framework for the same insight that I said Rahner helps us to court: that self-interpretation and meaning-making are responsive and responsible to something we (to borrow from Paul Ricoeur) do not invent but discover.[51]

The question implied by human being, then, is asked by the human and can be answered by her because she experiences the ontological structure of this answer immediately and directly in her own self-awareness. Recall that Tillich designates this structure as self and world. As a self, the human is separated from everything else but at the same time is aware of belonging to that from which she is separated. For this reason, the self transcends her environment, and thus, has a world. The world includes and transcends all possible environments; it is the structure by which the self grasps and shapes her environment. The world allows the self to encounter herself.[52] The self-world ontological structure, then, is the existential correlate to the subject–object character of reason. In this way, Tillich parallels the epistemological and ontological polarities of reason/revelation and being/God. Indeed, Tillich explicates the self-world structure in terms of different symbols and concepts which correlate to different analyses of human being, (e.g., he specifies the meaning of being as power, freedom, and love).

---

[50] Ibid., 113. Tillich speaks about the questions of being and nonbeing as one of ontological shock. This shock is preserved yet overcome in ecstasy.

[51] Paul Ricoeur, *Interpretation Theory: Discourse and the Surplus of Meaning* (Fort Worth, TX: Texas Christian University, 1976.) Of course, philosophically speaking, Tillich's ontological approach may appear just as unpromising as Rahner's transcendental Thomism. Certainly, it seems incommensurable with non-substantialist metaphysics like those found in Eastern approaches. Engagement with those projects lies well beyond my expertise. A helpful book, however, is Joan Stambaugh, *The Formless Self* (Albany, NY: SUNY, 1999). Stambaugh explores several Japanese Buddhists. See especially 55–97 in which she explores Tillich's dialogues with Shin'ichi Hisamatsu.

[52] See Tillich, *Systematic Theology*, vol. 1, 168–71.

In contrast to the thematization and correlational models of understanding that Rahner and Tillich employ, a hermeneutical approach models understanding as an event. As I noted earlier in this chapter, events of understanding connect knowing and valuing, the knowing entailed in sensory perception and in praxis, and the value that confronts us and that we bestow. This model is more basic than Rahner's and Tillich's and can accommodate them both. Rahner's thematization model, for instance, suggests that understanding is a process whereby the real arises in beliefs, symbols, practices, while Tillich's correlational model suggests a process of being grasped. Recognizing that understanding is an event emphasizes human agency in the constitution of meaning but does not render the agent as a singular source of value. In this way we can reckon with the particularity and contingency of knowledge without doing so at the expense of realism. Moreover, recognizing that understanding is an event highlights the fact that the self comes to itself under the demand to recognize what is other. Yet, importantly, the self's awareness of the other is not free of distortions, prejudice, and callousness. Love for self and others entails the purification of and sensitization of our moral affections as part of the task of knowing oneself and others truly and for discerning what concrete acts and relations embody that love suitably. Growth in love enables us to "see clearly," to "know as we are known." (cf. 1 Cor. 13:12) The completion of knowledge expresses itself in what love does and how love does it. Knowledge of oneself becomes complete as we abide in love, and the fullness and clarity of this knowledge expresses itself in the work of love, especially as it "rescues" our efforts and acts, rescues our very selves, from nothingness.

The self as creature

Rahner and Tillich begin with knowledge/reason because they want to respond to the epistemic revolution of modernity as part of their respective ontologies. At stake is the connection between knowledge (of oneself) and knowledge of God. This properly epistemological question brings us to the theological anthropological claims that accompany it. For Rahner, to be human is to be able to respond to God (because creation is always already graced) and so to be oriented to God. For Tillich, to be human is to participate in being and nonbeing and so to be ultimately concerned about what determines our being or nonbeing. We can note the way their respective models of understanding influence their analyses of being and of the divine–human relation in particular.

According to Rahner, the person's orientation to God is grace, "and it is an inescapable existential of man's whole being even when he closes himself to it freely by rejecting it."[53] That is to say, God has given God's self to the person as an offer such that the divine–human relation, prior to the person's exercise of freedom in response to that offer, has become constitutive of the person. Rahner captures this claim in the concept of the supernatural existential. The supernatural existential designates prevenient grace as an abiding existential of the person.[54] It is precisely because of such claims that some critics fault Rahner's understanding of nature and grace for undermining the difference between God and creature.[55] Because creation is always already graced, Rahner calls nature a "remainder concept" in order to refer to what creation would have been like apart from grace.[56] In other words, there is nothing about the human which demands or requires God's self-communication. Rather, God freely offers God's self.[57] Because

[53] Rahner, *Foundations*, 57. See Rahner, "Concerning the Relationship Between Nature and Grace," in *Theological Investigations*, vol. 1. See *Theological Investigations*, vols. 1–14 (vols. 1–6, Baltimore, MA: Helicon; vols. 7–10, New York: Herder and Herder; vols. 11–14, New York: Seabury; 1961–1976).

[54] See William Dych, *Karl Rahner* (London: Geoffrey Chapman, 1992) especially chapter 3; J. Cawte, "Karl Rahner's Conception of God's Self-Communication to Man," *Heythrop Journal* 25:3 (1984), 260–71. See also Richard J. Beauchesne, "The Supernatural Existential as Desire: Karl Rahner and Emmanuel Levinas Revisited," *Église et Théologie* 23 (1992), 221–39, especially 324–39. Beauchesne draws on Levinas's category of Desire as a way to preserve the difference of God from the person.

[55] See W. Hill, "Uncreated Grace – A Critique of Karl Rahner," *Thomist* 27 (1963), 333–56. Hill argues that Rahner's doctrine of grace "must involve either an unthinkable fusion of God with creature, or a transformation of the creature into the divine by way of hypostatic union or glorious vision." See 356.

[56] Rahner also says that God's self-communication presupposes creation as its deficient mode. See Rahner, *Foundations*, 122. Rahner does not want to deny the freedom of the Incarnation, so he insists that there could have been humans without the Logos having become human. Nevertheless, by calling human creatureliness the deficient modality of God's self-communication, Rahner means to claim that the possibility of there being humans is grounded in the greater possibility that God could express God's self in the Logos which becomes a human. See ibid., 223.

[57] As will become clear in Chapter Six this understanding of the relation of nature and grace proves important for the question whether there is a distinctive Christian ethics.

there is nothing about the person which demands grace, but the person has been created so as to be capable of receiving grace, Rahner speaks of obediential potency, or the *potentia obedientalis*.[58] The concept of obediential potency suggests the commensurability between human being as such and relation to the divine. To be sure, God's offer is the condition for the possibility of and bears the person's response, but the distinction is necessary in order to preserve the gratuity of God's grace. God remains free in God's offer, and God's offer empowers the person in knowledge, freedom, and love to transcend the particular toward the divine horizon which gives value and coherence to the particular.

For Tillich "man" is finitude that is aware of itself as such, and therefore experiences the threat of nonbeing as anxiety.[59] Finite freedom is what makes the transition from being to existence possible. In essential being, the ontological elements that constitute the basic structure of self and world are organized in balanced polarities; individuation is balanced by participation, dynamics by form, freedom by destiny.[60] But finitude transforms these polarities into tensions and threatens to disrupt the balance. If one of the polar elements is lost, the self faces disintegration. For example, when freedom loses its polarity with destiny, it ceases to be freedom and becomes arbitrariness. Because nonbeing is a threat but not a necessity, the human asks the question of God, the question of what can conquer nonbeing. The question of God is implied in the structure of being, then, and is present in the human's awareness of her finitude. Put differently, finitude drives being to the question of God.[61] Tillich speaks of the question which finitude poses as the human's ultimate concern. One is concerned ultimately about that which determines one's being or nonbeing. Tillich argues that one cannot be concerned about something which one does not encounter concretely, that is, something that is not real. Yet, neither can one be concerned ultimately with something that does not transcend preliminary finite concerns.[62] God is the name for

---

[58] See Rahner, "Concerning the Relationship Between Nature and Grace." See also Rahner, *Foundations*, 132 and 218.

[59] Tillich, *Systematic Theology*, vol. 1, 192.   [60] See ibid., 174–86.   [61] Ibid., 166.

[62] Of course, Tillich grants that such finite concerns can be attributed an ultimacy which does not belong to them; this is the force of his analysis of idolatry and the demonic.

that which concerns the human ultimately. God is absolute and ultimate because God is the power of being, and God is concrete and personal because God is the ground and aim of being.[63]

Each approach expresses and illumines some features of experience and neglects others. Each implies (as we will see) different pictures of self-determination and of redemption. Importantly, each ontology connects epistemologies and axiologies in a version of the basic claim that God has created us, and that our creaturehood entails differentiation from and belonging to God. The language of creaturehood places the self within an antecedent order of value. Substance metaphysics may construe this order statically and may neglect the role interpretation plays in identifying and responding to value. Yet it also affirms the value of the natural world and the goodness of existence even in the face of evidence to the contrary. By bringing hermeneutical theory to bear on Rahner's and Tillich's anthropologies we can re-cast their respective accounts of being from attempts to specify from a theological perspective the "essence" or "nature" of the self to claims about the meaning of existence. The self as question is always already set within a domain of value. The self as creature arises in acts of knowledge and concern, suggesting that creaturehood refers not to some substratum but to the praxis of understanding oneself in a world.

As I noted in Chapter One, the self may become a "new creation." She lives by another and in another because she lives for another. Her loves animate her. She participates in, becomes like the object of her love. The question is, for whom does she live? This brings us to the self as free.

The self as free

Setting self-relation in a theistic ontology counters the dominant reduction of freedom to autonomy that Chapter One noted. Freedom is the mode of our creatureliness, our capacity for

See Donald F. Driesbach, *Symbols and Salvation: Paul Tillich's Doctrine of Religious Symbols and his Interpretation of the Symbols of the Christian Tradition* (Lanham, MD: University Press of America, 1993), 11.

[63] Tillich, *Systematic Theology*, vol. I, 211. See also Tillich, *Dynamics of Faith* (New York: Harper Torchbooks, 1957). For God as absolute and ultimate see *Systematic Theology*, vol. I, 230 and for God as concrete and personal, see 245.

self-determination in relation to God and others and in the world. This is not the hermetically sealed autonomy that modernity so prizes. Freedom has conditions. Some of these conditions consist in freedom's situation, historically and socially, its psychological and appetitive conditioning and so forth. Within this situation, freedom finds a more basic condition, that for which freedom is created.

According to Rahner, freedom is neither an individual human power alongside others which can be observed empirically, nor is it neutral. The person's transcendence is opened and borne by absolute mystery and thus is not at the person's disposal; it is because of this, perhaps ironically, that the person experiences herself as, and really is, free to decide, and responsible for deciding, her posture toward this horizon. As will become clearer later, Rahner ties such self-actualization (the exercise of transcendental freedom) to self-acceptance, which is thematized in the self's categorical acts; in my judgment he thereby opens the door to a picture of self-relation in terms of a self-interpretation which is mediated in the self's moral and religious activity.

Rahner wants to avoid some conception of transcendental freedom as layered onto or extrinsic to its categorical objectifications. He argues that transcendental freedom is always situated categorically, that is, historically and socially. Indeed, it is only because the person experiences his historical conditioning that he can be confident that he also transcends such determination. Historicity and sociality are not qualities of the person alongside her freedom, but rather provide the arena for freedom.[64] Thus, being situated is constitutive of the person as such and indicates that "man even as doer and maker is still receiving and being made."[65] Thus, the person's capacity to respond to God is situated and embedded within a history which co-determines it as guilt.[66] Rahner maintains that guilt and redemption need not be understood as temporally sequential. In fact, if the cosmos is always already graced by God, the saving self-communication of God precedes the determination of freedom in guilt. For this reason guilt and forgiveness need to be understood in light of one another. Guilt is "closing oneself to this

---

[64] Rahner, *Foundations*, 41.   [65] Ibid., 43.
[66] See, for example, Rahner's "Does Traditional Theology Represent Guilt as Innocuous as a Factor in Human Life?" in *Theological Investigations*, vol. 13.

offer of God's absolute self-communication" and yet, the enduring validity of this offer in Christ discloses God's self-communication *as* forgiving.[67] Accordingly, Rahner appropriates the doctrine of original sin to express the "historical origin of the present, universal and ineradicable situation of our freedom as co-determined by guilt" and claims the possibility of sin is an existential of the person.[68] Yet Rahner in effect contextualizes sin within claims about God's antecedent relation to the person, to the cosmos, in grace. Because freedom is situated yet open to further determination, the person experiences her freedom in ambiguity and as hidden. Her exercise of freedom cannot be brought to reflection completely.[69] Rahner's description of freedom as transcendental and categorical has some fans and many critics. The two insights behind it are first, that freedom is exercised in categorical choices but also in the choice of oneself and second, that freedom is the mode not only of our difference from everything else, our separation, but our relationality. This is the point of speaking of freedom's horizon and of its co-determination by guilt.

Tillich picks up these points as well in his description of the transition from being to existence. The transition from essence to existence is possible because of finite freedom. Tillich argues that man is free "in so far as he has the power of contradicting himself and his essential nature. Man is free even from his freedom; that is, he can surrender his humanity."[70] According to Tillich, as compared to existence, essential being is best understood in terms of dreaming innocence, a state of non-actualized potentiality. Essential being cannot be understood as perfection because otherwise the Fall is unintelligible. Rather, it must be that essential freedom is uncontested, undecided freedom, and thus, that it must be actualized. Given this, Tillich argues that in freedom creation and the fall coincide because

being a creature means both to be rooted in the creative ground of the divine life and to actualize one's self through freedom. Creation is fulfilled in the creaturely self-realization which simultaneously is freedom and destiny. But it is fulfilled through separation from the creative ground

---

[67] Rahner, *Foundations*, 93.   [68] Ibid., 114. See also, 104.   [69] See ibid., 97.
[70] Tillich, *Systematic Theology*, vol. 1, 32.

through a break between existence and essence. Creaturely freedom is
the point at which creation and the fall coincide.[71]

Despite the fact that creation and the fall coincide, and thus, the
human makes the transition from essential unity with being to
estrangement from it, estrangement is not a structural necessity.[72]
It is a universal fact but it is also a personal act. In existence,
the individual's freedom is embedded in a universal condition of
estrangement, but does not thereby cease to be a matter of personal
responsibility and guilt.

Freedom's co-determination by guilt means, from a hermeneutical perspective, that the self understands herself in a situation and
with resources that are not of her own making, that include distortions and blindness and violence and despair. It is not simply that
our acting implicates us in a world marked by sin, but that in the
very springs of our own agency, we are not alone, nor are we our
own. If we live by and in something other than our selves because
we become selves by living for some other, our self-relation is always
a matter of loves and loyalties that animate us. Yet our freedom is
also the mode of our difference from everything else, which allows
for and requires our responsible self-determination.

SELF-DETERMINATION BEFORE GOD

Freedom relates closely to the person's capacity for self-
transcendence. So freedom might seem to be the capacity for self-
alteration, and as I noted in Chapter One, this picture of freedom
is offered in many quarters today. Freedom, in this view, is unfettered. It is the power of self-determination and it is exercised in
a neutral space. Freedom is severed from, takes no direction or
content from the agent who exercises it. Freedom is the capacity
to escape its own conditions. But if freedom always operates in a
space of value, and if in its very depths it is shaped by desire, then
freedom is fundamentally responsive. So freedom cannot be the

[71] Ibid., 256. See Peter Slater, "Tillich on the Fall and the Temptation of Goodness," *Journal of Religion* 65 (1985), 196–207, especially 205. See also Donald F. Dreisbach, "Essence, Existence, and the Fall: Paul Tillich's Analysis of Existence," *Harvard Theological Review* 73 (1980), 521–38.
[72] For this reason, Tillich speaks of the transition in terms of a leap. See Tillich, *Systematic Theology*, vol. 2, 44.

capacity to escape its own conditions. Rather, freedom resides in the configuration of those conditions. Rahner helps us to grasp this point. God, as the condition for freedom's possibility and as the providential and saving agent who reconfigures freedom, sets our freedom free. Lest this seem to distance freedom from its material, social, and cultural location, Tillich gives us some purchase on the intersubjective and material arena of freedom. Freedom is not the absence of all determination. Rather, it is a capacity to actualize oneself within one's material specificity. If freedom is the capacity for self-actualization (in particular choices and as the choice of oneself in those choices), then to be free is to be what one is created to be, to actualize one's potentialities, to enjoy the conditions for human flourishing, to choose and act in accordance with the human good.

For Rahner, freedom is both a capacity and a task, a possibility and a demand. According to Rahner it is because freedom is situated and co-determined, that is, because the person experiences herself as a product not at her own disposal, that freedom is not so much the exercise of some faculty as it is the achievement of her self. "In real freedom the subject always intends himself, understands and posits himself. Ultimately he does not do *something*, but does *himself*."[73] Rahner writes elsewhere, "although it exists in time and in history, freedom has a single, unique act, namely, the self-actualization of the single subject himself. The subject's individual acts must always and everywhere be mediated objectively in the world and in history, but he intends one thing and he actualizes one thing: the single subject in the unique totality of his history."[74] Freedom so conceived is not a capacity for arbitrary choices which can be made and then changed. It is the capacity for something final and definitive.[75]

For Rahner the question about personal existence is a question about salvation. Salvation is a matter of the "final and definitive validity of a person's true self-understanding and true self-realization in freedom before God by the fact that he accepts his own self as

---

[73] Rahner, *Foundations*, 94. See Andrew Tallon, "Personal Becoming," *Thomist* 43 (1979), 1–77, especially 129–33 on this point.

[74] Rahner, *Foundations*, 95. See also 38, and Rahner, "Theology of Freedom," *Theological Investigations*, vol. 6, 182.

[75] See Rahner, "Theology of Freedom," 179.

it is disclosed and offered to him in the choice of transcendence as interpreted in freedom."[76] The exercise of freedom is a practical self-interpretation; we realize and understand ourselves truly as we respond to God's self-offer. This relation between God's self-communication and human freedom can be explained by means of the metaphysical principle of causality.[77]

Rahner adopts and transcendentally modifies the Aristotelian–Thomistic model of causality. His account is certainly not the only resource for construing the divine–human relation, though it has some merits. As a heuristic device it can bring into relief and fund thinking about nature and grace, divine and human agency, freedom as determined and as open to determination. Rahner uses efficient causality to speak about creatureliness and formal causality (sometimes called quasi-formal causality) to speak of God's self-communication to the human.[78] Efficient causality explains creation as the "free establishment by God of what is other precisely as other" but it does not explain or require God's self-communication to that created existent.[79] Formal causality, however, designates God's self-communication to the creature wherein God becomes a constitutive principle for the created existent yet remains free and completely intact.[80]

As a heuristic device the model of causation turns on a more basic theological claim about how and why the person has been created, a claim about what is most essential to the person, namely that freedom has grace as its condition of possibility and that the actualization of freedom is itself an event of grace. The full and final actualization of freedom constitutes a response to that offer. The person's self-determination does not simply coincide with a

---

[76] Rahner, *Foundations*, 39.

[77] The "metaphysical principle of causality is not an extrapolation from the causal thinking that we use in everyday affairs. It is grounded rather in the transcendental experience of the relationship between transcendence and its term . . . it only points to the transcendental experience in which the relationship between something conditioned and finite and its incomprehensible source is immediately present, and through its presence is experienced" (ibid., 70).

[78] "The nature of the spiritual creature consists in the fact that that which is 'innermost' to it, that whence, to which and through which it is, is precisely *not* an element of this essence and this nature which belongs to it" (Rahner, "Immanent and Transcendent Consummation of the World," *Theological Investigations*, vol. 10, 281). See Paul de Letter, "Divine Quasi-Formal Causality," *Irish Theological Quarterly* 27 (1960), 221–28.

[79] Rahner, *Foundations*, 122.   [80] Ibid., 121.

response to God. But the person's self-determination has God as both its origin and its telos. Freedom is set free by God for God.[81] Thus self-relation finds its source and power in something other than oneself which transcends the self, and moreover, the meaning of life is found in relation to the divine. This claim provides an important moral critique of self-realization ethics which tend toward egoism or which define fulfillment with respect to finite goods or projects. God is the primary agent within the person's self-determining exercise of freedom.

This construal of freedom shows that we cannot understand self-relation descriptively or normatively apart from the basic claim that we are created by God for God. Just as a yes to God's offer of grace is itself an instance of grace, a no to God's offer also depends upon this antecedent relation of grace in order to be a no.[82] Although the character of freedom is such that its fulfillment is in God, self-determination constitutes a response to God, whether that response is a yes or a no. Rahner maintains that freedom requires us to hold that a no, a personal decision against God, is a real possibility. However, given the character of freedom, a yes to God and a no to God are not parallel possibilities. Rahner writes,

since freedom's "no" to God is based on a transcendental and necessary "yes" to God in transcendence and otherwise could not take place, and hence since it entails a free self-destruction of the subject in an intrinsic contradiction in his act, for this reason then this "no" must never be understood as an existential-ontological parallel possibility of freedom alongside of the possibility of a "yes" to God. This "no" is one of freedom's possibilities, but this possibility of freedom is always at the same time something abortive, something which miscarries and fails, something which is self-destructive and self-contradictory.[83]

All of this intimates how Rahner recoups the classical claim that God is the good of the human as such, that is, how Rahner commensurates the being and flourishing of the person with her relation to God.

---

[81] See ibid., 79.   [82] See ibid., 118. See also 97–106.
[83] Ibid., 102. See also Rahner, "Theology of Freedom," 181–82. Some thinkers contend that Rahner's understanding of sin as a free and definitive no to God is inconsistent. See for example Ron Highfield, "The Freedom to Say 'No'? Karl Rahner's Doctrine of Sin," *Theological Studies* 56 (1995), 485–505. Highfield, like other critics of Rahner, charges that Rahner eclipses the difference between God and the person. See 504.

Rahner's construal of self-determination as self-disposal fits his thematization model of understanding and transcendental-causal analysis of being. Tillich's correlational model of under-standing and bipolar analysis of being shape his account of self-determination. Tillich speaks of self-determination as centeredness and integration. The self, like all beings, drives toward its actualiza-tion and toward reunion with essential being. Nevertheless, a spe-cial dimension of life, the dimension which is particularly human, is the dimension of spirit.[84] Spirit, divine and human, is the unity of power and meaning; it includes awareness and intentionality, eros and reason. Tillich argues that spirit has three functions: religion, culture, and morality. Because the dimension of spirit is particularly human, the functions of spirit are constitutive for human life. To describe the self-actualization of life under the dimension of spirit, Tillich correlates self-integration with morality, self-creativity with culture, and self-transcendence with religion.

Self-integration depends upon the polarity of individuation and participation. An individuated self is a centered self.[85] Yet, the cen-tered self, by virtue of being separate from her world, is capable of relating herself to it. Centeredness is both a reality and a task.[86] Centeredness is given in essential being, but it is not actually given "until man actualizes it in freedom and through destiny. The act in which man actualizes his essential centeredness is the moral act. . . . Morality is the function of life in which the centered self constitutes itself as a person."[87] The actualization of centeredness is a moral act under the norm of essential being; this is Tillich's concept of theonomy.

Theonomy means that one's essential being constitutes a moral imperative which is experienced as categorically binding within the ambiguities of life.[88] To disobey the moral imperative is to live in fundamental self-contradiction.

Man is able to respond to these commands and . . . this ability is what makes him responsible. Every moral act is a responsible act, a response

---

[84] See Tillich, *Systematic Theology*, vol. 3, 21.   [85] Ibid., 32–38.   [86] Ibid., 30.
[87] Ibid., 38.
[88] "The moral imperative is valid because it represents our essential being over against our state of existential estrangement" (ibid., 44). See Charles J. Sabatino, "An Interpretation of the Significance of Theonomy within Tillich's Theology," *Encounter* 45 (1984), 23–38.

to a valid command, but man can refuse to respond. If he refuses, he gives way to the forces of moral disintegration; he acts against the spirit in the power of the spirit. For he can never get rid of himself as spirit. He constitutes himself as a completely centered self even in his anti-essential, antimoral actions. These actions express moral centeredness even while they tend to dissolve the moral center.[89]

What Tillich recognizes here is that self-relation can take a variety of forms, some of which are destructive and morally invalid. Thus, for Tillich, as for Rahner, disobedience or resistance to the person's primordial relation with God depends upon this very relation. Later I will argue that Tillich does not provide adequately for moral differentiation among forms of self-relation. These norms are experienced in the person's encounter with other persons. The centeredness of the other person, their inviolability as such, places a limit on the self's attempt to integrate everything into itself.[90] The person responds to God in her self-actualization; this process of centering is a moral process.

Self-integration is a matter of establishing self-identity, but a crucial aspect to this process is self-alteration or self-creativity. The function of self-creativity depends upon the polarity of dynamics and form. Self-creativity is actualized under the dimension of spirit in the function of culture. In culture, the human creates the new by the basic functions of language and technology. The self is determined by others and determines others, even as genuine self-determination occurs. Thus, self-creativity is always ambiguous. Self-transcendence denotes the person's quest for unambiguous life, the person's reach beyond herself and beyond finite life. Tillich argues that the human begins the quest for unambiguous life in religion and that it is in religion that the human receives the answer.[91] The person can reach for unambiguous life but cannot grasp it. Rather, she must be grasped by it.

[89] Tillich, *Systematic Theology*, vol. 3, 39. See also ibid., vol. 1, 284 where Tillich writes, "A finite being can be separated from God; it can indefinitely resist reunion; it can be thrown into self-destruction and utter despair; but even this is the work of the divine love. . . . Hell has being only in so far as it stands in the unity of the divine love. It is not the limit of the divine love. The only preliminary limit is the resistance of the finite creature."

[90] See M. W. Sinnett, "The Primacy of Relation in Paul Tillich's Theology of Correlation: a Reply to the Critique of Charles Hartshorne," *Religious Studies* 27 (1991), 541–57.

[91] Tillich, *Systematic Theology*, vol. 3, 107.

For Tillich, as for Rahner, self-determination depends upon God even though the exercise of human freedom within it is and must be genuine. Moreover, for Tillich, as for Rahner, the person's self-determining response to God is clearly religious in character. "The act of faith and the act of accepting the moral imperative's unconditional character are one and the same act."[92] Tillich speaks of participation in New Being as faith. But faith leads him to love, for "in relation to God the distinction between faith and love disappears. Being grasped by God in faith and adhering to him in love is one and the same state of creaturely life. It is participation in the transcendent unity of unambiguous life."[93]

Self-determination before God stands in marked contrast to the norm of self-realization. It shifts us away from an ethics of "success" and it emphasizes human agency without valorizing the power to act or the will to power. Moreover, given the responsive and responsible character of self-determination, the particular concrete acts and relations by which the self determines itself and the symbolic and linguistic resources through which she understands herself need to be evaluated morally. The moral import of our creatureliness is that we evaluate these acts, relations, and resources in light of some account of what the person is created to be. As we have already seen, attempts to specify some human nature or essence confront a number of challenges. And it is here that Rahner's and Tillich's attempts to rework conceptual frameworks of being in light of modern criticisms of them seem to retain some of the difficulties they sought to avoid. A hermeneutical approach to self-relation, however, promises a way to develop an account of what the person is created to be, and on its very terms demands and allows for the ongoing criticism and revision of such an account. In a hermeneutical account the claim that the self is known in God does not require a single and static nature, but articulates the truth about the person in a way that orients her practically. It does not end the question of what the self is created to be by supplying a tidy answer that is supposedly applicable in all times and places. Instead it enjoins a critical and collective process of self-understanding. The conceptual language of being here becomes a means to index self-interpretation to the material conditions in which we live and to our flourishing as bodily, social, and reflective creatures. This materiality funds and can correct self-interpretation, even as the interpretive process prohibits naïve movements from our embodiment to prescriptive moral claims.

LOVE AND MORAL BEING

If we ought to understand self-relation with reference to relation to God, why is it appropriate to speak of this intersection in terms of love? Why does this properly religious response to God comprise a moral obligation? Christian theologians claim that God is love. The divine self-disclosure is also a self-offering. God's creativity establishes what is other but does so for the sake of relationship with it. Nowhere is the divine self-offer more concrete than in the person of Christ. God's self-offer in Jesus Christ suggests a different account of love than Nygren thinks it does. To be sure, to make a gift of oneself may require the sacrifice of certain pursuits, interests, and possibilities. But it does not suggest the violent and denigrating connotations self-sacrifice could carry, nor does it imply the juridical and hierarchical relations that self-sacrifice can. Love as a gift of self expresses more positively the self's "coming to be" in relation to another and as gift. It affirms simultaneously the self's freedom and individuation, as well as that of the other. So, the point here is not why this portrait of self-relation is a love relation, but what it shows lovers to do. A lover knows and accepts the truth about the beloved, affirms the value of the beloved (by acknowledging it as already there and/or by bestowing it) and acts for, on, and with the beloved toward her good and in a manner faithful and fitting to her truth and value. This is what God does in loving us.

The contemporary problem of self love is one of identity, of meaning, in which aversion to and skepticism about normative anthropologies create various practical dangers insofar as it becomes difficult to identify concrete actions and relations as incompatible with the self's flourishing. As both Rahner and Tillich recognize, self-determination is ambiguous. The person's self-relation can take a number of forms, some of which are morally invalid. This is why the person's self-determining response to God is a moral obligation.

As it began to become clear in the previous section, the person's self-determining response to God is a matter of love for her self and for God because of the commensurability between her own flourishing and the acceptance of God's self-offer to her. The character of this response will be considered in detail in Chapter Four. Self-determination is not a crass ethical egoism in which the self affirms God in order to pursue her own interest. Instead, her synthetic character demands that the person establish herself as such, thereby differentiating herself from God who creates and sustains that difference.

Rahner maintains that "man is responsible, that he is accountable, that at least in certain dimensions of his existence he has the experience of being able to come and of actually coming into conflict with himself and his original self-understanding."[94] The experience of such contradiction and ambiguity, like the experience of a particular moral demand, is indicative of human transcendence and its term in God; according to Rahner specific moral laws and specific values point to the absolute value of freedom, and, therefore, to the dignity of the person.[95] Because freedom is a task and a demand, it comprises a personal ought, a moral obligation.

Morality is the free personal acceptance of one's own pre-established nature, confidently coming to grips with one's own dynamic reality in all its united though multiple dimensions and precisely coming to grips also with that nature which realizes itself only when it turns lovingly to another person and when it accepts its own nature as the nature of the mystery of love.[96]

Rahner insists that the flight from freedom's task is immoral. The person's responsibility for her freedom is a moral demand.

On Tillich's account, while self love and love for God are united in essential being, separated in existence, and mixed with un-love

---

[94] See Rahner, *Foundations*, 91–92.

[95] Rahner, "The Dignity and Freedom of Man," *Theological Investigations* vol. 2, 249.

[96] Rahner, "The 'Commandment' of Love in Relation to the Other Commandments," *Theological Investigations*, vol. 5, 441. Note how similar Rahner's definition of morality is to his definition of salvation as "the final and definitive validity of a person's true self-understanding and true self-realization in freedom before God by the fact that he accepts his own self as it is disclosed and offered to him in the choice of transcendence as interpreted in freedom," Rahner, *Foundations*, 39. See Ronald Modras, "Implications of Rahner's Anthropology for Fundamental Moral Theology," *Horizons* 12 (Spring 1985), 70–90, especially 72–73.

in actual life, their reunion remains a norm for the person. The person's response to God is a matter of her own self-determination because love involves "the whole being's movement toward another being to overcome existential separation. As such it includes a volitional element under the dimension of self-awareness, i.e., the will to unite. Such a will is essential in every love relation, because the wall of separation could not be pierced without it."[97] Tillich calls love the most radical concern. Recall that a concern must have something concrete as its object. As the most radical concern, love's object must be the completely concrete being, the person.[98] This claim indicates the deep connection in Tillich's thought between love and the moral act of establishing oneself as a person and comprises the moral imperative. Tillich coordinates morality, the person's self-relation, and the person's response to God because "love, as faith, is a state of the whole person."[99]

It is important to emphasize the purely responsive character of the person's self-determination. Proper relation to God and proper self-relation are only enjoyed by grace. The absolute need for grace does not make self love morally irrelevant. It accounts for the intimate connection between self-relation and relation to God. The following chapter will explore the relation of self love to love for God and neighbor.

We can already note the ways a reappropriation of transcendentally/ontologically grounded anthropologies enables us to respond to contemporary demands for an account of self love. Rahner and Tillich share an awareness of the embeddedness and embodiedness of the self. Rahner, for instance, points out that the person experiences herself as a product. He even argues that some aspects of the person are not at the person's own disposal. Tillich takes up the person's creation of and shaping by technology and language in his analysis of culture. Both recognize that freedom is situated historically and therefore socially. Tillich calls the situatedness of freedom destiny while Rahner speaks of freedom as categorically objectified. Freedom determines itself vis-à-vis its own prior self-determination and the self-determination of other persons. The situated or categorical character of the person's free response to God points to

---

[97] Tillich, *Systematic Theology*, vol. 3, 136.   [98] Ibid., vol. 1, 211.   [99] Ibid., vol. 3, 137.

the unity of person and identity. To the extent that Rahner and
Tillich insist that the person's flourishing as such requires her self-
determination, they accommodate the concern that inordinate self
love is accompanied by a roughly equivalent danger of the self's
failure to establish itself as a self. In the following chapter, however, I
will show that the character of self-determination may include some
elements which seem at odds with such a positive endorsement of
self-determination, elements like surrender and sacrifice. For the
moment, however, their anthropologies at least promise to provide
resources to address the concern that the self achieve a proper self-
realization. Each thinker resolutely maintains that certain things
can be predicated of the person as such; neither is bashful about
specifying some account of "human nature." Furthermore, each
thinker insists that the person exceeds the sum total of characteristics which can be empirically observed. This stands to reason, given
the mysterious horizon (Rahner) and holy abyss (Tillich) to which
subjectivity points, and it indicates that both thinkers would reject
positions which extend insight into the specificity of the individual
to a denial of the self.

Does this mean philosophical hermeneutics is a legitimate resource for Christian ethics? As Schweiker notes, Christian ethics
should provide properly theological reasons for employing philosophical resources. These reasons also suggest how Christian ethics
can contribute to secular ethics because theological discourse
shapes consciousness in light of the affirmation that God establishes
and affirms the value of creation. Consider, for instance, some of
what is implied by the claim that (as Rahner and Tillich stress) creation entails the differentiation of the Creator and creature. This
may seem to be an obvious claim for all but a committed pan-
theist, but the import of the claim should not be overlooked. This
differentiation means that while the person's fulfillment as such is
in God, the self is not dissipated into God. God's love unites the
person with God's self but does not obliterate the person; rather,
God thereby creates the person and enables her to establish herself as such. Moreover, God's creative differentiation indicates that
classical concepts such as *imago Dei* and *imitatio Christi* do not denigrate the creature. That is to say, while such concepts have been
understood to locate human goodness in the soul or mind and

thereby to devalue the embodied self, God's creative differentiation affirms the human's *created* goodness. Essential being is experienced in existence as a moral imperative, moral goodness is a matter of self-acceptance because in this God-relation lies the good of the human *as such*. Creative differentiation also points to the tension between what one is and what one ought to be. That is, it has experiential resonance. And finally, even as it expresses God's creative and saving activity, it preserves human freedom. The person's differentiation from God does not thwart relation to God but is a necessary condition for it; this claim is important morally for the criticism of forms of religious activity and thought which denigrate the self or dissolve the self into God.

CONCLUSION

To recognize the unity of person and identity is to recognize that the self who exists before God has the determination of her religious existence as a moral obligation. Such a claim does not deny the gratuity of grace or obscure the pervasiveness of sin, but, rather, points to the intersection of the religious and moral dimensions of the person in the realities of grace, freedom and love.

The insight that the person is created to love God opens and normatively directs theoretical reflection on the self. Moreover, it speaks to the deepest longings of the human heart, our most profound aspirations for meaning and our relentless drive for unity and wholeness. This insight resonates with the resilience of the human spirit – our instinct for self-preservation as well as our desire to flourish. And it resonates with our smallness, our sense of contingency and helplessness in the face of suffering, the acuteness of our limitations and failings. It resonates with our wonder at and gratitude for the goodness of life and it sparks a proper anger and indignation when that goodness is denied or violated. The theological insight that we are created to love God makes sense of the fact that we encounter ourselves as something given to us, determined by others, not entirely at our disposal. But it also speaks to the fact that we experience our agency, freedom, and self-transcendence. The insight that we are created to love God suggests that the project of our selfhood has its origin and term in the divine. And this in turn reveals something about the divine: the God for whom we have been created gives God's very self to us for our fulfillment. We realize ourselves in our participation in (Tillich) and acceptance of (Rahner) God's offer of relation. Human being is fundamentally moral and religious being. Because right self love is a mode of being in which the person actualizes herself in a response to God, the moral life is a distinctively religious one. This moves us from the account of self-relation offered in this chapter to the next, where I consider right self love as the morally proper form of self-relation.

CHAPTER 4

Right self love

An adequate account of right self love must begin with an analysis of the self who is to love herself because the moral life is not simply a matter of doing good, but of being and becoming good.[1] Chapter Three argued that as the person takes up her self-relation she responds to God's offer of the divine self. Self love can be rightly or wrongly enacted. Right self love, then, designates the morally proper form of self-relation. This chapter (1) explores the relation of self love and love for God; (2) argues that right self love is only actualized and assessed socially and historically, and, accordingly, explores the relation between self love and love for neighbor, and between self love and social justice; (3) and argues that self love is actualized and assessed in one's concrete acts and relations, such that right self love consists in the moral good of embodied integrity.

This chapter continues reading Rahner and Tillich hermeneutically. By thinking with them we arrive at two insights into moral goodness. First, we see how the very structure of the person's experience of herself, mediated through what is other, arises in her asking about herself: the person comes to herself by understanding herself in relation to her world and to others. The mediated character of self-relation offsets solipsism and subjectivism, because the

---

[1] Much of contemporary ethics draws a distinction between questions of the right and questions of the good, and, moreover, confines ethics to the former. Given the epistemic difficulties entailed in specifying some universal account of the good, many thinkers, especially in the Kantian tradition, argue that ethics should specify duties to be performed rather than goods to be sought. Such positions can fail to realize that deontological prescriptions nonetheless imply some desirable state of affairs to be realized or respected. Questions of the right imply questions of the good. When deontological and teleological dimensions of ethics are severed from one another ethics become internally inconsistent and promote anemic moral anthropologies.

self's relation to itself can only be evaluated morally in terms of her acting in the world, and, specifically, in her relations with others. The person comes to be a person in her interpersonal encounters, and moreover, the moral quality of her self-relation is wrought and assessed in these encounters. Put differently, this chapter suggests that the obligation to love God and neighbor resonates bindingly in the self's experience of herself.

The second insight into moral goodness can be gleaned from the fact that both Rahner and Tillich consider the person's self-constitution under the threat of its negation. Rahner constructs a theology of death whereby the finality and meaning of the person's freedom is achieved in her death; when the person befriends her death she surrenders or abandons herself to the horizon of mystery. Tillich speaks of the person's self-determination in terms of a self-affirmation which is coupled with self-acceptance, that is, with the faith which accepts that one has been accepted. Rahner and Tillich thus indicate that at bottom the moral good is a matter of faith, of trust, and of hope. This act of faith actualizes a distinctive way of being, one which affirms the goodness of life and of oneself despite evidence to the contrary, one which enacts the meaning of life not in a self-mastery which makes sense of everything, but in an embrace of the plurality, complexity, and final incomprehensibility of life. I marshal Rahner and Tillich to address a contemporary version of the threat of negation, namely the absorption of the self into relations and systems. Both thinkers open up the person's self-determination as it is tied to her self-understanding, though neither develops this insight into the fundamentally interpretive character of self-relation. By thinking *beyond* Rahner and Tillich toward such an interpretive account of self-relation, we can discern how the very conceptual frameworks which foster these insights also encourage voluntaristic and intuitionistic pictures of self-relation.

SELF LOVE AND LOVE FOR GOD

I have been arguing that Christian ethics needs to recoup classical connections between self love and love for God and that doing so speaks to problems that attend the contemporary norm of self-realization. Here I specify the relation of the two loves and affirm their difference. I argue that love for God is a norm for self love, and that self love bears normatively on love for God.

Love for God is a norm for self love. As Stephen Pope, working from the Thomistic perspective, insists, "true self-love and neighbor love are possible only to the extent that we love God above all."[2] But too often this appears to mean little more than that love for God prohibits idolatry and pride; it then seems that love for God sets negative boundaries for self love, or that it prohibits self love altogether. But love for God can actually contribute some positive content to a proper conception of self love. To begin, the person loves herself when she loves God. Thomas Aquinas argued this because the person loves God as the principle of good and loves oneself as a partaker of this good.[3] Søren Kierkegaard argued that to love God is true self love; he makes this claim in the context of arguing that God teaches that the content of love is self-sacrifice.[4] Edward Vacek argues that through love for God "we come to love and hate, in our finite and differentiated way, what God loves and hates and in accord with the preferential order of God's loves and hates."[5] A number of relevant theological and moral claims operate here. The person loves herself – that is, she is rightly related to herself – when she lives and loves as she was created to do, when she is faithful to God's purposes for her, when her concrete acts and relations and her dispositions and affections are ordered to her good, who is God. The person loves herself when she orients and offers herself not around some future object or concern, but in response to a transcendent, sovereign God who surpasses and relativizes all such objects and concerns, including that of her own well-being. The person loves herself when she participates in God's life and love for the world.

If God is the highest good of the person, love for God is in some measure constitutive of self love. Yet if love for God is not a component or feature of self love but is in fact a norm for it,

2 Stephen Pope, "Expressive Individualism and True Self-Love: a Thomistic Perspective," *The Journal of Religion* 71 (July 1991), 384–99, 399.
3 See his *Summa Theologia* II II Q. 26 art. 4.
4 Søren Kierkegaard, *Works of Love*, eds. and trans. Howard V. Hong and Edna H. Hong with introduction and notes (Princeton, NJ: Princeton University Press, 1995), 107.
5 Edward Vacek S. J., *Love, Human and Divine: the Heart of Christian Ethics* (Washington DC: Georgetown University Press, 1994), 133.

in what might love for God consist? It is not first and foremost a matter of religious observances and practices, though these have an important place as expressions and embodiments of love. Love for God is a relationship of profound personal intimacy. Like all relationships, it consists in a particular history – seasons of sweetness and of difficulty, movements into deeper intimacy and evasions of it. Because the person's relationship is with a living God, love for God has an open-ended character.[6] In love for God the person ventures her very self.

Man is . . . obliged to love God with his *whole* heart. This one heart which man has to engage – the innermost centre of his person (and on this basis also everything else found in the individual) – is something unique: what it contains within its uniqueness, what is engaged and given gratuitously in this love, is known only once it has been done, when the person has really caught up with himself and hence begins to know what is in him and *who* he is in the concrete. By this love, therefore, man embarks on the adventure of his own reality, all of which is at first veiled from him. He cannot comprehend and evaluate from the very start what is actually demanded of him. He is demanded, he himself is staked in the concreteness of his heart and of his life lying still before him as an unknown future and revealing – once it has been accomplished and only then – what is this heart which had to wager and expend itself during this life.[7]

Love for God asks and exacts everything, calls one into question, challenges one's understandings and loyalties. Love for God continually discloses the person to herself in all her poverty, discloses the futility of her attempts to justify or secure herself or to do so through some finite object or pursuit. H. Richard Niebuhr argued that God is "the enemy of all our causes," and "the opponent of all our gods," the slayer of that with which we separate ourselves from God.[8] In this way God shows the divine self to be our friend.

6 Kathryn Tanner notes that God's transcendence does not counter but makes possible God's immediacy and intimate presence. See her *God and Creation in Christian Theology* (Oxford: Blackwell, 1988), 46.
7 Karl Rahner, "'The Commandment of Love,'" *Theological Investigations*, vol. 5, 453. See *Theological Investigations*, vols. 1–14 (vols. 1–6, Baltimore, MD: Helicon; vols. 7–10, New York: Herder and Herder; vols. 11–14, New York: Seabury, 1961–1976).
8 H. Richard Niebuhr, "Faith in God and in Gods," *Radical Monotheism and Western Culture, With Supplementary Essays*, foreword by James M. Gustafson (Louisville, KY: Westminster/John Knox, 1960), 122.

Christian ethics cannot separate the open-ended character of love for God from God's self-disclosure in the person, work, and resurrection of Jesus Christ. Particular love relations with God find shape and life in the concrete response of discipleship and in ecclesial life.[9] In an encounter with the totality of Jesus' word, life, and death, God becomes present in an offer of forgiveness. Moreover, this offer in Jesus is final and irrevocable. The person understands herself most properly when she realizes that she has been created, disposed of, and forgiven, when she accepts herself as one not wholly at her own disposal. Such a self-acceptance constitutes a surrender to God. Jesus Christ is the model for such a surrender; Jesus reveals that the person really achieves herself when she exercises her freedom in an act of definitive self-disposal.[10] But only Jesus of Nazareth has surrendered his existence to God absolutely and unconditionally. On Rahner's account the person's encounter with Jesus mediates the immediate, unthematic offer God has made always already. A personal relationship with Jesus constitutes, then, mediated immediacy.[11] This mediated immediacy indicates that for Rahner "salvation does not mean a reified state of affairs, but rather a personal and ontological reality. . . . This takes place in and through an abiding personal relationship to the God–Man in whom and in whom alone immediacy to God is reached now and forever."[12] The loss or gain of God unfolds in the person's experience, changing her, yielding the abundant life Christ brings (John 10:10). Similarly, for Tillich one can be certain that in Jesus as the Christ the conditions of existence have been conquered because this faith is based on the experience of the conquest itself. The experience of New Being grounds faith in New Being, but the experience need not be an explicit experience of Jesus Christ. Tillich denies the claim that there is no salvation apart from Christ. Rather, the uniqueness and universality of the Christ event indicate

[9] See, for example, Stanley Hauerwas, *A Community of Character: toward a Constructive Christian Social Ethic* (Notre Dame, IN: University of Notre Dame Press, 1981) and Charles Curran, *The Catholic Moral Tradition Today: a Synthesis* (Washington DC: Georgetown University Press, 1999).

[10] Rahner links this act to the person's death.

[11] Note that the encounter with Jesus, then, need not occur in an explicitly religious act.

[12] Rahner, *Foundations of Christian Faith: an Introduction to the Idea of Christianity*, trans. William Dych (New York: Crossroad, 1993), 309.

that Christ is the criterion for all saving experiences. In the Christ the healing power is complete and unlimited, but Tillich maintains that the person of the Christ cannot be separated from that which made him the Christ; "the being of the Christ is his work and . . . his work is his being, namely, the New Being which is his being."[13]

What is the moral import of love for God for self love? The foregoing already indicates a moral prohibition of idolatrous religious affections and a moral exhortation to a religious encounter and relation with God. Love for God can also remind us of the religious depths of moral actions. Our moral actions are means (though surely not the only means) through which we take up our relation to our selves, to others, and to God. Thus, to act in ways and nurture attitudes and dispositions that are morally self-destructive separates us from God and from others. And to sin against God is to behave in ways and persist in attitudes and dispositions that are self-destructive. This does not mean that salvation or damnation designate God's reaction to the person in reward or judgment, but that the loss or gain of God is itself performed in the person's free self-determination before God.[14] Properly understood, love for God comprises a norm for self love that rules out works righteousness; it also rules out a quietism that reduces love to a faith that supposes that the priority and efficacy of God's grace nullifies human freedom. Christian thought and tradition are marked by disputes about the relation between faith and love, the Reformation being in many respects the escalation of such early disputes. Is faith formed by love, particularly works of love, as many Roman Catholic theologians have suggested? Or as many Protestants have insisted, Martin Luther vociferously so, does faith flow into love? The former position courts works righteousness, the latter risks neglecting the self-constituting character of (works of) love. If, as Jean Porter notes, acting comprises a kind of knowledge and, as John Finnis notes, is a way we participate in goods, then works of love can flesh out faith, deepen or re-enliven it, even purify it by connecting it with the hard realities of human life, or restore it by connecting

[13] Paul Tillich, *Systematic Theology*, 3 vols. (Chicago: University of Chicago, 1957–63), vol. 2, 168. Tillich seeks to mediate Incarnational and Adoptionist Christologies. See 149.
[14] See Karl Rahner, "Theology of Freedom," *Theological Investigations*, vol. 6, 186–87.

it with experiences of goodness, communion, and hope. If faith changes us, the way we understand ourselves and the world, then of course faith will flow into and inform our acting. The real worry in disputes about faith and love is to avoid the erroneous claim that the person's acts of love somehow demand a favorable response from God. This worry should not dissuade us from stressing that the person's acts of love do affect and effect (if not exhaust) her response to God. They do not effect God's response to her.[15]

Love for God also highlights and relativizes the inevitability of moral uncertainty and risk.[16] Because love for God has an open-ended quality, to say that the person loves herself when she lives and loves as she was created to do (and loves others when she affirms and promotes their creaturely goodness and well-being) is to gesture at the real yet dynamic moral value of creation. As Kathryn Tanner argues, "the stress is therefore on the manifestation of God's will in a moral *ordering* rather than in a moral *order* with some static and immutable character."[17] Moral codes, decisions, and relations carry an ineradicable risk, yet this risk need not paralyze us because God's love is not a verdict on our moral efforts. And the very open-ended quality that highlights the risk also relativizes it. The final meaning of our moral efforts is hidden, because we are hidden, in Christ.

Moreover, because love for God is open-ended and because it asks and exacts everything, it requires us to face the costs of discipleship. The commensurability of self love and love for God does not make for a facile self love or a vacuous love for God which reduce either or both loves to a lame and general esteem or affirmation, or to a blind, defensive protection of our causes and interests. Love for God can require self love to express itself in various and ongoing forms of self-denial and self-sacrifice. And yet, love for God cannot permit a narcissistic martyrdom in which one can evade the responsibility of being oneself. Intimacy with God can be a fearful experience, one shirked by resorting to self-expenditure as well as self-assertion. Love for God shows self love to involve a distinctive way of being in the world in which the moral good is a matter of faith; faith does not eradicate the moral risk, or nullify the possibility

[15] Vacek insists that the person's works do affect God's response. See *Love, Human and Divine.*
[16] I will take this up at greater length in Chapter Five.
[17] Kathryn Tanner, *The Politics of God* (Minneapolis, MN: Fortress, 1992), 101.

of a self-sacrifice that extends to martyrdom, or dissolve the fear of venturing oneself. It affirms in love that God is the highest good, and as such is one's own good.

In light of all this, is it possible or desirable to speak of a person loving God disinterestedly? Nygren and Ramsey offer powerful criticisms of the sort of enlightened selfishness that makes love for God a project of self-fulfillment or self-improvement. Yet the commensurability of love for God and self is not simply an eschatological one, or a matter of contingent, unintended side effects (such that love for God can *happen* to contribute to the self's flourishing). Others like François Fénelon urge a disinterested love for God. But human love for God cannot be wholly disinterested. How could the person be disinterested about the one who is her ultimate concern? James Alison notes that Jesus taught in terms of heavenly rewards and expected these to be motivational forces in the lives of the disciples.[18] Loving God as one's good need not subordinate God to the project of seeking one's good.[19] As Vacek insists, God creates and sustains us *for* the divine self-gift. "A gift of one's self, love, is the act of uniting one's self with the beloved. When someone gives himself or herself to us, we become aware that we do not live our lives alone. . . . God's love means that God transcends God's *aseity* and enters our life. God unites God's own self with our self and thereby makes God's own self available to us."[20] Loving God as one's good can and should be a process of devotion, of surrender and self-disposal towards and participation in the divine. Loving God as one's good is compatible with and should accompany loving God for God's own sake. Indeed, love for God yields fruits we reap in this life, but it also demands a great deal of us. Love for God and self entail an often painful and inevitably humbling process of self-discovery and self-criticism. Loving God for God's own sake is part of this process and can sustain us through it.

Now that we have considered, in brief, the normative bearing of love for God on self love, let us consider what if any normative bearing self love might have on love for God. In light of the

[18] James Alison, *The Joy of Being Wrong: Original Sin Through Easter Eyes* (New York: Crossroad, 1998), 229.
[19] Cf. John Burnaby, *Amor Dei* (London: Hodder and Stoughton, 1947).
[20] Vacek, *Love, Human and Divine*, 122.

commandment to love God with one's whole heart, mind and strength (Matt. 22:37), it would seem that self love cannot bear normatively on love for God, at least not if normative bearing suggests that self love is in any respect a prior or higher norm than love for God. But there are at least two respects in which self love bears normatively on love for God insofar as it can counter distortions of love for God as such.

The first concerns the difference between self love and love for God. The profound and abiding commensurability of self love and love for God does not mean that they can be collapsed into one another without remainder. Because they are commensurable but not coextensive loves, there are duties proper to each. A regular life of prayer yields many benefits for the self, but prayer is properly about expressing and growing in love for God, not about those benefits.[21] Similarly, there are duties proper to self love that, while not isolated from the self's love for God, are not properly or directly acts of love for God. Practices of caring for oneself, like regular exercise or a good diet, could *express* gratitude to God as one's creator and may *prompt* gratitude inasmuch as they call to mind one's creatureliness. But they are not directly or necessarily acts of love for God. More to the point, because self love entails proper duties, it counters a distortion of love for God that would permit *no* room for the self to pursue her own interests and projects. Susan Wolf has argued against a moral sainthood that crowds out non-moral pursuits and traits, ones that either do not contribute to sainthood or cut against its grain.[22] Interpreting love for God in a similar fashion would be just as erroneous as Wolf's version of moral sainthood. Her worry is legitimate – that a morality (or religiosity) conceived without limits can devalue legitimate and good pursuits and personality traits that do not seem to contribute to the project of morality or to one's religious life. Right self love, as a positive and independent moral obligation, counters such moral and religious distortions of love for God by affirming the goodness of creaturely

---

[21] Petitionary prayer can serve this end, too, fostering reliance on God and providing clarity about and room for criticism of what we ask from God.

[22] For the latter Wolf gives the example of cynical wit. This only serves to show how false her conception of moral sainthood is; it is a caricature of goodness. Susan Wolf, "Moral Saints," *The Journal of Philosophy* (August 1982), 419–39. See also Robert M. Adams's response to Wolf, "Saints," *The Journal of Philosophy* (July 1984), 392–401.

life and the propriety of pursuits like recreation. Right self love can fund reflection on the difference between a worldliness or sensuality that is, say, isolating and concupiscible from a creatureliness that delights in the pleasures of creation in a way that opens one to and affirms others and the world. Right self love can fund reflection on the mean between a self-indulgent and unjust life of consumption and a scrupulous asceticism that devalues our bodily existence and earthly blessings. It makes room for a joy chastened by justice and a justice mellowed (but not mitigated) by joy.

The second respect in which self love bears normatively on love for God is the theoretical correlate of the first. Self love helps us to see the need for moral criticisms of religious beliefs. I will develop this argument in Chapter Six. For now we can note helpfully a distinction that Christian theology draws between *fides qua* (the faith by which one believes) and *fides quae* (the faith that is believed). The distinction captures a point important for a contemporary account of self love because it can illuminate the fact that different symbols and claims can mediate an existential posture and relation of faith. The *fides quae* mediates the *fides qua* and can do so in better and worse fashion. So, on the one hand, the existential commitment of faith, the *fides qua*, is primary. On the other hand, because the *fides quae* comprises more than a set of propositions to affirm, it constitutes a cognitive, affective, moral world in which grace operates. In this respect, it is primary. A hermeneutical account of self-relation grasps both of these points. It is possible and important to reflect critically on the adequacy of the *fides quae* to the *fides qua*. This reflection should include moral criticism of religious beliefs and practices. We might, for example, ask after the anthropocentrism or sexism of various doctrines and seek to revise these doctrines so that they express more faithfully and correctly the God whose self-disclosure in Jesus Christ secures our faith. Yet this reflection on the adequacy of the *fides quae* proceeds according to criteria that emerge in the *fides quae* itself.

SELF LOVE AND LOVE FOR NEIGHBOR

Chapter Two noted that some thinkers, such as Paul Ramsey, argue on behalf of self love as a duty legitimately derived from love for the neighbor. I argue that self love is a positive moral obligation in its own right. I also argue that self love is actualized and identified in love for the neighbor. Do these two claims conflict? How can self love be an independent duty and yet depend upon love for the neighbor in order to be actual? How are love for God, neighbor, and self related? Is neighbor love simply a litmus test for self love and love for God? This section will show that the triadic love obligations to God, neighbor and self are united in God and in the person as such. The complex dynamics between love for God, neighbor, and self cannot possibly be done justice in the brief space which this chapter allows; this section neither pretends nor endeavors to exhaust the topic. Rather, it explores the inter-relation of self love and neighbor love in order to show the essentially differentiated relation among love for God, self, and neighbor as well as their essentially related differentiation. Rahner and Tillich contribute a number of insights important to a contemporary account of right self love. But their transcendental and ontological approaches also risk displacing the neighbor and diverting moral attention away from our concrete social and moral existence. They also risk over-emphasizing either the differentiation or the relation of love for God, self, and neighbor. A hermeneutical approach fares better.

Self love and love for God are actualized in neighbor love because the self is an embodied and social person. We cannot identify, much less morally assess self-relation or our relation to God apart from our being and acting in relation to others and in the world. Otherwise self-relation and relation to God would consist solely of states in the mind, divorced from our embodiment, our actions, our determination by and of others. The social character of the person is not some quality alongside others but touches every dimension of the person. Thus, the person comes to know herself, to be herself in relations with others. The person's self-determining response to God is not achieved over against others but within these relations. It is not something won by self-assertion, but is discovered when she gives herself away. This is the paradox of the moral life, that to lose oneself is to find oneself.[23] Just as God created by giving God's

[23] Rahner writes, "only if one thus abandons oneself, and lovingly sinks into the other, does one succeed in finding oneself. Otherwise, a person languishes in the prison of his or her own selfishness," (*The Love of Jesus and the Love of Neighbor*, trans. Robert Barr (New York: Crossroad, 1983), 17). This is not a new theme in Christianity. And it is on this point that an account of self love which is culled from Rahner seems at odds with the feminist wariness

self, thereby establishing something different, so too does the person actualize herself in surrender to the incomprehensible other. Nevertheless, to say that self love and love for God are enacted in a world and in relation to others still leaves much to be said, descriptively and prescriptively. One important point is that self-relation and relation to God are not reducible to or exhausted by the self's relations to and with her neighbors. But first let us see how Rahner and Tillich account for the relation between love for God, self, and neighbor.

Rahner's appropriation of Thomistic causality allows him to link self-realization with dynamic relationality. According to Rahner "man is a social being, a being who can exist only within such intercommunication with others throughout all of the dimension[s] of human existence."[24] For Rahner love of neighbor is the "actualization of Christian existence in an absolute sense."[25] In other words, love for the other is the basic act of Christian life. As such, it is the basic act of the human being.[26] Love of neighbor is not just another moral act among many but is the "basis and sum total of the moral as such."[27] This is because the "one moral (or immoral) basic act in which man comes to himself is also the (loving or hating) communication with the concrete Thou in which man experiences, accepts or denies his basic *a priori* reference to the Thou as such."[28]

Rahner insists on the unity of love for the neighbor and love for God. "Wherever a genuine love of man attains its proper nature and its moral absoluteness and depth, it is in addition always so underpinned and heightened by God's saving grace that it is also love of God, whether it be explicitly considered to be such a love by the subject or not."[29] Not every act of love for God is also formally

---

of sacrifice which I detailed in Chapter Two; one need only recall Beverly Harrison's emphatic rejection of sacrifice to see the disparity. The place of sacrifice, surrender, and obedience will be considered in the next section. Rahner's claim that in Jesus Christ, the God–Man, the divine and human stand in solidarity with one another will provide important symbolic means with which the role of sacrifice can be made amenable to, if not commensurate with, feminist critiques of sacrifice like Harrison's. See Beverly Wildung Harrison, *Making the Connections: Essays in Feminist Social Ethics*, ed., Carol S. Robb, (Boston, MA: Beacon, 1985).

[24] Rahner, *Foundations*, 323.   [25] Ibid., 308.
[26] For Rahner to be Christian is to be a human being.
[27] Rahner, "Reflections on the Unity of the Love of Neighbor and Love of God," *Theological Investigations*, vol. 6, 240.
[28] Ibid., 241.   [29] Ibid., 237.

neighbor love.[30] But all interhuman love is also love of God, provided it is already of a moral quality, "since it is oriented towards God, not indeed by an explicitly categorised motive but...by its inescapably given transcendental horizon, which is given gratuitously by God's always prevenient saving grace."[31] Thus, the unity between love for neighbor and love for God is not on Rahner's account a matter of directing one's intentions. Rather, "the categorized explicit love of neighbour is the primary act of the love of God....It is radically true, i.e., by an ontological and not merely 'moral' or psychological necessity, that whoever does not love the brother whom he 'sees,' also cannot love God whom he does not see, and that one can love God whom one does not see only *by* loving one's visible brother lovingly."[32]

The unity consists in the fact that love for God and love for neighbor share the same horizon. Love for neighbor is love for God because the person is in the world and realizes her love for God insofar as in her love for neighbor she accepts the conditions of its possibility, namely, the grace which supports both loves. Moreover, love for God is love for neighbor because explicit religious acts are taken up by the transcendental and inclusive experience of God which is only found unreflectedly in our interaction with the world, that is, with other persons. Rahner, then, would reject the notion that the person can have a privatized relation with God, that the person can attain God interiorly in an unmediated fashion.[33]

But the claim that love for God, neighbor, and self are radically united entails serious risks. Does their unity abolish any distinction between them? Is the God–self relation that is actualized in neighbor love co-extensive with it (i.e., is love for God exhausted by neighbor love)? This may constrict love for God. Granted, the unity of love for God and neighbor may open Rahner's position to the claim found in some feminist and liberation theologies (such as

[30] For example, the concrete act of prayer is not formally an act of neighbor love. See ibid., 238.
[31] Ibid., 238.   [32] Ibid., 247.
[33] Rahner of course was not unappreciative of mysticism; the role Ignatian spirituality plays in his thought attests to this. The point, however, is that the person is a unity of spirit and matter. See Andrew Tallon, "The Heart in Rahner's Philosophy of Mysticism," *Theological Studies* 53 (1992), 700–28. For a constructive use of Rahner's spirituality see Annice Callahan, "The Relationship between Spirituality and Theology," *Horizons* 16 (1989), 266–74.

Beverly Harrison's) that God is known in the struggle for justice. Recall that in Chapter One I argued that such a claim sometimes confines the person's relation with God to a fruit of or moment within interpersonal relations. I want to show the abiding unity between the person's relation with God and the person's relations with neighbors, but argue that, while relation to God is always mediated categorically, it is not exhausted by interpersonal relations. Moreover, the radical unity of love for God and neighbor threatens the self inasmuch as it implies that surrender to God occurs in surrender to the neighbor. Consider for example how the unity of love for God and neighbor pose the problem of right self love anew:

> what we are commanded by the "commandment" to love our neighbor, in its oneness with the commandment to love God, is the demolition of our own selfishness – the overthrow of the notion that love of neighbor is basically really only the rational settlement of mutual claims, that it demands only giving and taking to the mutual satisfaction of all parties.... When one really understands the unity of the love of God and neighbor, the latter shifts from its position as a particular demand for a delimited, verifiable achievement to a position of total fulfillment of one's life, in which we are challenged in our totality, wholly challenged, challenged beyond our capacity – but challenged in the only way in which we may gain the highest freedom: freedom from ourselves.[34]

How can freedom *from* self, especially when understood as our highest freedom, be compatible with a command to love ourselves? In light of the feminist critique that the basic sin of women is the failure to establish themselves as selves, can we endorse the role which surrender plays in Rahner's account?

Rahner's insistence on this unity also threatens to displace the neighbor. Johannes Baptist Metz, Rahner's student and critic, has forwarded what has become a stock criticism of Rahner, namely that because of his transcendental approach Rahner fails to deal

---

[34] Rahner, *The Love of Jesus*, 84. I do not mean to equate selfishness with establishing oneself as self; indeed, it is precisely such an equation which feminists reject. That is why Rahner's understanding of self-realization in terms of surrender may be problematic. More amenable to the feminist critique would be Rahner's specification of self-realization in terms of self-acceptance or self-disposal. This language may suggest a valuation of the self which the feminist critique finds necessary to offset traditional ethical wariness of self-assertion. Yet, it is important to note that self-acceptance and self-disposal do not differ from self-assertion for Rahner; this is the force of his ontology of symbols.

adequately with the historical and political character of human existence.[35] Edward Vacek also argues against Rahner that human consciousness "is not so necessarily open to the infinite that in every act of self-transcendence we always intend an infinite or absolute horizon."[36] We generally live our lives within the finite horizon of our world. Some even experience life as absurd rather than meaningful. Moreover, even if love for neighbor does affirm God, it "is not the same thing as a conscious, free act of loving God."[37] According to Vacek, "the neighbor is not God, and so love for the neighbor is not love for God. Our neighbors deserve a love that is directed directly to them."[38] We can love neighbors for their own sake and also love them as part of our cooperation with God.

Tillich encounters problems as well. Recall that Tillich understands morality as the constitution of the self as a person and that spirit is the dimension of the self which characterizes the person as such in a community of persons. Given this, the person experiences the norms of essential being in the encounter with another person. The other self "is the unconditional limit to the desire to assimilate one's whole world, and the experience of this limit is the experience of the ought-to-be, the moral imperative. The moral constitution of the self in the dimension of the spirit begins with this experience."[39] The person-to-person encounter implies a moral imperative of unconditional validity, the demand to acknowledge and respect the other person as a person. This imperative is experienced as the other's resistance to the self's attempts to assimilate everything into itself.[40] The interpersonal encounter is illuminated by the polarity of individuation and participation. The individuated self is a centered self; a centered self is one who successfully actualizes some potentialities and, in doing so, integrates them such that no single potentiality dominates the self. As a centered self, the person

---

[35] See Metz's *Faith in History and Society: toward a Practical Fundamental Theology*, trans. David Smith (New York: Seabury, 1979). A condensed version of his critique can be found in his "An Identity Crisis in Christianity? Transcendental and Political Responses," *Theology and Discovery: Essays in Honor of Karl Rahner*, ed., William Kelly (Milwaukee, WI: Marquette University Press, 1980), 169–78.

[36] Vacek, *Love, Human and Divine*, 144.   [37] Ibid., 145.

[38] Ibid., 266.   [39] Tillich, *Systematic Theology*, vol. 3, 40.

[40] Tillich, of course, does not deny that the self can ignore or violate the other's claim to respect, but he insists that the claim of the person to be acknowledged as such can never be eradicated. Here is Kant's influence on Tillich.

remains separate from everything other than itself; the self *has* a world. Yet, the self also *belongs to* her world. Thus, the self participates in a world. But the self cannot participate in such a way that the self loses its centeredness, or else it ceases to be a self. Thus, the person-to-person encounter must be of such a kind that the separateness of the persons is maintained in the midst of interpersonal participation. "It is the superiority of the person-to-person relationship that it preserves the separation of the self-centered self, and nevertheless actualizes their reunion in love."[41]

There are several reasons why for Tillich love for God, neighbor, and self intersect. First, these three loves are united in the ground of being, that is, in God. The self participates in being-itself, is separate from it, and seeks reunion with it. This is the ontological movement of love. In the urge toward reunion, the self negotiates its self-relation vis-à-vis its relation to being-itself, that is, to God. Second, and relatedly, Tillich maintains that right self love and love for others are interdependent.[42] The reunion to which love drives is not only a reunion of one's actual self with one's essential being and a reunion of the person with the divine but a reunion of the person with other persons. "The other person is a stranger, but a stranger only in disguise. Actually he is an estranged part of one's self. Therefore one's own humanity can be realized only in reunion with him – a reunion which is also decisive for the realization of his humanity."[43] Thirdly, love for God, self, and neighbor intersect because power, love, and justice are only made real in interpersonal encounters. Every encounter between persons is an encounter in which individual bearers of power engage each other.[44] In the person-to-person encounter, the power of being actualizes itself in the form of justice. Tillich insists that the "intrinsic claim

[41] Paul Tillich, *Love, Power and Justice* (Oxford: Oxford University Press, 1954), 27.
[42] Ibid., 22.
[43] Tillich, *Systematic Theology*, vol. 3, 261. Such a passage responds nicely to the poor criticism made against Tillich by Glenn Graber, who argued that Tillich's thought is afflicted by monism. See Glenn Graber, "The Metaethics of Paul Tillich," *Journal of Religious Ethics* 1 (1973), 113–33, especially 125–26.
[44] Tillich, *Love, Power and Justice*, 41. For a defense of Tillich against the charge that his theology is individualistic, see M. W. Sinnett, "The Primacy of Relation in Paul Tillich's Theology of Correlation: a Reply to the Critique of Charles Hartshorne," *Religious Studies* 27 (1991), 541–57, especially 555. See also Joseph Keller, "Mysticism and Intersubjective Creativity," *Studia Mystica* 8:4 (1985), 36–46.

in everything that is cannot be violated without violating the violator."[45] This is because the self, as an ego, cannot be an ego without some other, some thou, in relation to which it establishes itself. To ignore the other's claim and treat the other as an object is to surrender one's own ego.[46] Thus, the failure to love the neighbor constitutes a failure to love oneself.

The acknowledgment of the other person qua person is not an abstract respect; at least, it cannot remain abstract if it is truly to be love for the other. This is because the "immediate expression of love is action."[47] So a fourth and final reason why love for God, self, and neighbor are interdependent is the relation of faith and love. Faith, as ultimate concern, implies both love and action. This is because an ultimate concern includes the "passionate desire to actualize the content of one's concern. 'Concern' in its very definition includes the desire for action."[48] Tillich argues that ethical faith seeks to transform estranged reality; in it the agape quality of love is dominant, which means that the person accepts her neighbors yet seeks to transform them into what they potentially are. Because Tillich understands love as the reunion of the separated, self love, love for God, and love for neighbor drive toward the actual manifestation of essential being.

But, does the drive toward essential being conflate or collapse love for God, neighbor, and self? If these three loves are united in essential being, and separated under existence, how are they related in the actual conditions of life? Are they coextensive? Does the argument that love reunites the estranged undermine the person's self-determination? Critics like Judith Plaskow would argue this because, as Chapter Three noted, they attribute a monistic character to Tillich's thought. While such charges of monism ignore the emphasis Tillich places on individuation, they nonetheless indicate that some elements of Tillich's system seem at odds with the claim that in self love the person achieves her identity. While these critics fault Tillich for a monism that may eclipse the self, others like Schweiker and James Gustafson fault him for an intuitionism that

[45] Ibid., 68.   [46] See ibid., 78.
[47] Paul Tillich, *Dynamics of Faith* (New York: Harper Torchbooks, Harper Brothers, 1957), 115.
[48] Ibid., 116.

may eclipse the neighbor. Schweiker argues that because Tillich understands the self's moral task of integration "in terms of the relation between the essential and actual self, his real concern is not the integrity of diverse goods in historical and social life. This means that his ethics verges on intuitionism in the appeal to the 'silent voice' of conscience about what to do, rather than examining the range of questions which constitute the field of morality in terms of the actual values and disvalues of life."[49] Not only does this intuitionism divert attention from the actual values and disvalues of life, the overall quest for fulfillment and authenticity requires a maximization of power that "leads to further fragmentation and frustration. It pits life against life in a circle of fear."[50] Notwithstanding Tillich's claims about justice toward other persons, his very emphasis on self-actualization risks making the neighbor a rival. Therefore, concludes Schweiker, an ethics must affirm the goodness of the person's power to act but avoid making it the good of life.

Because self love is mediated through love for the neighbor, does the person instrumentalize others in her endeavors to love her self, to seek her own *bonum*? I argued that self love is not exhausted by neighbor love. But, have neighbors become stepping stones toward her own self-realization? In my judgment, the claim that self love is not exhausted in love for the neighbor protects and preserves the neighbor as much as the self. The same irreducibility which belongs to the self must be attributed to other persons; to recognize this is to capture in the form of a principle for action the force of the self's experience of herself as mediated through others. Moreover, the person's self-determination is not achieved over against others, but in relation with them, and these relations entail a certain sacrifice from the person. While Rahner and Tillich construe the place of sacrifice differently, each thinker contends that the person in some way sacrifices or surrenders the desire to master herself. Rahner develops this in terms of the person's surrender to the incomprehensibility of her divine horizon. Tillich develops this sacrifice in

---

[49] William Schweiker, *Responsibility and Christian Ethics* (Cambridge: Cambridge University Press, 1995), 84. See also James M. Gustafson, *Protestant and Roman Catholic Ethics: Prospects for Rapprochement* (Chicago: University of Chicago, 1978), 42.

[50] Schweiker, *Responsibility and Christian Ethics*, 225.

terms of the person's relinquishment of her own goodness. Despite these differences, it may be said that the person's sacrifice of her own mastery prevents her, at least theoretically, from a kind of concupiscible assimilation of other persons and things into her self. The person cannot violate the other person's claim to be acknowledged as such without violating herself, and God must be loved for God's own sake. Right self love entails the surrender (Rahner) and sacrifice (Tillich) of self-mastery; this surrender or sacrifice offsets tendencies of self-realization ethics to glorify power or truncate the self. In this surrender or sacrifice, the person acknowledges that her identity is bound up with her relation to the divine. Because proper self-relation cannot be won by her own efforts, its goodness is not her own creation or achievement. Rather, it is the work of grace. But to the extent that the person engages her freedom in her response to God's offer, the person actively seeks her own realization and flourishing. Self love is centrally a matter of love for God. Human actualization and flourishing consist in a coherence or integrity the self achieves through grace.

Whatever the difficulties of Rahner's insistence on the unity of love for God and neighbor, it cautions against the privatization of the person's love for God. And it reminds us of the religious import of neighbor love. Tillich reminds us that self love and love for neighbor actually require one another. A love for the neighbor that obliterates the self is not really love, nor can the self be properly related to itself while failing to do justice to others. Yet it seems the language of being threatens to instrumentalize the neighbor, and fails to sustain attention to concrete life. In these transcendental and ontological approaches the tensive relation between self and other is either collapsed (either the self is instrumentalized by the neighbor or vice versa) or made into a rivalry. A hermeneutical approach can retain the insights of transcendental and ontological approaches while maintaining more adequately than they do the tensive relation between self and other. It renders being in more embodied, social, historical, and linguistic directions. Importantly, a hermeneutical account of self-relation emphasizes that the person is embedded in a world of import and value, in social relations and linguistic–symbolic systems. Yet it also emphasizes the

person's capacity to transcend her situation, to reflect on it critically. The person exercises her agency in and on the moral space
in which she lives. The dialectical relation of being and thinking,
or self-enactment and self-understanding, means that the person
actualizes her self-relation and her relation to God in her transactions with others and in the world. As a lover, she travels the
tension between her unity with and difference from others in an
ongoing process of discerning the truth and affirming the value of
self and other. And this process occurs in and for the sake of orienting her actions and relations. In this respect, the self-understanding
and self-enactment that belongs to right self love differs from the
norm of self-realization that I sketched in Chapter One. Under this
norm the self seeks to understand and realize herself in a process
of excavating some true identity that flits elusively in her interior
life. Or she creates, discards, and tailors her identity at will. Under
this norm others are absent or appear as rivals to the self's realization. By contrast, a hermeneutical account of self-relation construes the moral obligation of self love as a process undertaken in
and through relation to God, with and for God and others and in the
world.

This approach to self love indicates that at times the self may
legitimately pursue her own interests, just as it indicates that at
others she must exercise self-denial. Recently, Gerald Schlabach
has made this point, but he permits the pursuit of the self's interests
in order to re-charge the self for further self-denial.[51] I wonder if this
instrumentalizes self love and our delights in particular goods and
pursuits in the name of ordering them. Moreover, I do not think that
an ethics of self love is first and foremost a matter of adjudicating
what is owed to others against the threat of self-preference, as much
of Christian ethics has rendered self love.[52] Nor is the primary
concern to legitimate the self's pursuit of its own interests against
exhaustive obeisance to others, as many feminists have treated self
love. Inquiry into the order of love, the adjudication of love relations

---

[51] Gerald W. Schlabach, *For the Joy Set Before Us: Augustine and Self-Denying Love* (Notre Dame,
    IN: University of Notre Dame, 2001).
[52] For a recent work that explores such matters of adjudication, see Garth L. Hallet,
    Priorities and Christian Ethics (Cambridge: Cambridge University Press, 1998). See also
    Hallet's earlier work *Christian Neighbor Love: an Assessment of Six Rival Versions* (Washington DC:
    Georgetown University Press, 1989).

in situations of conflict, remains important, as does the recognition that a person's identity and moral obligations are not identical with the expectations and needs of others. We must not invoke too quickly or cheerily the claim that the inter-relation of self and other means that there is no ultimate conflict between their interests. Much of our daily moral lives will consist in adjudicating just such conflicts, and in negotiating conflicts between the interests of those who are near and dear to us and those who are remote and perhaps unknown. But in a hermeneutical approach to self love the order of love is less a crib sheet for navigating the moral life than a crucible of understanding and action. The demand to purify love (e.g., to develop virtuous dispositions, to see oneself and others truly) meets the demand to exercise love appropriately (e.g., to know when to prefer oneself, when to prefer others, when to offer a reproof and how to accept one, to know when and how to offer friendship and when as an act of love to withhold it, etc.). With grace, this tensive relation between askesis and praxis is not enervating but productive. Indeed, with grace, as a grace, this crucible redeems self and others.

In this way a hermeneutical approach avoids two dangers: an emphasis on acts of neighbor love that ignores fundamental dispositions, and an emphasis on dispositions that neglects the power of acts to build up or destroy others. It avoids these dangers because it construes understanding as an event in which knowing and valuing intersect for the sake of orienting action. The intersection of knowing and valuing highlights the importance of cultivating moral sensitivity and dispositions. An ethics of self love is a conversion ethics. Love for neighbor requires overcoming moral prejudice and callousness and egoism. But because this understanding occurs for the sake of orienting action, a hermeneutical approach can stress dispositions involved in loving without obfuscating the importance of concrete acts and relations.

SELF LOVE AND SOCIAL JUSTICE

If we reduce self love to selfishness, self love and social justice certainly seem opposed to one another. If personal selfishness often dissuades one from acts of charity and service, the self-interest of groups (as Reinhold Niebuhr and Karl Marx noted in their respective ways) proves a much greater obstacle especially when it takes on institutionalized and systemic forms and especially when justice requires not simply charity and service, but a transformation of the status quo. Structural forms of self-interest are especially problematic because individual agents acquire in them a kind of (false) anonymity – their specific choices and lifestyles seem of little account and their responsibility to others seems dispersed into the machinery of the status quo. But because self love is actualized in love for one's neighbors, does proper self-relation entail solidarity with the poor and the oppressed? Notice this question differs from asking whether neighbor love properly entails a commitment to social justice. I judge that it does, but here I am concerned to explore whether and how a commitment to social justice belongs properly to self love. I argue that it does.

We can see why this is so from the vantage point of the oppressed as well as from the vantage point of oppressors. Who are the oppressed? The oppressed include those who are economically poor, who are socio-politically marginalized, who suffer discrimination on the basis of race, ethnicity, creed, gender, sexual orientation, and/or class. We can determine who the poor are through an analysis of social, economic and political power relations, through the deconstruction of cultural and religious ideologies that mask and warrant injustice and by listening to those who experience injustice in its manifold forms. For one who is oppressed, self love entails a commitment to social justice because the struggle for liberation from oppression is a process of claiming one's humanity against that which and those who deny it. Ada María Isasi-Díaz rightly claims that to become fully human is to be in a love relation with God and others.[53] To do this, justice must prevail. Isasi-Díaz defines sin as alienation from God and others. Similarly, Gustavo Gutiérrez argues that sin is not only an impediment to salvation in the afterlife. Sin is a historical reality, a breach of communion among persons, withdrawal from others and a break with God.[54]

[53] Ada María Isasi-Díaz, "Solidarity: Love of Neighbor in the 1990s," in *Feminist Theological Ethics*, ed. Lois K. Daly (Louisville, KY: Westminster/John Knox, 1994).
[54] See Gustavo Gutiérrez, *A Theology of Liberation*, rev. edn., trans. and eds. Sister Caridad Inda and John Eagleson (New York: Orbis, 1990).

By contrast, salvation is the communion of human beings with God and among themselves. It embraces all human reality, transforms it, leads it to its fullness in Christ. According to Gutiérrez, understanding salvation in this way shows that the world beyond this one is not the true life, not something opposed to this one, but rather is the transformation and fulfillment of the present life. The absolute value of salvation does not devalue this world but rather gives it authentic meaning and independence – salvation is already latent in this world.

Isasi-Díaz notes that the oppressed often depend upon oppressors for their survival. Breaking the cycle of dependence and charity in order to transform exploitative relations is a risky enterprise. This fact sheds light on the courage and self-possession that right self love entails. Moreover, to struggle for the transformation of the world is in some measure to experience that transformation in oneself. Says Isasi-Díaz, *"La vida es la lucha."*[55] To engage in the struggle for liberation is to be about justice and self-determination. Recall a point made in the previous chapter about the practical character of ethics: ethics is practical because it is reflexive (that is, self-involving) and participatory (to reason practically is in some measure to participate already in the good life about which one reasons). Realizing that struggling for liberation yields a taste of it here and now can sustain us. We must avoid what Thomas Merton calls the fetishism of immediate results.[56] Merton recognized rightly that our attachment to quick and clear results can cause us to flag in our work for justice and peace and can distort the meaning of the work itself.

So for those who are oppressed, right self love includes a commitment to social justice. Fair enough. But in what way might an oppressor's self love require such a commitment? Is it not her self love that needs to be set aside in order to make such a commitment? Who, in fact, are oppressors? They are those who discriminate against others and who enjoy power and privilege in economic and socio-political relations and do not stand in solidarity with the oppressed in a commitment to transform those structural relations.

[55] Isasi-Díaz, "Solidarity: Love of Neighbor in the 1990s," 78.
[56] Thomas Merton, *The Nonviolent Alternative*, ed., Gordon Zahn (New York: Farrar, Straus, Giroux, 1980), 213.

Love for God and love for neighbor require such a commitment, but does self love require it as well? Yes, and for some of the same reasons that self love requires the oppressed to struggle for their liberation. If to become fully human is to be in a love relationship with God and with others, and an oppressor is one who is alienated from God and others by virtue of her participation in exploitative institutions and relations, a commitment to transform these institutions and relations is an exercise of self love as well as love for God and neighbor.[57]

Further, right self love requires one to understand oneself truthfully and to reckon with one's concrete acts and relations. Given the collective and conflictive character of oppression, right self love involves a process of conscientization, critical reflection on the structural causes of oppression and one's role in sustaining these structures. Christian theologies of liberation like those Gutiérrez and Isasi-Díaz offer express the dialectical relation between being and thinking as the unity of theory and praxis. Liberation theologians relate seeing or perceiving the truth to doing the truth. We need to understand better and to transform the reality of the oppressed. Liberation theology seeks to reveal the false ideologies that conceal and justify privilege and construct a social order which is free of such inequity (e.g., natural differences in aptitudes cannot be used to justify economic disparity).

It seems, then, that few people practice right self love in this respect. Of course a commitment to social justice can take different expressions and should, given one's particular commitments and responsibilities. And of course, the analysis of systemic oppression and the transformation of it are incredibly complex, concrete tasks about which there will inevitably be much disagreement. And of course, the reality of sin prevents any complete realization of justice and peace in this world. But these facts should prompt a readiness for self-criticism, a willingness to name injustice as such without self-righteousness but also without reservation. All too often, as I have experienced in conversation with friends, in teaching in undergraduate and adult-education programs, these facts elicit instead self-defense, complacency, despair, appeals for caution and

---

[57] Cf. Tanner, *Politics of God*.

patience. When we are tempted in these directions we would do well to remember Martin Luther King's letter from a Birmingham jail, in which he stated that the civil rights movement's real opponent was not the rabid segregationist so much as the white moderate. King recognized that the white moderate's devotion to "order" and appeals for patience rest on misunderstandings of the plight of blacks and the nature of justice. Such devotion and such appeals can mask both cowardice and a reluctance to surrender the benefits the white moderate enjoys in the status quo.

Arguments for social justice are sometimes grounded in the experience and epistemological privilege of the poor and oppressed, sometimes in the self-disclosure of God in the struggle for liberation, and, sometimes, especially in secular arguments, in human rights discourse. In addition to grounding such reflection and praxis on these resources we ought to attend to the demand for social justice as a part of proper self-relation. This is not a crass appeal to self-interest such that improving the lot of those less fortunate benefits us as well as them. My point is that self-relation is in part a matter of deciding the kind of person one should be (I say in part because we depend on grace) and right self-relation means, among other things, being about justice in our concrete acts and relations.

A hermeneutical approach to self love deals more adequately with the relation between self love and social justice than the transcendental and ontological approaches exemplified by Rahner and Tillich. As I noted above, Metz is one of a number of thinkers who criticize Rahner for neglecting the socio-political dimensions of theology. Thinkers like Carter Heyward criticize Tillich for similar reasons. There are resources in each for responding to these criticisms, e.g., Rahner's arguments on behalf of the unity of love for God and neighbor, Tillich's privileging of the person-to-person encounter, the fact that both recognize the person as situated in a mortgage of guilt and a heritage of collective wisdom. A hermeneutical approach recognizes the self as embedded in symbolic, linguistic, and social systems, and recognizes that these systems are sites of power. It demands and provides for the criticism of such systems according to a standard of goodness that is objective yet internal to consciousness. This is akin to the practice of radical interpretation. In order to appreciate the relation between self love and social justice, though, it is important to stress the collective practice of such criticism and the primacy of social and communal praxis as a source of insight and understanding. The criticism of social conventions that is required for social justice cannot occur without the self's capacity to transcend morally the conventions that shape her, but often communal practices and resources foster and enable such transcendence. Indeed, the extent to which they do so can serve as a criterion for criticizing their particular conventions. As we will see in Chapter Six, it is because Christian ethics provides for its self-criticism that it can criticize other moral systems. It is also why Christian ethics can be internally validated even as it is shown to be true through its liberating and transformative effects here and now.

SELF LOVE AND EMBODIED INTEGRITY

This section will indicate that the identity achieved in right self love is interpretive or hermeneutical in character. This allows me to conclude the chapter by specifying the moral good which right self love achieves, the good of embodied integrity. The distinction between the identity any person has and the moral good of embodied integrity (1) allows an ethics of right self love to address the contemporary problems of fragmentation and incoherence without sacrificing the complexity of the self; (2) allows for the moral evaluation of forms of self-relation, especially because it attends to the concrete acts and relations through which the person takes up relation to herself, others, and God; and (3) divests a hermeneutical account of self-relation of the voluntarism and intuitionism that can accompany the conceptual language of being.

Thus far I have argued that self love consists in a self-determining response to God that is actualized in but not exhausted by neighbor love. This is a formal statement of my thesis. It expresses the interdependence of self-relation with relation to God and neighbor. This account of self love applies whether a person loves herself rightly or not. The problem, Chapter One showed, is that our contemporary Western moral situation is characterized by an uncritical endorsement of self love, what I called the norm of self-realization. The norm of self-realization is a contemporary version of the basic problem of identifying what kind of life is worthy of living. Persons can be related to themselves in better and worse fashions. Despite the bad press many in Christian tradition gave self love, even thinkers like John Calvin, Søren Kierkegaard, and Reinhold Niebuhr agree with Augustine and Aquinas that proper self-relation is found in God. The issue is what kind of content is given to "proper self-relation." This means that my formal claim about self love must be specified materially. Right self love designates the morally proper form of self-relation characterized by the moral good of integrity and governed by the moral norms of love for God and neighbor. Integrity consists in true self-understanding embodied in one's acts and relations with others and in the world, so I refer to the moral good as embodied integrity. This material thesis testifies to the contributions that recent work in philosophical hermeneutics and theories of practical reason make to conceptual frameworks of being in a moral anthropology.

A hermeneutical account of self-relation not only reconceptualizes the problem of self love, it reconceptualizes the moral good. Integrity means that self love is not about fixing the self, either as correcting what is broken in the self or as getting the self right and keeping it still. Charles Taylor's study of modern identity traces this concern to fix the self back to Locke's "punctual" self. Paul Lauritzen notes that this concern is shared by heirs as disparate as Richard Rorty and Ernest Wallwork.[58] Integrity replaces this concern to fix the self with a complex process of free self-acceptance. What distinguishes this process of self-acceptance from appeals to authenticity (and thereby keeps it from devolving into a process of self-creation or self-realization not unlike fixing the self)? What distinguishes self-acceptance from fatalism about oneself? What distinguishes it from self-justification? The self-acceptance that belongs to integrity includes truthfulness of and to the self. But this observation brings us back to where we began. How does one know who she is or ought to be? Even if one does know this, how does one go about being true to oneself? Persons are complex, erratic creatures, and contemporary culture often fragments persons further. The pluralism of human existence confronts the

---

[58] Paul Lauritzen, "The Self and its Discontents: Recent Work on Morality and the Self," *Journal of Religious Ethics* 22:1 (1994), 189–210.

human aspiration for meaning and coherence. Culture, politics, arts and sciences, biology and nature all confront the person and cannot be manipulated into a comprehensive system. The person is tempted to integrate everything else into some inner-worldly value, to make some value which she encounters absolute. The person's temptation to center her existence on a finite value indicates that she determines her identity relationally, vis-à-vis some defining value. And if this fragmentation, complexity, and multiplicity are not enough, attempts to respond to them not only fail, they constitute efforts to fix what is wrong with ourselves. Is there a way out of this conundrum?

Here we can appreciate the importance of a Christian ethical perspective. Christian ethics transforms the idea of integrity. I have expressed the meaning of integrity as knowing the truth about oneself and embodying this in one's acts and relations. Of course, a person can know he is a scoundrel and be a scoundrel with remarkable consistency, and this is a kind of integrity. But when integrity is used to designate the moral good that belongs to proper self-relation, and when proper self-relation is governed by the norms of love for God and neighbor, two points become apparent. First, we come to and know ourselves truly in the Lord. Second, truthfulness to our selves is empowered by grace. Integrity is not the point of the moral life, not something at which one can aim directly. Indeed, it comes only through a self-surrender. So integrity, from a Christian ethical perspective, is not the quest for one's true self that contemporary Western culture celebrates and encourages. We do not discover the truth about ourselves by spelunking in the caverns of our psyches. We discover it when we venture ourselves in relation to others. In other words, to recoup a classical insight, the person becomes what she loves. The difference between any particular form of self-relation and the self-relation which occurs in right self love depends, then, on that with respect to which the person determines herself. Rahner argues that "love is not the end of the integration of these partial moments of man's self-realization; rather, love is this self-realization itself as such and as a whole, without this wholeness being merely the sum-total of moments. . . . Love has nothing by which it could be explained except the one person who himself, however, only learns who and what he is (as a whole person) when he loves."[59] The person has been created for and commanded to love God. But the unity of Christian existence lies beyond its pluralism, even though it is mediated in this pluralism. Unlike love for some inner-worldly value, love for God does not confer the person's identity in relation to something tangible or created but in relation to absolute mystery. In love for God one's identity is given as beloved and yet remains to be achieved as the task of one's freedom.

Because the self comes to and knows the truth of herself in God, she cannot aim directly at truthfulness to herself. Integrity encompasses dialectically both the constitution and determination of the self by what is other than her (the divine, other persons, institutions and systems, contingent personal factors, etc.) as well as her self-determination (her self-transcendence, freedom, responsibility, and creativity). The hermeneutical character of self-relation suggests that the person must go out of herself in order to possess herself. We cannot aim directly at our own good but receive it indirectly in a commitment to others; so the obligation of self love is not to seek our own flourishing directly. Indeed, right self love demands us to surrender or sacrifice this good as a direct pursuit. Still, if we are to take seriously the feminist critique of traditional Christian accounts of self love, projects of self-realization must not denigrate the self or valorize the self's well-being. As my analysis of the contemporary moral outlook showed, the feminist critique and the deconstruction of the self raise the problem of how to specify the relation of the self's good to that of others without exhausting or subsuming the self into others and without instrumentalizing others for the sake of oneself. This is why self-transcendence is central to right self love; when we transcend ourselves we understand ourselves in an affirmation of something beyond us in power and worth. This self-transcendence is a grace, not our own creation, not produced at will. Yet it engages our freedom since it requires us to trust the paradox that we achieve ourselves when we sacrifice the direct pursuit of our own good. I take it that this insight is the moral force behind Rahner's appeal to mystery and Tillich's claim that "this surrender of one's

---

59 Rahner, "The Commandment of Love," 443. See Andrew Tallon, "Rahner and Personalization," *Philosophy Today* 14 (1970), 44–56.

own goodness occurs in him who accepts the divine acceptance of himself, the unacceptable. The courage to surrender one's own goodness to God is the central element in the courage of faith."[60] The concept of integrity expresses that the dignity and coherence of the person's life are known in relation to God. Self-relation has its source and power in the divine other.

We can formulate this in a norm under which the obligation of right self love falls. The norm which best articulates it is nothing else than the law of love: "Thou shalt love the Lord thy God with all thy heart and thy neighbor as thyself."[61] This norm for right self love obliges the person to love God and neighbor because proper self-relation is mediated and actualized in love for God and neighbor. It recoups the classical commensuration of self love and love for God. Moreover, it indicates that the neighbor is to be loved in God, for like the self, the neighbor's dignity and coherence is found in relation to God. Thus, it specifies love for God and neighbor as criteria for self love. As a norm for self love, the law of love offsets both egoism and the instrumentalization of others for the sake of one's own fulfillment. The two criteria of love for God and for neighbor allow for a creative tension in which the self is neither exhausted in love for the neighbor nor denigrated in her relation to God. That is, the law of love fosters moral evaluation of the person's relations to her neighbors and the person's religious relation to God. Finally, as a norm for self love, this law avoids the subjectivism of Rahner's and Tillich's accounts while still accounting for the affective, passional elements of the moral life. This is not to say that the question of how to specify the law of love in particular moral decisions is without

---

60 Tillich, *Systematic Theology*, vol. 3, 226. Tillich notes that the justice which belongs to divine love destroys what is not love in the person so that the person can be reunited with the divine. It is not the destruction of evil in the person, since the person has been created good, but rather the person's *hubris*, the person's attempt to reach reunion on her own efforts.

61 See the gospels of Mark 12:28–34 and Matthew 22:34–40. The Markan pericope includes the following: "'Which commandment is the first of all?' Jesus answered, 'The first is, "Hear, O Israel: the Lord our God, the Lord is one; you shall love the Lord your God with all your heart, and with all your soul, and with all your mind, and with all your strength." The second is this, "You shall love your neighbor as yourself." There is no other commandment greater than these'" (Mark 12:28b–31). For some treatments of the love command in scripture see Victor Furnish, *Love Command in the New Testament* (New York: Abingdon, 1972) and Ernest Wallwork, "Thou Shalt Love Thy Neighbor As Thyself: the Freudian Critique," *Journal of Religious Ethics* 10 (Fall 1982), 291–92.

difficulties. Chapters One and Two made this much clear. The law of love appeals to the structures of self-relation as normative and translates these structures into a specific moral principle. This principle addresses the pluralism of existence without sacrificing the complexity of the self. It reconceptualizes the good, or self-realization more generally by directing moral attention to what, whom, why, and how the self loves. In doing so it casts the moral problem of self love as one of evaluating forms of self-relation as they take concrete shape in relations to and with others.

At this point the difficulties of Rahner's and Tillich's positions emerge. To see why, and to appreciate how a hermeneutical approach can read them in ways faithful to their insights and without their problems, let us consider briefly how each thinker's treatment of symbols illustrates the difficulties of their respective positions. This foray into symbols is important for understanding the relation between self love and love for God for reasons I will develop in the remainder of the book. Because love for and faith in God are mediated by symbolic resources and in our actions and relations, self love requires the moral criticism of religious constructs. Because right self love does not require explicitly Christian or even theistic faith, it is important to understand how non-theistic symbols and encounters with others mediate the self's relation to Christ, the Mediator. And because persons not only use symbols but, like symbols, realize themselves by expressing themselves, we cannot construe self-relation adequately apart from such acts of understanding and expression.

Being and using a symbol

For Tillich symbols do not possess an intrinsic relation to that which they symbolize. Symbols have an objective and subjective side – the object present to the person and the person's response to it. The symbol grasps the person and provides the person with ecstatic participatory knowledge of that which is symbolized. But the person is not dissipated into or merged with the symbolized; rather he retains a capacity to assess the adequacy of the symbol. Not all objects function as symbols. In a symbol the object becomes translucent, manifesting the ground of being. Tillich characterizes and classifies types of symbols in various ways throughout his corpus. Regardless, all symbols reveal or manifest the power of being-itself. According to Tillich, symbols function to express and occasion being-itself. The expression occurs in an original revelation, such as the picture of Jesus as the Christ. The occasioning function occurs in temporally later, dependent revelations which evoke the original revelation. Critics like David Kelsey and Donald Driesbach have noted that Tillich fails to make clear how these occasioning symbols are related to the expressing symbols. Tillich draws expressing symbols from the biblical picture of Jesus as the Christ. He draws occasioning symbols from his ontology. He does not clarify how temporally later, dependent revelations evoke the original revelation in Jesus as the Christ.[62]

Driesbach notes that Tillich operates with two different understandings of faith. Sometimes Tillich speaks of faith as being grasped by the power of being that conquers estrangement; at other times, Tillich speaks of faith as being grasped by an ultimate concern.

One is the state of being ultimately concerned about the genuine ultimate, so that the personality is made coherent, and inadequate and potentially destructive ultimate concerns are rejected. The other is an altered state of self-understanding, so that one has the sense of not being abandoned to reliance on one's own power, that one is sustained by the power of being-itself. These two different but not incompatible notions, taken together, imply response to a religious symbol as producing a coherent personality that is empowered to confront the deepest structural problems of human existence.[63]

The different definitions of faith play off the tension between a salvation experienced in the present as unambiguous yet fragmentary and the person's eschatological fulfillment. On the one hand the Christ is a symbol which provides courage for self-affirmation in

---

[62] David Kelsey makes this point. See his *The Fabric of Paul Tillich's Theology* (New Haven and London: Yale University Press, 1967). See also Donald F. Driesbach, *Symbols and Salvation: Paul Tillich's Doctrine of Religious Symbols and his Interpretation of the Symbols of the Christian Tradition* (Lanham, MD: University Press of America, 1993); H. D. McDonald, "The Symbolic Christology of Paul Tillich," *Vox Evangelica* 18 (1988), 75–88. See also James J. Buckley, "On Being a Symbol: an Appraisal of Karl Rahner," *Theological Studies* 40:3 (1979), 285–98. Buckley contrasts Tillich's ontology of symbols with that of Rahner's. See 455–57.

[63] Driesbach, *Symbols and Salvation*, 45.

the threat of nonbeing, and on the other hand, Christ is a power of being, and thus more than a symbol, which conquers the threat of nonbeing *qua* threat. A similar tension can be seen in Tillich's treatment of Spiritual Presence. Because symbols mediate the act of faith, the problematic relation between symbols which express the power of being and symbols which evoke it corresponds to a problematic relation between the symbol which produces a coherent personality and the symbol which empowers the person to confront the deepest structural problems of existence.

This tension highlights the difficulties of Tillich's ontology for a contemporary account of self love. Tillich suggests, and rightly, that life is characterized by ambiguity; it is this ambiguity that makes self love a moral problem. But Tillich's account is not adequately equipped to confront the task of morally evaluating the forms self-relation can take. Put differently, it contributes to rather than addresses the way contemporary ethics neglects the concrete acts and relations through which the person takes up relation to herself, others, and God. The tension in Tillich between the conquest of estrangement and courage in the face of it yields an account of conscience as the "silent voice" of essential being, and an approach to ethics that, notwithstanding its merits, courts subjectivism in the form of intuitionism. Moreover, as Schweiker noted above, Tillich's emphasis on self-actualization risks a valorization of the power to act that threatens respect for other persons. Finally, the tension in Tillich's handling of symbols (which illustrates a broader tension in his system as a whole) makes his ontology ill-equipped to deal with attention to concrete acts and relations if we were to give it. The tension makes it difficult to understand the continuity of the person in her acting, and complicates attempts to account for moral change. Resources in Tillich for addressing such matters (e.g., his discussion of self-alteration, self-creativity, and self-transcendence) only illustrate the way his system is beholden to the ontological polarities he identifies.[64]

Tillich's difficulties center on how symbols function in self-relation. For Rahner, however, the point is not that persons use symbols, but that they *are* symbols. According to Rahner, a real

[64] See Tillich, *Systematic Theology*, vol. 3, 30–110.

symbol "is the self-fulfillment of a particular being in another that
is constitutive of the essence of that particular being."[65] This means
that the person's self-fulfillment is achieved when she gives herself
away "to that which is other and finds [herself] in the other through
knowledge and love."[66] For Rahner a being has being to the degree
that it is present to itself (*Beisichsein*). The person is a symbol because
his self-possession is always mediated through the material world.
The person is a synthesis of spirit and matter. Rahner's ontology
of symbols highlights the person's embodiment and fundamentally
relational (or as Rahner sometimes says, dialogical) character. By
claiming that all beings are symbols Rahner attempts to transform the static substance metaphysic of Aristotle and Aquinas and
show that beings are "dynamically self-mediating realities."[67] But
Rahner's attempts to revamp the Aristotelian–Thomistic substance
metaphysic continue to struggle against this conceptual ontological framework. As James Buckley notes, this claim raises the question of where personal identity is located. Buckley argues for what
he calls a performative anthropology based on Rahner's ontology
of symbols. A performative anthropology accounts for the self's
establishment of itself in self-avowals through which it expresses
itself to an other. A paradigmatic example of such a self-avowal
is the utterance, "I love you." Because the person's self-possession
is achieved in self-expression, Buckley notes that "it is of the very
essence of human subjects to 'express themselves in the other,'
to utter a performative 'I love you' to God and to neighbor."[68]
Buckley questions the merit of localizing personal identity in such
performative acts: "Granted that I am a symbol in certain performative moments, how can I follow through on this identity in a
historically patterned way? Rahner's notion of symbol deals with
the self-involved 'I' in individual moments without dealing with

[65] Karl Rahner, "The Theology of the Symbol," *Theological Investigations*, vol. 4, 234.

[66] Ibid., 285.

[67] Stephen Fields, S.J., *Being as Symbol: on the Origins and Development of Karl Rahner's Metaphysics* (Washington DC: Georgetown University Press, 2000), 3. For additional treatments of Rahner's ontology of symbols, see Annice Callahan, "Karl Rahner's Theology of Symbol: Basis of his Theology of the Church and the Sacraments," *Irish Theological Quarterly* 49 (1982), 195–205 and Thomas Sheehan, *Karl Rahner: the Philosophical Foundations* (Athens, OH: Ohio University Press, 1987).

[68] Buckley, "On Being a Symbol," 285–98, 468. He offers here a version of the criticism that Rahner's anthropology is individualistic and voluntaristic.

the ongoing moments of personal identity which are not always performative."[69] So Rahner's position, too, finds itself beholden to a (transcendental) conceptuality of being that generates some problems. Like Tillich's, Rahner's position is ill-equipped to account for the continuity of the person's identity in her acting and, so, is ill-equipped to account for moral change. Moreover, Rahner's resources to address this problem only exacerbate another – inasmuch as Rahner's emphasis on the self's exercise of freedom in a decision provides for the continuity of her identity and can help to account for moral change, it also heightens the voluntarism of his position. And, as I noted before, notwithstanding Rahner's insistence that the person comes to herself only in a concrete other, the transcendentalism of his position drags attention away from concrete acts and relations.

In Chapter One I argued that the norm of self-realization fails to evaluate morally the forms that self-relation may take. In Chapter Three I suggested that conceptual frameworks of being are a more valuable resource for this evaluation than many might think. But these frameworks, as in Rahner and Tillich, can begin to choke and not simply flesh out our moral evaluation. As the next chapter will show, a hermeneutical approach can make good use of these frameworks. It incorporates Rahner's and Tillich's respective insights, for instance, by rendering the moral good as embodied integrity. Because embodied integrity consists in true self-understanding embodied in one's acts and relations, it attends to the use of symbolic systems through which we understand ourselves and by which we live (Tillich) and the concrete acts and relations through which the self takes up relation to her self, others, and God (Rahner).

This line of reasoning differs from the other arguments made on behalf of right self love which I detailed in Chapter Two. I noted that contemporary thinkers who commend self love do so for several reasons: as a derivative duty of neighbor love, for the same reasons which warrant love for the neighbor (e.g., each person is the *imago Dei*), and because of structural self-responsibility. The moral obligation of self love, or put differently, the task of establishing oneself as a self, is experienced by the person in her freedom and

---

[69] Ibid., 471.

responsibility. The person experiences the gap between what she is and what she ought to be. The moral obligation to right self love arises in the person's experience of herself. It is experienced as the demand to actualize oneself. As I have suggested, however, the difficulty lies in specifying the proper form of self-relation, that is, designating in what right self love consists. That is why the next chapter explores moral action and Chapter Six explores the moral criticism of religious claims and relations.

CONCLUSION

This chapter has supplemented the analysis of moral being offered in Chapter Three in order to advance my thesis: right self love consists in a self-determining response to God which is actualized in but not exhausted by neighbor love. In doing so, Chapters Three and Four explored self love as a moral problem. The following two chapters change gears and take up self love as a moral principle. In that way, I seek to warrant my thesis and test its adequacy with respect to other problems in ethics: how to account for moral development and the relation that pertains between religion and morality. Respectively, Chapters Five and Six ask, "What does the idea of right self love contribute to an account of the moral life?" and, "what insight does the idea of right self love lend to the relation between religion and morality?"

CHAPTER 5

Self love and moral action

Previous chapters showed that the person freely decides about herself in relation to God. This decision, in its material specificity, constitutes the person's identity. This chapter asks how the person's categorical moral choices and actions condition and constitute her response and how her response shapes and directs her categorical choices, even her capacity to reason morally. It explores the status of concrete acts and relations by engaging conceptual frameworks of being and by appealing to the norms of love for God and neighbor. This chapter suggests that (1) moral action entails a creative self-constitution in light of particular situations; (2) moral development consists in a fundamental self-interpretation of oneself in relation to God, who has acted on behalf of the person first; and (3) a hermeneutical account of self-relation helps to specify the kinds of acts and relations that are/are not ordered to the self's authentic good.

IDENTITY AND INTEGRITY

My description of embodied integrity is indebted to and departs from the account of integrity that William Schweiker offers. Schweiker's account of integrity begins with the claim that there are two levels of goods. The first, lower level of goods includes bodily, social, and reflective goods. It is multi-dimensional. Persons encounter and recognize these goods in their sensory experiences of values and disvalues (e.g., pleasure and pain). They also encounter and recognize them in social roles and relations by which they identify themselves and are identified by others. And persons experience reflective goods in their capacity to reflect on their lives, paradigmatically in their linguistic self-designation in a space of value.[1] Schweiker insists on a second, higher level of goods because persons transcend these lower goods in the act of self-criticism (or conscience or radical interpretation). This higher good consists in a commitment to respect and enhance the integrity of lower goods. This commitment constitutes the ethical good of integrity. "Christian ethics makes this distinction between levels of value simply because it understands questions of faith to be basic to human existence. Faith is about what one trusts in and is loyal to in all actions and relations."[2]

The good of integrity entails what Schweiker terms an integrated theory of value. He distinguishes it from the axiology offered by John Finnis, who collaborates with Germain Grisez. Schweiker, Finnis, and Grisez agree that a range of diverse and basic goods characterize human existence. Finnis and Grisez argue that these goods are not commensurable. Many Roman Catholic and Protestant ethicists dispute this claim. According to Finnis and Grisez, the incommensurability of goods means that it is wrong to act directly against any of them. To be sure, as finite creatures we cannot pursue all goods at all times. The project of writing this book, for instance, requires me to neglect other goods, chiefly rest and recreation. Neglecting goods or allowing disvalues like pain to occur in the pursuit of a good (e.g., obtaining vaccinations for one's child) differ from directly attacking a good. Finnis puts it this way: "Make one's choices open to human fulfillment: i.e. avoid unnecessary limitation of human potentialities."[3] Grisez argues, "In voluntarily acting for human goods and avoiding what is opposed to them, one ought to choose and otherwise will those and only those possibilities whose willing is compatible with a will toward integral human fulfillment."[4]

Schweiker claims to offer a different theory of value. "Moral integrity demands truthfulness *of* self *to* the project of respecting

[1] William Schweiker, *Responsibility and Christian Ethics* (Cambridge: Cambridge University Press, 1995). See Chapter Five and 160–69 for the multi-dimensionality of value.
[2] Ibid., 115.
[3] John Finnis, *Fundamentals of Ethics* (Washington DC: Georgetown University Press, 1983), 72.
[4] Germain Grisez, *Christian Moral Principles*, vol. 1 of *The Way of the Lord Jesus* (Chicago: Franciscan Herald Press, 1983), 184.

and enhancing the integrity of all life."[5] This means that while "that which directly and intentionally destroys or demeans the meaningful coherence of diverse goods and aspirations is categorically prohibited"[6] nevertheless "in some circumstances we are justified in acting against certain goods, like pre-moral goods, in the name of the whole of life."[7] Schweiker defends this latter claim because the moral life is ambiguous and sometimes tragic, but he also thinks it is more adequate a response to and account of the multi-dimensionality of goods. By contrast, he claims that Grisez's and Finnis's insistence on the incommensurability of goods means that they are concerned not with the whole of life, as Schweiker is, but with "the sum of its constitutive goods in isolation from one another."[8]

Still, Schweiker's argument for integrity rests not only on a theory of value but on a claim about persons as agents. Because axiologies entail claims about agents, "any statement about what to do must presuppose and also bear upon the coherence of the life of the agent who is trying to act on that principle."[9] This means "that the idea of the integrity of an agent is logically and ontologically prior to the goods which he or she can or ought to seek; it means that an act of commitment to live with some integrity is prior to the quest to secure certain values in existence."[10] An imperative about integrity can be the kind of moral imperative that Kant called categorical. "The idea of integrity articulates the relation between identity-conferring projects and the acting person" which means that it concerns the conditions for choosing and acting.[11] The logical and ontological priority of integrity makes an imperative about integrity categorically binding, but it also means one can maintain a commitment to the project of respecting and enhancing the integrity of life even as one acts against some of the basic goods that constitute human life.

While there is much to commend Schweiker's account of integrity, a modification is in order here. Schweiker's idea of integrity corresponds to his account of conscience as the activity of radical interpretation. Integrity identifies the values and goods that persons

---

[5] Schweiker, *Responsibility*, 121. [6] Ibid., 125. [7] Ibid., 121. [8] Ibid.
[9] Ibid., 123. [10] Ibid., 124. [11] Ibid., 124–25.

and communities ought to seek, including the commitment to the moral project of respecting and enhancing these goods. This is expressed in the imperative to respect and enhance the integrity of life before God in all actions and relations. Radical interpretation is the person's or community's appropriation of this imperative into her or its self-understanding.[12] In Chapter Three I argued that the idea of radical interpretation does not provide adequately for the temporality of the person's identity. Schweiker does mention temporality as important for the moral life; temporality here refers to constancy in one's commitment to respect and enhance the integrity of life.[13] Moreover, because the concept radical interpretation weds a natural law ethics to an ethics of conversion, it implies an ongoing transformation. Schweiker's use of philosophical hermeneutics makes him attentive to the person's socio-linguistic situation, and because hermeneutics recognizes that understanding involves knowing and valuing for the sake of orienting life, radical interpretation involves the perception of value and the reformation of moral sensibility in the activity of assuming and ascribing responsibility.[14] Still, the emphasis is on orienting action through the education of moral sensibilities less than the exercise of agency in a personal history of freedom. That is, on Schweiker's account, moral identity appears in acts of self-critical reflection on and the direction of one's acts rather than in the acts themselves.

But because self-understanding and self-enactment are dialectically related, it is important to recognize that persons constitute themselves in their acts. There is, of course, no strict separation that we can make between our awareness of ourselves and our acting even as the moral problem is one of division or fragmentation. But, the problem of self love requires us to amplify certain aspects of self-relation and accordingly, certain questions in moral theory. We must wrestle with the temporality of our acting in order to explore the ways self-relation is negotiated in and through our ongoing relations to God and neighbors in the world. We must ponder the disparity that often exists between a person's self-understanding and her concrete actions and relations. When we say that persons do things they do not want to do, or never thought they were

---

[12] Ibid., 178.   [13] Ibid., 167–68.   [14] Ibid., 183.

capable of doing, or that they can deceive themselves, we state the obvious. Nevertheless, given Christian tradition's tendency to treat self love as a problem of selfishness, postmodern denials of the self, and Western culture's norm of self-realization, we must explore this problem *as* the problem of self love. So the primary concern with this "space between identity-conferring commitments and the acting person" is not that of ascribing and assuming responsibility but whether and how the person's acts and relations are ordered to her flourishing.[15] Can the person act directly against some of the goods that constitute human existence and maintain a commitment of her self to the moral project? Is that commitment sustained in her self-understanding even while her actions seem to belie it? Or are such actions ways in which the self affirms, even re-commits herself to respecting and enhancing the "meaningful coherence of diverse goods"? Projects and commitments do confer a person's identity, but in some measure persons constitute their identities in their acting. Can the person act directly against some of the goods that constitute human existence and love her self? Might so acting be, paradoxically, necessary for her to love her self? This question is important in order to respond to the norm of self-realization – without critically assessing this norm we cannot identify acts and relations that are self-destructive. We need to find ways to evaluate morally the ways in which persons seek to realize themselves. And since the person works out her self-relation (and relation to God and neighbor) continually in her decisions and actions, we need to look more closely at her moral actions, their relation to identity, to particular norms, and to faith. How ought we to construe moral change and development, and how ought we to understand the continuity of the self in her various actions?

THE RELEVANCE OF MORAL ACTIONS

There are a number of reasons why a contemporary account of self love requires attention to the status of concrete acts in the moral life and ethics. To begin, the person takes up her self-relation in her acting. She posits her self in response to various given features that

---

[15] Ibid., 125.

situate and shape her freedom but do not exhaustively determine
it. Another reason why we need to specify the status of moral acts is
because right self love concerns more than self-esteem, more than
how we feel about ourselves. Indeed, persons can and often do
deceive themselves. They can be in denial, they can be relatively
unreflective, they can be overly self-critical. Persons can exhibit
false consciousness. As I have been revising these pages I have seen
two different news programs that treated the sex industry. Both included interviews with women working in the sex industry as porn
stars and prostitutes, women who claim their work is fun, that it
not only pays well, but lets them make people happy, that they feel
free and/or powerful. The contemporary norm of self-realization
is unable to respond to these claims – they can only be taken at
face value. A range of feminists argue for the decriminalization
of sex work and for the right of sex workers to unionize. Drucilla
Cornell constructs her arguments on the insistence that the person
is an abstraction, a node of choice and source of value; as such,
persons (be they sex workers or not) have the right to sexual self-
representation.[16] Never mind that these women are encouraged to
think of their work in such terms by an industry that, and by cus-
tomers who, profit from their labor. Never mind that these terms
allow us to ignore or to address as an afterthought the harsh social and economic realities that can force women to work in the
sex industry. Never mind that our cultural readiness to deconstruct
(and so to invalidate) negative attitudes about sex finds little readiness to deconstruct as well our glorification of sex, or that both
the denigration and the glorification of sex operate with terribly
impoverished and confused understandings of human sexuality. If
these women claim to be happy, fulfilled, even proud of their work,
who are we to say otherwise?

   This line of reasoning sustains women's unwillingness to confront the reality of their degradation. It sustains the industry's and
consumer's unwillingness to stop exploiting women for profit and
pleasure. It sustains our collective unwillingness to address the social
and economic factors that sustain the sex industry. And it sustains
personal confusion and cowardice in the face of such a complex

[16] Drucilla Cornell, *At the Heart of Freedom: Feminism, Sex, and Equality* (Princeton, NJ: Princeton
University Press, 1998). See Chapter 2.

socio-economic reality, in the face of the complexity of human sexuality, and in the face of the tension between facile self-righteous moral judgments and enervating moral relativism. Other less dramatic examples can illustrate the importance of defining self love more richly than emotional or psychological states. My point is that a hermeneutical approach to self love retains the importance of self-understanding (which of course has emotional and psychological dimensions) yet sets self-understanding in the history of her moral freedom and in a truthful and fitting relation to the actions and relations through which the person constitutes herself.

It is also important to specify the status of moral acts for one's self-relation because self-relation is actualized in relation to God and neighbor and in the world. We negotiate these relations through what we do, although they are more than a series of discrete, identifiable deeds. In a hermeneutical account of self-relation, moral acts are objects of understanding and interpretation – the person deliberates over what to do and retrospectively interprets her actions. Moral acts also express the person's self-understanding. They disclose her commitments and values, her compassion or her callousness, the perceptions and beliefs and desires that prompted her so to act, etc. Moral acts are also part of the media of understanding, ways the person posits her self-relation and relation to others and ways she affects and effects these relations.

Rahner's concept of the fundamental option helps us to chart the connections among identity, action, and faith. Recall that Rahner understands identity as a free decision of finality vis-à-vis God. The person achieves her very self in the mode of an acceptance of God's offer of self-communication. If the person realizes herself in love, then moral change and development consist in an ongoing self-disposal in love for God and neighbor, whereby the person really comes to be as such. Rahner offers an ethics of transformation, one in which the moral good is a matter of being and becoming (and not simply doing) good. Nevertheless, it would be a mistake to restrict right self love to an interior attitude or solipsistic self-interpretation; given the unity of person and identity, self love must be mediated and actualized concretely. Because the person's free decision about herself before God is mediated concretely through her moral life, Rahner can distinguish growth in ontic sanctity from growth in

174   *Self Love and Christian Ethics*

moral sanctity. Growth in ontic sanctity refers to growth in sanctifying grace.[17] This growth is not the Christian perfection that is
incumbent on the person as a duty. Growth in *moral* sanctity is.
Because Rahner eschews any quantitative understanding of grace,
growth in ontic sanctity is not the accumulation or accrual of grace,
but a deepening relationship, which means that ontic and moral
sanctity are related. This distinction between ontic and moral sanctity points to a tension between Rahner's perfectionist motif and
the transcendental condition of the person.[18] Rahner asserts that
God has communicated God's self (at least as an offer) to the person and that this self-communication is an abiding existential of
the person. But the perfectionist motif seems at odds with such a
claim; if the person is always already graced, what need is there
for transformation? In order to understand the relation between
one's deepening relation with God and moral progress, we must
look at the relation between being and doing, or, put differently,
the relation between the person and her actions.

According to Rahner, freedom accomplishes something that
cannot be undone. One becomes something. Namely, one becomes
what one loves. "This means that man does not merely perform
actions which, though they must be qualified morally, also always
pass away again (and which after are imputed to him merely ju-
ridically or morally); man by his free decision really is so good or
evil in the very ground of his being-itself that his final salvation or
damnation are really already given in this, even though perhaps
in a still hidden manner."[19] Thus, without denying the person's

---

[17] For example, growth in grace via reception of the sacraments.
[18] This tension is not helped by the fact that Rahner sometimes uses the terms "transcendence" and "transcendental" in a less than precise fashion, making it difficult to
distinguish the two. Another way to put this difficulty is in terms of the relation between
nature and grace. The secondary literature on how Rahner understands this relation is
immense, and very often critical. The criticisms tend to be versions of the main charge that
Rahner's understanding is contradictory or inconsistent, and that this is generally due to
the static framework which Rahner adopts from scholastic Thomism. See, for example,
Mark Lloyd Taylor, *God is Love: a Study in the Theology of Karl Rahner* (Atlanta, GA: Scholars
Press, 1986); William Dych, *Karl Rahner* (London: Geoffrey Chapman, 1992) especially
chapter 3. R. R. Reno defends Rahner's account of nature and grace along Barthian
and Wittgensteinian lines. See *The Ordinary Transformed: Karl Rahner and the Christian Vision
of Transcendence* (Grand Rapids, MI: William B. Eerdmans, 1995).
[19] Rahner, "Theology of Freedom," *Theological Investigations*, vol. 6, 184. See *Theological
Investigations*, vols. 1–14 (vols. 1–6, Baltimore, MD: Helicon; vols. 7–10, New York: Herder
and Herder; vols. 11–14, New York: Seabury; 1961–1976).

absolute dependence on grace and the utter gratuity of God's self-communication, Rahner nevertheless can say that "man disposes over the totality of his being and existence before God and this either towards Him or away from Him. Man does this in such a way that his temporal decisions determine the eternal finality of his existence either in an absolute salvation or damnation: on account of his freedom, man is responsible for his eternal salvation or damnation."[20] The transcendental horizon is the condition for the possibility of the person's temporal decisions, but it is not immediately clear how these decisions condition the transcendental horizon. The fact that the person is always already graced appears to undercut the radical claim Rahner makes, that the person is responsible for his salvation or damnation. For Rahner the various moral decisions the person *makes* thematize the decision that she *is*; and because the person is a symbol, the categorical decisions do not simply arise out of and express the singular, final decision, they constitute it as well, but not in a straightforward or quantitative manner. For "there exist decisions which are objectively wrong but which do not destroy a man's positive relationship with God, so-called 'objective' sins which carry no 'subjective' guilt."[21] And, conversely, "a particular categorical object of choice, even if it is materially correct and conforms to the objective structure of man and the world, cannot guarantee for certain that its choice will bring about a positive relationship to human transcendence and its goal."[22] These important claims can account for the fact that a person's moral conduct can be erratic and contradictory, and that different actions vary in terms of the moral gravity of their object. Rahner maintains that one's existential decision about God cannot

---

[20] Rahner, "Guilt–Responsibility–Punishment within the View Of Catholic Theology," *Theological Investigations*, vol. 6, 200.

[21] Rahner, "Experience of the Spirit and Existential Commitment," *Theological Investigations*, vol. 16, 26. It is important to read this in light of Rahner's essay "On the Question of a Formal Existential Ethics," *Theological Investigations*, vol. 2. I will use this essay later in this section, but note here that Rahner insists therein that a moral act can never contradict a universal moral norm. Given this, the statement that an objectively wrong act can carry no subjective guilt should be understood to mean that there can exist a discrepancy between the moral status of an act and the ethical designation of the act according to moral principles which may or may not adequately express a universal moral norm. It may also mean that the extent to which a person's action is conditioned by ignorance, coercion, internal dispositions, etc. co-determines the extent to which the act expresses and establishes her relation with God.

[22] Rahner, "Experience of the Spirit and Existential Commitment," 27.

be directly produced or undone by an objectively moral or immoral act.[23] This is because, as we will see, the person's existential decision is made over the course of her lifetime, because multiple motives operate and help to determine the morality of an act, and because a morally good act may or may not conform to particular moral norms. These reasons will be explored in what follows.

Thus far we have seen that Rahner understands the person as a transcendental being oriented toward God and that he understands morality as free self-realization. The response to God which is at the heart of self love engages the entirety of the person. Rahner calls this total engagement the fundamental option. It refers to the person's exercise of freedom, not at the categorical level as the selection among available objects, but transcendentally. This transcendental exercise of freedom is neither irreversible, nor the unambiguous object of human reflection. It both arises out of and is constitutive of the direction in which the person is moving – the yes or no one gives to God. The categorical choices one makes arise from and express it. Yet, these categorical choices can be incongruent with the fundamental option; it is the chief act of the person, her surrender to or refusal of God, and is not located in a single act. This is important because it allows Rahner to say that a fundamental option toward God is not necessarily and immediately reversed by a particular sin. The person cannot make her fundamental option in and through a singular categorical act; it refers to the inclusive totality of her life and death. Nonetheless, one's categorical actions do, over time, both affect and effect the fundamental option. Although it cannot be brought wholly to reflection it cannot exist apart from the categorical acts which mediate and objectify it. The fundamental option is not simply the sum total of the moral weight of categorical acts, but these acts and the ineffable response to God they suggest and betray are mutually interdependent.[24]

There are a number of difficulties with the fundamental option. Because the fundamental option designates the transcendental exercise of freedom, yet Rahner maintains a categorical dimension

---

[23] Pope John Paul II disagrees with this in his encyclical *Veritatis Splendor*.

[24] Rahner, "Experience of the Spirit and Existential Commitment," 203–04. Rahner preserves here the traditional Catholic teaching that one cannot be certain about one's salvation.

to freedom, he seems to equivocate. If categorical freedom arises out of one's free transcendental decision, is it really freedom? If categorical freedom can contradict the transcendental dimension, why ought we to understand that dimension as freedom? That is, if transcendental freedom is decisive, does it undermine or negate categorical freedom, and if categorical freedom can be at odds with transcendental freedom, does this qualify its character as the capacity to posit something definitive? Rahner contends that the transcendental and categorical dimensions constitute a unity-in-difference of the one human freedom. Charles Curran criticizes the fundamental option because "in this approach salvation and grace take place on the transcendental level, but salvation should involve persons totally in all their relationships and in working for justice and the transformation of the world."[25] John Finnis argues that there is no evidence for the fundamental option; what is offered as evidence is "questionably metaphorical."[26] Moreover, both Curran and Finnis find the language of "choice" problematic, but for different reasons. For Curran too much emphasis on choices eclipses the moral importance of relationships and threatens to construe the moral life too atomistically. For Finnis, the fundamental option seems to be a choice that is not a choice to do anything, or is made, ostensibly, apart from particular choices of actions. Instead of a single fundamental option Finnis argues that "each serious and deliberate choice made with awareness of what is being chosen, and directly affecting a basic human good, is itself a fundamental option for or against practical reasonableness or, if you prefer, against virtue. It is fundamental because it makes a change in the self by which all future choices will be made, whether reasonably (virtuously) or unreasonably (wrongly)."[27] So, the voluntarism of the fundamental option may direct moral attention away from the person's concrete acts and relations and away from the socio-political conditions that situate us and that deserve our moral attention. In this way Rahner's account of how persons are related to their actions begs the very question the problem of right self love presses: in what sorts of actions does the person relate

[25] Charles Curran, *The Catholic Moral Tradition Today: a Synthesis* (Washington DC: Georgetown University Press, 1999), 97–98.
[26] Finnis, *Fundamentals of Ethics*, 142.   [27] Ibid., 144.

properly to herself, her neighbors and God and in what sorts does she not? Does Rahner's voluntarism and the ineffability of her fundamental option permit us to answer this question in any way other than by resorting to moral subjectivism? Moreover, a defense of the fundamental option must clarify how it is that we can reconstitute the condition for the possibility of acting.

We can respond to these difficulties by attending to the self-constituting character of moral acts and to the temporal character of agency, points a hermeneutical account of self-relation highlights. The relation between transcendental and categorical freedom is illumined helpfully by what I call the principle of accretion. This principle shifts the emphasis in Rahner from the voluntaristic tenor of the fundamental option as a choice or act of freedom to the strands in Rahner which stress the asymptotic character of personal becoming and the fact that the person's experience of and relation to God unfold in her personal history. Let me explain what I mean by the principle of accretion.

Given the unity-in-difference between the fundamental option – the person's transcendental decision – and categorical moral action, moral development can only be undertaken, if not finally accomplished, in the stuff of human life and society. For Rahner, moral value is not entirely located within a given situation. Neither is it wholly attached to a particular choice. Rather, specific situations and particular choices effect a ripple of moral value and are themselves prescinded by previous choices in previous situations. "The intensity, the existential depth, the freely acquired personal characteristic, all of which have developed in one's life up till then, all enter as intrinsic elements into the new act of decision and put their stamp on it. In every moment of the free, personal achievement of existence, the past becomes an inner, essential principle of the present and its acts."[28] The events and choices comprising the life of an individual prior to a particular moment thus co-determine both the given situation and the capacity of the individual to act morally in it. For this reason, the accretion of earlier choices made by an individual both create the individual and affect the following situations. The individual, then, in each given situation, makes a

---

[28] Rahner, "The Comfort of Time," *Theological Investigations*, vol. 3, 146.

decision not simply to do this or that, but to continue the course set by earlier decisions or to abandon it, to choose in favor of God and the self or against them.

Such a decision does not only determine the disposition of the whole person (since it determines its eternal destiny as a whole and not merely a part of our existence, merely "implicating" everything else); it also acts as the result of the always present totality of the person and thus out of the latter's previous life, because only the whole person can master the whole. It risks the life which has gone before; it works with the gains of its previous life.[29]

The individual makes a decision to *be* this or that. One's person-hood is either promoted or contradicted.

In this manner each singular moral choice relates not only to the overall *moral* sanctity of the individual, it affects the individual in such a way that *ontic* sanctity has a greater or lesser potential for realization as well. Particular moral choices dispose the individual, accumulating in such a way over time so as to effect an orientation, indeed, a mode of existing and apprehending. Morality itself, then, is a matter of process and progress, insofar as previous actions affect one's capacity for moral behavior in following situations. The more one sins, the more one becomes disposed to sinning. Indeed, the more one sins the more one becomes sinful; practicing sin results in the distortion of one's perspective and capacities. On the other hand, the more one acts morally, the more free, the more *human* one becomes. Moral action, then, like physical training, hones the agent for future and final self-commitment to being.

The principle of accretion does not undermine the freedom of the individual by allowing for her to become something in spite of her own will and effort. For Rahner one is not entirely what one does, and in this sense one does not become in spite of one's will, such that one becomes less human and holy because of sin despite a genuine and fervent desire to become otherwise. Every decision one makes leaves room for further decisions, which, to be sure, are conditioned and determined by those that have gone before them, but are not simply a linear expression of them.[30] A bad

---

[29] Ibid., 145.
[30] See Rahner, "On the Question of a Formal Existential Ethics."

choice, a series of bad choices comprise only moments in a lifetime response to God. Despite the uncertainty that one has acted morally and despite the ultimate ineffability of one's fundamental option in the person's moral reasoning and self-examination "man accepts himself in his own self-understanding and hands himself over – precisely as the one who understands himself in this or that way – to the mysterious judgment of God."[31] This indicates that the very activity of moral deliberation and that moral action itself mediate a self-interpretive process. Importantly, this self-interpretation entails a basic self-acceptance. Furthermore, this self-acceptance is an acceptance of God, whose self-communication is the condition for the possibility of our deliberation and action.

Rendering the fundamental option as a process of self-understanding that is embodied in one's actions and relations tempers the voluntarism of the fundamental option and specifies the continuity of the person's identity in her actions. It shares with narrative and virtue ethics an emphasis on the person's formation in practices and in her social relations amidst given objective realities. Indeed, Stanley Hauerwas argues that "at most, agency names the skills that enable us to make our own the things that happen to us – which includes 'decisions' we made when we thought we knew what we were doing but in retrospect seem more like something that happened to us."[32] Hauerwas recognizes that the moral meaning of a particular act or decision is not temporally located or confined – the person wakes up to her decisions. Moral understanding and decisions have as much to do with retrospective reflection (and repentance!) as they do with prospective deliberation (because we cannot and do not always deliberate before choosing, because we cannot foresee all the consequences of our acting, etc.) Other ethicists, philosophical and religious, stress the importance of practices in the formation of the self. Martha Nussbaum urges a "therapy of desire" that frees the soul from false and tyrannous socio-political influences. Others adopt the discourse of virtue to

---

[31] Rahner, "Guilt–Responsibility–Punishment Within the View of Catholic Theology," 206.

[32] Stanley Hauerwas, "Agency: Going Forward by Looking Back," in *Christian Ethics: Problems and Prospects*, eds., Lisa Sowle Cahill and James F. Childress (Cleveland, OH: Pilgrim, 1996), 191. Hauerwas states that "morally our lives are more properly constituted by retrospective rather than prospective judgments," 185.

counter the abstract rationalism of some (e.g., Kantian) forms of ethics; habituation in the virtues counters disinterested legalism with a richer dispositional ethics.

Against Rahner's use of the fundamental option to specify the relation between identity and action, these narrative and virtue approaches seem to deal more adequately with the concrete and socio-political dimensions of the moral life and their influence on identity. Relatedly, by eschewing any talk of transcendental conditions for acting, they also provide what may be a more palatable picture of moral change and development. Hauerwas construes identity in terms of the life and practice of the church; his position is one of internal realism. The truth of Christian ethics is validated within the Christian community and not by appeal to metaphysics or to human nature. Integrity here would mean consistency or fidelity to the community's defining characteristics. Nussbaum looks to human capacities and needs to reform reason and desire such that "the truths needed to correct errors of belief are to be found within our human condition, rather than beyond or outside our condition."[33] In different ways, then, these positions truncate self-transcendence.

Whatever its difficulties, Rahner's account captures the radical reflexivity of human consciousness (our self-awareness unfolds in an awareness of the divine and in the world with others) and the radical reflexivity of human action (in our actions we take up some relation to the condition for the possibility of our acting). There are resources in Rahner that allow his concept of the fundamental option to be rendered moral hermeneutically; recall that the person is a symbol because she comes to be herself by expressing herself.[34] A hermeneutical reading of the fundamental option is faithful to Rahner and can respond to some of the criticisms that are offered against it. The self works out her self-relation and her relation to God in her concrete actions and relations with others.

[33] Maria Antonaccio, "Contemporary Forms of Askesis and the Return of Spiritual Exercises," *Annual of the Society of Christian Ethics* 18 (1998), 69–92, 79–80. Martha Nussbaum, *The Therapy of Desire: Theory and Practice in Hellenistic Ethics* (Princeton, NJ: Princeton University Press, 1994).

[34] See Andrew Tallon, "Rahner and Personalization," *Philosophy Today* 14 (1970), 44–56. For a lengthier discussion see Andrew Tallon, "Personal Becoming," *Thomist* 43 (1979), 1–177, especially 149–77.

The embodied and temporal qualities of agency are stressed such that the self always acts within a history of free, self-constituting acts yet her relations and her freedom remain open to determination. Because the self understands herself in and through her acting, her self-relation is not severed from its material social and historical conditions. In fact, this hermeneutical approach helps us to think about the relation between an agent's intentions and the concrete actions and relations that are to embody them.

This approach markedly contrasts the cult of self-creation that Chapter One described. Our capacities to fashion new selves through technology and psycho-pharmacology tempts us to believe that persons can adopt and discard new identities at will. Because some of these technologies increase our capacities to compartmentalize our lives, they also tempt us to believe that some of our actions and relations do not impinge on other parts of our lives or do not "count" at all. Sherry Turkle's exploration of cyber-activities like MUD-rape illustrates this point; by understanding what the MUD-rapist does as a "game" in which "no one gets hurt," we cut short moral reflection on why one's sexual desire "plays" with that particular expression of power over another, or conversely how one's desire for power is expressing itself in sexual acts or acts of anger. What is going on in the life of the MUD-rapist that prompts such an act? How else is his or her sexuality expressing itself? In what other ways is that person grasping for power?

Cornell's argument for the decriminalization of prostitution also shows the difficulty of maintaining that one's acts and relations simply are what one understands them to be. Cornell argues that a liberal society must protect freedom of conscience, by which she means the freedom of a person "to claim herself as the 'self-authenticating source' of what the good life is for her."[35] Cornell admits that our (sexual) self-representation does not start from scratch, so we cannot be fully the source of our own values. But we should be politically recognized as if we were. What kind of regulation, then, is appropriate "when a woman insists that she is involved in the self-representation of her sexuality by becoming a porn worker and/or prostitute? What does it mean for a feminist to advocate

---

[35] Cornell, *At the Heart of Freedom*, 37–38.

that the state should save a woman from herself?"[36] After all, some prostitutes argue that they only sell part of themselves for a period of time. Even if this understanding of their profession is partly the result of having been sexually abused, prostitutes should decide for themselves the meaning of their prostitution. This is a matter of personal responsibility.

Here again, substantive moral reflection is cut short by an impoverished understanding of freedom. It separates the prostitute's decision about the meaning of her prostitution from the social, political, and cultural circumstances and effects that surround it. Granted, Cornell claims that our immersion in a world is why we individuate, and that self-representation is a lifelong process we negotiate relationally. But the fact that our (sexual) self-representation does not start from scratch is more important than she recognizes. The self that Cornell describes negotiates her immersion with a will that is somehow detached from the conditions of willing, conditions that are political in character. On what grounds can the person reflect critically on the materials that fund and direct her own self-representation, that move her will and desire in intimate relation to her self-understanding?

We can address these matters more adequately by appeal to a hermeneutical account of self-relation and the moral good of embodied integrity. With those who compartmentalize and discount certain actions ("What goes on in Cancun stays in Cancun"), a hermeneutical approach recognizes that some actions depart from our usual behavior. We can do things in which we do not recognize ourselves; at least we might reject certain descriptions of the acts in favor of others, which may be more true, or may be more palatable to our self-understanding (e.g., a prostitute only sells part of herself for a period of time). But a hermeneutical approach sets these in the context of a history of freedom, asks after the needs, and failings, and aspirations that prompt even isolated and uncharacteristic deeds, and asks how these needs, failings, and aspirations are shaped by one's socio-historical context. The moral good of embodied integrity provides an ideal that directs moral reflection. It counters the voluntarism and subjectivism of the cult of

---

[36] Ibid., 47.

self-creation by prompting us to ask how our concrete actions and relations are ordered to the diverse goods that characterize human life. Here again, a conceptual framework of being can fund reflection on what sorts of actions are ordered to the self's flourishing, precisely because such reflection is inescapably indebted to (but not exhausted by) social consensus and practices, shared meanings and values, collective experience and insight.

Moral actions are "relevant" to self love because in them we posit and negotiate our relations to self, others, God, the natural world. Beverly Harrison is right to proclaim the awesome power of acts of love or lovelessness to build up or destroy others. A contemporary ethics of self love must provide a way to identify the kinds of actions and relations by which we promote our authentic good. I have done this with the love command and the good of integrity. Of course, ethics that specify our authentic good in too static or naïvely naturalistic terms, or by an uncritical promotion of convention are inadequate and even dangerous. A hermeneutical account of self-relation notes the provisionality of accounts of the human good without lapsing into moral relativism. A Christian ethical perspective asks and endeavors to articulate the truth about human beings as it is revealed in Jesus Christ. And it depicts and fosters the dispositions and practices that fit the life of one who becomes a "new creation" in Christ. So the principle of accretion does more than address the voluntarism of Rahner's fundamental option. It helps us to consider how the choices we make to pursue or violate particular goods in our acting build up or destroy ourselves, our neighbors, and the world.

THE IRRELEVANCE OF MORAL ACTIONS

A greater emphasis on concrete acts and relations involves certain risks. It courts scrupulosity and legalism. It can prompt on the one hand a self-righteousness that is blind to one's failings and moral callousness and is harmful to others. It can prompt, on the other hand, a despair that faithlessly neglects one's gifts and God's blessings. Thus it is important to reflect on the irrelevance of moral actions in an ethics of self love.

Paul Ramsey argues that self love is paradigmatic for neighbor love because of its constancy. On Ramsey's account persons love themselves and remain steadfast in their self love quite apart from whether they merit that love. Common ideas of self love as self-esteem or other largely psychological definitions of self love capture Ramsey's point not as an indictment but as an exhortation. Persons need to accept their limitations, even embrace and love their flaws in order to love themselves. So some argue (as Nietzsche did and as some postmodernists do) that we need to jettison ethics altogether. Others insist that we formulate ethics that meet the "principle of minimal psychological realism." Owen Flanagan formulates this principle as an injunction: "make sure when constructing a moral theory or projecting a moral ideal that the character, decision processing, and behavior prescribed are possible, or are perceived to be possible for creatures like us."[37] For Flanagan, psychological realism leads to these "exhilarating" and "liberating" conclusions: that there is no single idea of moral personhood but rather varieties of morally good personalities; that high degrees of and virtuosity in reflectiveness or self-understanding need not accompany moral goodness, mental health or happiness and may actually obstruct them; and that our "radical plasticity" in this regard provides ever present opportunities for "change, growth, and improvement" while cautioning against over confidence about our prospects and intolerance toward others.[38]

Christian ethics offers a psychological realism that can yield similar conclusions. Despite the fact that some critics fault Christian ethics for mongering guilt through systems of reward and punishment or oppressive and suffocating pictures of morality, it not only describes the person's deliverance from an uneasy conscience, from sin, it proclaims the good news which can effect that deliverance. St. Paul writes of our three-fold freedom from the law, the flesh, and sin. John Calvin, Jonathan Edwards, and H. Richard Niebuhr each describe the transformation of the person's way of being in the world through faith. Calvin argued that faith transforms our experience of God from a God of wrath to one of graciousness.

---

[37] Owen Flanagan, *Varieties of Moral Personality: Ethics and Psychological Realism* (Cambridge, MA and London: Harvard University Press, 1991), 32.
[38] Ibid., 335–36.

Similarly, Niebuhr argues that "the human problem is this: how can we interpret all actions upon us, especially the decisive action by which we are, and all things are, by which we are destroyed and all things are destroyed, as divine actions, as actions of affirmation and reaffirmation rather than as actions of animosity or of indifference?"[39] Christians understand themselves and the world in light of God's affirmation of creation, particularly as this is manifested in Jesus Christ.

A hermeneutical account of self-relation recognizes the connections among moral anthropology, moral ontology, and axiologies. It can explain how explicit faith offers more than a particular perspective for the agent; it re-constitutes the conditions for her acting. But it does this by disclosing the limits of agency. Tillich is instructive on this point, for he suggests that we are affected positively in our religious and moral being by realities which are not produced or deserved by us. Good things happen. People do right by one another and themselves. We can, too. We are gifted with and by others, in intimate relations and in anonymous, mundane encounters in check-out lines, in literature, and in art. The dog wags its tail when we enter the room. The friend catches our eyes and what is unspoken is deeply understood. Our acts of love are not our own creation, but a gift whereby we overcome our self-seclusion and participate in another, whereby we affirm being. We actualize ourselves in love for something other. Tillich speaks of these moments as common grace. This common grace operates in all realms and relations of life. As grace, it is independent of any merit and cannot be produced or willed. This grace permeates life; it is experienced whenever one loves, regardless of the object of that love (another person, an idea, a thing) and regardless of the quality of love which dominates (philia, eros, agape). This love reunites being with being, and, to the extent that it does so, fulfills the moral imperative. This reunion is given and can be lost. Indeed, Tillich insists that it will be lost. Its character as grace may be forgotten, its seriousness may be eclipsed or trivialized. We can forget that our love is a gift, a grace which grasps us and reunites us with the object of our love; we can think mistakenly that we will and control such participation.

---

39 H. Richard Niebuhr, *The Responsible Self* (San Francisco, CA: HarperSanFrancisco, 1963), 175.

Because we inevitably overlook this common grace, our relations become sites of struggle – we feel the pain of separation from those with whom we seek union. We feel divided within ourselves. We become problems to ourselves. Tillich argues that both the demand of essential being and the norms which one's culture formulates, bequeaths, and modifies tend to be expressed in laws. He formulates the person's experience of the demand of essential being in the concept of conscience. The conscience, however, witnesses to this unconditional, absolute demand through the cultural contents which tradition and authority provide. When the law is internalized, it creates conscience and, according to Tillich, the feeling of guilt. Guilt is inevitable because "the law is not able to create its own fulfillment."[40] When grace is experienced and operative, the law ceases to be a law, for one need not struggle to give what the law commands. But when grace is lost, the law acquires its commanding character. It reveals the person's separation from essential being and the person's impotence to overcome this separation. Because one realizes painfully that one is not what one should be and is incapable of becoming so, the law creates anxiety and guilt and despair. According to Tillich, "this suffering under the moral law finally drives us to the question of the meaning of our existence in the light of the unconditional moral command which cuts into our finite and estranged predicament."[41]

This human questioning receives its answer in the Christian message. "The response of Christianity is the message that a new reality has appeared with the coming of the Christ, a power of being in which we can participate, and out of which true thought and right action can follow, however fragmentarily."[42] The Christian message is the message of grace; it forgives sins and offers the fulfillment of reunited being. Those who are grasped by the New Being receive a special grace, one which conquers the painful loss of common grace and infuses the person with love. The fulfillment which this grace effects is fragmentary and paradoxical. It is fragmentary because it occurs within the ambiguities of actual life. It is paradoxical because it accepts the unacceptable. The paradox of forgiveness must be

---

[40] Paul Tillich, *Theology of Culture* (Oxford: Oxford University Press, 1959), 142.
[41] Paul Tillich, *Morality and Beyond* (Louisville, KY: Westminster/John Knox, 1963), 62.
[42] Tillich, *Theology of Culture*, 145.

accepted by the person; she must accept that she has been accepted. This is no easy task. Indeed, this acceptance is itself the work of grace. "*The good, transmoral conscience consists in the acceptance of the bad, moral conscience*, which is unavoidable whenever decisions are made and acts are performed."[43]

When the person accepts that she has been accepted in spite of the fact that she is unacceptable, she transcends her guilty conscience and experiences what Tillich calls the transmoral conscience. According to Tillich, "grace unites two elements: the overcoming of guilt and the overcoming of estrangement."[44] Only grace can forgive one of the guilty failure to obey the law and only grace can fulfill the law; hence, grace liberates one from the convicting power of the law. "A conscience may be called 'transmoral' if it judges not in obedience to a moral law, but according to its participation in a reality that transcends the sphere of moral commands. A transmoral conscience does not deny the moral realm, but is driven beyond it by the unbearable tensions of the sphere of the law."[45] There is in Tillich no perfectionist motif. The transmoral, or joyful, conscience allows the person to look at her failings and her conflicts without denying them or despairing over them. Thus, the transmoral conscience does not produce an anti-nomian lawlessness, but genuine freedom.

The transmoral conscience reveals the limits of moral actions. "Moral self-discipline and habits will produce moral perfection although one remains aware that they cannot remove the imperfection which is implied in man's existential situation, his estrangement from his true being."[46] The person cannot save herself. And while the ambiguities of the moral life result from this religious problem of estrangement, progress in the moral life does not resolve the religious problem. For Tillich "there is reunion with the eternal 'Ground of our being' without 'right' action on our part, without our being 'good people,' or the 'people of good will.'"[47] Self love is a moral problem that arises out of a religious predicament. Thus, right self love is a moral obligation that finds both its possibility and its limits in a religious "solution," grace. This means that right

[43] Ibid., 80.   [44] Ibid., 142.   [45] Tillich, *Morality and Beyond*, 77.
[46] Paul Tillich, *The Courage to Be* (New Haven: Yale University Press, 1952), 75.
[47] Tillich, *Morality and Beyond*, 14.

self love is not finally equivalent to being a morally good person. As both Ramsey and Outka noted in their treatments of self love, we must surrender our moral goodness as an instrument of self-justification, as a source of complacency or sloth, as a rod with which to beat ourselves. This surrender frees us for a proper moral seriousness.

But there are difficulties with Tillich's construal of conscience as the "silent voice" through which we apprehend the demand of essential being. It renders conscience apart from the concrete social and historical situations in which we recognize that things are not as they should be. Sin threatens to become only existential malaise.[48] We can specify more adequately the irrelevance of moral actions. They are irrelevant in three ways. First, our moral actions are irrelevant to right self love because they do not merit or earn salvation. They do not merit, but they do matter. In them we take up a relation to real goods, to ourselves, to one another, to God. The positive duty of self love is not the direct pursuit of moral goodness or only the love of God and neighbor. Responsible and faithful and joyous participation in the goods of this world are required as responses to God, who gives them graciously.

Second, our moral actions are irrelevant because they are provisional. They accomplish or transact something definite but in just this way they propel us forward into what is open and unknown. Their moral meaning can be described (e.g., as disloyalty but not treachery) with some accuracy, and they can give a more or less reliable reading of how the person stands in relation to herself, others, God. But their religious significance is hidden in the counsel of God.

Third, our moral actions are irrelevant because of the commensurability of self love and love for God. Right self love is really about a deeply intimate, particular, and personal relation with God. This means that the descriptions and judgments that are the stock in trade of (Christian) ethics are abstract and incomplete when they are isolated from the history or story of this relation of love. Moral acts may be intelligible in properly ethical terms; Christian ethics can describe the moral character of a given act or relation as it

---

[48] Carter Heyward, "Heterosexist Theology: Being Above it All," *Journal of Feminist Studies in Religion* 3 (1987), 29–38.

fits in the personal history of an agent and as a complex event in the agent's broader historical, cultural, and political situation. And, inasmuch as these descriptions identify and articulate how a given act or relation is or is not ordered to objective goods, they can be true. So the point I am making differs from moral subjectivism, which suggests that the person determines for herself the moral meaning of her acts and relations. It also differs from the intuitionism of Tillich's account of conscience as the "silent voice" of essential being. The truth of moral realism is a glimmer, a sight "in a mirror, dimly." (I Cor. 13:12) And the call of that "silent voice" is a call to a relation that ethics can help us to understand and enter more resolutely and well. But these moral descriptions are only part, however crucial, of what is essentially a love story. In this love story the ethical intelligibility of our moral acts and relations is fulfilled and surpassed by understanding, and the moral knowledge ethics provides is fulfilled and surpassed by wisdom. As Psalm 51 asks, "Teach me wisdom in my secret heart." (Ps. 51:6) Here we come to see the incompleteness of our morally proper acts and relations and the gratuity of whatever goodness inheres in them. Here we come to see the full horror and gravity of our sins and indiscretions. Here we experience the freedom of being judged justly and the utter gratuity of God's mercy. Here we recognize ourselves before God, and when this love story reaches its climax we will know fully as we have been known (1 Cor. 13:12).

This three-fold irrelevance of moral acts suggests the limits of an ethical response to the problem of self love. Indeed, it suggests the limits of the moral enterprise altogether. But just so, we can appreciate the importance and promise of ethics. What transpires between God and the person can prompt understanding and love of the law: "How sweet are your words to my taste, sweeter than honey to my mouth! Through your precepts I get understanding; therefore I hate every false way" (Ps. 119:103–04). So let us consider the role of moral norms and moral change.

MORAL ACTS, MORAL NORMS AND MORAL CHANGE

Any ethics confronts the ongoing task of navigating the tension between absolutism and relativism. In ethical theory, this tension often expresses itself in an ethicist's choice of and arguments about models or methods. H. Richard Niebuhr's important work *The Responsible Self* described three different models for ethics, each of which entails a picture of the moral agent. Deontological theories picture the person as man-the-citizen. "We come to self-awareness if not to self-existence in the midst of *mores*, of commandments and rules, *Thou shalts* and *Thou shalt nots*, of directions and permissions."[49] "For some the republic that is to be governed is mostly that of the multifarious self, a being which is a multiplicity seeking unity or a unity diversifying itself into many roles. It is a congeries of many hungers and urges, of fears and angers and loves that is contained somehow within one body and one mind, which are two, yet united."[50] Teleological theories picture the person as "the being who makes himself – though he does not do so by himself – for the sake of a desired end. . . . We act toward an end or are purposive; and, we act upon ourselves, we fashion ourselves, we give ourselves a form."[51] While teleological theories differ regarding what the human end is and how and why it is to be sought, these theories agree that human freedom appears as "the necessity of self-determination by final causes" and practical reason appears as the person's "ability to distinguish between inclusive and exclusive, immediate and ultimate ends and to relate means to ends."[52] Neibuhr's own theory is an alternative to deontological and teleological theories; it is a catechontic or relational-responsibility theory. "What is implicit in the idea of responsibility is the image of man-the-answerer, man engaged in dialogue, man acting in response to action upon him."[53] It pictures the person as a responder. Here the primary question is not "By what norm ought I to live?" or "What good should I seek" but rather "What is the fitting action?"

A number of Protestant and Catholic ethicists have adopted the relational-responsibility model Niebuhr articulated. A relational-responsibility approach nicely places the moral agent as one seeking goods and states of affairs and as one living under the law and with others. The tension between deontological and teleological moments in ethics must be sustained and rendered productive, especially if a relational-responsibility approach is to avoid two pitfalls: allowing the self's encounter with (and constitution by) the other to displace the self's goods and its duties to itself, and

---

[49] Niebuhr, *The Responsible Self*, 52.   [50] Ibid., 54.   [51] Ibid., 49.
[52] Ibid., 51.   [53] Ibid., 57.

allowing the self to instrumentalize the other in the pursuit of her own realization.

A hermeneutical account of self-relation has affinities with relational-responsibility theories, especially since it construes the relation between moral consciousness and moral agency in a way that negotiates the tension between absolutism and relativism. Moral consciousness is socially and linguistically mediated even as moral consciousness is itself the medium of our encounters with the reality of value (or put differently the commensurability of being and goodness). This dense flux of cognition and evaluation is the condition for moral agency. But, as I have argued here, moral acting can re-constitute these conditions. Moral identity arises in the dialectical relation of self-understanding and self-enactment in the world and in relation to others. This is why the moral good of integrity consists in knowing and accepting the truth about ourselves and embodying this in actions and relations that realize love for God and neighbor.

In what, then, does moral change consist? And how is the self's moral determination related to moral norms? In order to grasp the distinctiveness and the contributions of a hermeneutical approach to self-relation, let us return first to the arguments of Rahner and Tillich.

Rahner and moral change

In order to understand Rahner's account of moral change, let us gain some purchase on how he construes moral acts themselves. Rahner argues that moral acts consist in internal and external acts. The external act does not follow from an internal action, as though the categorical, material performance were subordinate to the person's intention or volition. Rather, the internal act in some manner depends upon the external act in order to be achieved.[54] For Rahner,

true Christian morality is therefore a balance between the internal intention of the heart and the external act, a balance which always goes from one to the other without resting or taking root in either one of them. It

---

[54] Rahner, "Some Thoughts on 'A Good Intention,'" *Theological Investigations*, vol. 3, 106.

does not rest in 'interiority', for this can be extremely thin and empty and deceptive if it does not continually 'inform' itself anew and powerfully into very real deeds. It does not rest in external deeds either – as if ultimately and after all only such sturdy, honest and solid things mattered and not just "feelings" and "moods" – for all "good works," no matter how good and right and beneficial they may be to one's neighbour, can also be empty of what alone endows them with true saving value, viz. the believing, hoping love of the heart. This love they cannot carry on their own; this love cannot completely enter into them, for it reaches out beyond every concrete act to the infinity of God in himself.[55]

Although the internal act (love) requires the external act, it cannot be captured or confined by the external act. Because love gives the external act its saving value, Rahner stresses the need for a good intention. Rahner calls a good intention the "practising effort to establish more and more perfectly the necessary unity between internal and external action, a unity always remaining a task to be achieved anew. This unity must be established in such a way as to make the external act always more concrete and perfect in this unity, by making it spring in ever-increasing purity and directness from the correct internal attitude and holding it, as it were, in its origin."[56] Of course actions can be prompted by multiple motives, and these can be contradictory and even unreflexively hidden from the person who has them. "The moral dignity of a motive is co-determined by its formal object, i.e. by what is intentionally and properly meant and willed, loved and sought. For a love is always worth as much as *what* is loved."[57] So it is not sufficient simply to announce to oneself that a particular intention motivates an act; it is a moral duty to purify and direct intentions and motives through prayer, reflection, and composure.

But, then, what role do moral norms play? Rahner develops a dialectic between essential ethics (which pertain to the immutable nature of the person and the universal, objective norms which follow from it) and existential ethics (which concern the mutable, unique

---

[55] Ibid., 109.
[56] Ibid. Rahner distinguishes actual and virtual intentions; an actual intention, for example, can be a mother's intention to wash her baby's diapers; the virtual intention of this act, presumably, is the love which prompts her to care for the baby. For an act to be supernaturally meritorious a virtual intention or motive of faith is sufficient. See ibid., 111–12.
[57] Ibid., 121.

engagement of personhood).[58] The difference may be illustrated as that between the norm "Do not kill" and the norm "Do not kill non-combatants in warfare." According to Rahner, essential and existential ethics may conflict. What holds them together in tension is his understanding of human freedom. The individual possesses the capacity to discern God's will for herself, and she exercises her freedom neither irrespective of nor in complete accordance with material moral norms and laws. The goal of growth in perfection is simultaneously the goal of self-realization by the transcendent individual within given objective realities. Because freedom has both transcendental and categorical dimensions, moral norms point to and express transcendent realities yet describe created structures. It follows that moral norms are lower than, and at the use of the person.[59] Because moral growth does accord with universal moral norms Rahner is free to argue for what superficially seems to be a variety of situation ethics.[60] At the same time, material norms cannot be disregarded, for they point to a transcendent, religious reality which cannot be violated without impinging on the person, on the person's relation to God. The person is bound to act in such a way to preserve and promote one's personhood, "to overcome or lessen in an upward direction the difference which belongs to his essence between what he is and what he can be and should be."[61]

---

[58] For more on Rahner's distinction between essential and existential ethics, see his *The Dynamic Element in the Church* (London: Burns and Oates, 1964), 84–170. For secondary literature on essential and existential ethics, see William A. Wallace, "Existential Ethics: a Thomistic Appraisal," *Thomist* 27 (1963), 493–515; James F. Bresnahan, "Rahner's Ethics: Critical Natural Law in Relation to Contemporary Ethical Methodology," *Journal of Religion* 56 (1976), 36–60; Ronald Modras, "Implications of Rahner's Anthropology for Fundamental Moral Theology," *Horizons* 12 (Spring 1985), 70–90. Bresnahan and Modras both consider Rahner's work with respect to a reformulated natural law. Bresnahan does so more adeptly. Particularly interesting is his consideration of the translation of "ought" to "is" and vice versa. See "Rahner's Ethics," 53–54. Modras argues that concrete moral norms are historically and culturally conditioned and therefore are not universal and absolute.

[59] Rahner, *Foundations of Christian Faith: an Introduction to the Idea of Christianity*, trans. William Dych (New York: Crossroad, 1993), 409.

[60] Situation ethics were quite popular in Germany during the 1950s, the time when Rahner wrote "On the Question of a Formal Existential Ethics." He charged that severe situation ethics amount to a "massive nominalism," but that situation ethics do admit of a truth, namely that the person, and thus his moral action, is not simply a particular instance of a universal.

[61] Rahner, *Foundations of Christian Faith*, 409.

The problem becomes, then, whether or not and which actions increase human freedom and which contradict it. Moreover, in the dialectic between essential and existential ethics, Rahner suggests that each situation demands something very particular and unique from the person confronted with that situation. This single moral choice is not reducible to the application of a material norm. Neither, however, can it conflict with the transcendent reality to which the norm points (which of course, is something quite different from the question of whether it can conflict with the norm itself). That for which the norm is a referent and sometimes inadequate expression is the inviolability of the person. Although Rahner maintains that a concrete imperative cannot violate universal moral norms, he nevertheless asks whether the moral obligation which pertains in a given situation might exceed simple obedience to an imperative.[62] The concrete situation cannot be analyzed into finite, general propositions. Particularly in a situation wherein several possible decisions are morally permissible, Rahner argues that there must be one action which alone is morally obligatory and binding. For Rahner "the concrete moral act is more than just the realization of a universal idea happening here and now in the form of a case. The act is a reality which has a positive and substantial property which is basically and absolutely unique."[63] Rahner speaks of this positive element within the moral act as the coming to light or the being-thus of the ineffable moral individuality of the person. Thus, the decision made within a range of permissible courses of action is not arbitrary and neutral but is the absolutely binding will of God.[64] The substantial nature of the person must achieve itself in positive, unique, concrete, individual

---

[62] Rahner, "Formal Existential Ethics," 222. Consider also the following: "Maturity is, first of all, the *courage* and the *resolve* to make decisions and to take responsibility for them even if they cannot be legitimized any longer by universal and universally accepted norms" (Rahner, "The Mature Christian," *Theological Investigations*, vol. 21, 119). Maturity also entails the readiness to inform oneself of norms which apply to a particular situation, to appreciate their complexity and to weigh them. Maturity also involves thoughtful consideration of church teachings and laws, an appreciation for distinctions between teaching and explanations and a knowledge of the hierarchy of truths in the Catholic faith. Moreover, maturity entails a willingness to criticize oneself. "Maturity means courage for greater freedom and this freedom means greater responsibility. Courage is anything but mere whim and subjective capriciousness. Maturity in its authentic form makes human beings lonely in a certain sense," (ibid., 128).
[63] Rahner, "Formal Existential Ethics," 225.   [64] Ibid., 227.

decisions; it is installed in the non-derivable qualitative properties of the individual act.[65] These acts are more than mere cases. There is a positive ethical reality which is untranslatable into material universal ethics. So there must be a formal existential ethics, that is, an ethics that treats the formal structures of perceiving such existential ethical realities.

"Life . . . is made up of a series of situations (in the main, dependent on one another up to a certain point), a series of tasks, each of which is different from the other with its own particular place in the course of life as a whole, each of them bringing with them a certain characteristic and ideal recipe as to how they ought to be mastered, and each of them being mastered in this or that way or not being fulfilled at all."[66] Situations encompass the vital statistics of the person, external circumstances not completely under one's control, including intervention by God through grace, and earlier situations which always co-determine following situations, not only with respect to the manner in which one experienced the prescinding situation but simply its having been experienced at all. Thus, what each situation demands of the person is also co-determined by the person.

Rahner distinguishes growth in moral sanctity from the mere acquisition of virtues. The facility for a virtuous act does not exhaust what is morally demanded in a given situation. In other words, Christian perfection is not collapsible with virtuous habituation. Rahner asserts this simply because of the potential for moral acts, which in the process of acquiring a virtue were spontaneous and genuine moral acts, to become instinctive reactions which lack what Rahner terms the "moral nucleus," the engagement of the moral agent. Acquired virtues do not of themselves indicate greater perfection. They free one from marshaling one's energy to respond to particular pressures of the moral life in favor of attending to other moral tasks; so the acquisition of virtues is the acquisition of the *possibility* for greater perfection.

Rahner, then, understands moral change as the possibility that the perfect person and the beginner perform the same moral act

---

[65] See ibid., 228 footnote 3.

[66] Rahner, "Reflections on the Problem of the Gradual Ascent to Christian Perfection," *Theological Investigations*, vol. 7, 20.

differently, that is, the possibility that a moral act may increase in intensity. "Hence we must distinguish two quite different dimensions of intensity in the case of a human act: one of these is the measure of the greater or lesser personal depth of an act, while the other measures the intensity and density of the act on a particular personal level . . . [T]here is evidently a development of man's capacity for an ever more total self-commitment by ever deeper personal acts."[67] In other words, acts may be distinguished with respect to what each objectively demands from the person (e.g., the decision not to tell a cashier he gave you too much change as compared with the decision to terminate a loved one's life support systems); and acts may be distinguished with respect to the existential depth with which the agent exercises her freedom (e.g., the decision to give alms may be done rather superficially or thoughtlessly or it may involve a very conscious and concerted self-commitment to the neighbor). The moral recipe of the situation, that which God demands of the person in that situation, is something unique to the agent and to the situation itself. This means that God has a will for the individual, not apart from the universal call of holiness, but the asymptotic approach to holiness as the self-realization of that individual. God's offer of God's self-communication means that *every* person is charged with the task of accomplishing his or her personality. In this sense, though a universal call, it is a highly individualized endeavor. This unique and personal ideal applies to the whole of the person's self-realization and to particular categorical situations. Moreover, one's relationships and occupations, as various types of vocation, comprise both the means and the arena in which the individual responds to the more fundamental vocation to holiness; through both providence and discernment the person travels his or her own pathway to perfection.

Here again we see the voluntarism that dogs Rahner's moral theology. His transcendental-categorical account of freedom permits him to argue that the moral significance of an act exceeds the act itself, that the morally binding character of a norm rises from a transcendental reality that the norm may express inadequately, that what God asks of the person in each moral situation is progress

[67] Ibid.

in what God asks of the person as such, her self-disposal in love. At each point, Rahner's account directs moral attention to the person's transcendental decision or choice and away from the categorical acts, norms, and situations. Still, we should not overlook Rahner's insistence that "true Christian morality is therefore a balance between the internal intention of the heart and the external act, a balance which always goes from one to the other without resting or taking root in either one of them." A hermeneutical approach can develop this insight. Rahner suggests that a properly moral act is characterized by a unity of the internal and external act, so that the intention is pure and the external deed springs from and holds the intention. In a hermeneutical approach this unity is a matter of "fit." An intention expresses itself in better and worse fashion in concrete acts (which can be interior acts by which we work on our perceptions of others and our affections as well as exterior, observable acts). There are some acts that cannot "fit" the intention they are meant to carry and express. Recent terrorist attacks in the United States on the World Trade Center and Pentagon contradicted the religious intentions of those who perpetrated them. Ascertaining the fit between intention and act requires reflection on circumstances, experience, social consensus, authoritative moral sources, and moral exemplars. It also requires attention to the objective goods that constitute human flourishing. Tillich's account of moral action affords some help on this point.

Tillich and moral change

Tillich constructs a "structure of moral action that embodies both the absolute and the relative, the static and the dynamic, the religious and the secular elements of ethical thought and moral experience."[68] For Tillich there is no progress in the moral act as such because what is demanded morally is not a state of affairs, but a person. Morality concerns the actualization of the person in community, the integration of the person's dimensions in a centeredness which is gained by participation in the New Being. Tillich shifts moral attention away from particular springs of action to the

---

[68] Tillich, *Morality and Beyond*, 36.

wholeness of the person and to community. Nonetheless, in order to become a person, the self must make moral decisions of her own. Because the moral act is a personal decision wherein the dimension of spirit appears, it is formally absolute and immutable. Tillich goes on to say,

> But there are two kinds of progress in connection with the moral function, the two kinds being those of ethical conduct and of educational level. Both are cultural creations and open to the new. The ethical content of moral action has progressed from primitive to mature cultures in terms of refinement and breadth, although the moral act in which the person is created is the same whatever content is actualized. . . . It is in the cultural element within the moral act that progress takes place, not in the moral act itself.[69]

Progress in educational level refers to individual and collective moral habituation. Such habituation can mature persons and groups, but this progress does not belong to the moral act. Moral habituation, clarity in moral reasoning, and the cultural content given to the moral act do not diminish or condition the constitutive moral conditions of freedom and responsibility. The person is free to deliberate and decide morally, but her very freedom sets the ontological parameters of genuinely moral action. Morality is rooted in being so moral reasoning ought to take the structures of being into account. Some thinkers argue that Tillich's ethics verges on intuitionism here.[70] Because the moral aim is the actualization of the person, which Tillich understands in terms of reunion with essential being, the person's moral attention is shifted away from the actual to the potential, to the dimensions of essential being. Such a move resonates with some natural law approaches in ethics, and natural law theory might offer resources with which one might begin to translate the "silent voice" of essential being into some

[69] Paul Tillich, *Systematic Theology*, 3 vols. (Chicago: University of Chicago, 1951–63), vol. 3, 333–34.
[70] The way in which my own account of self love presses beyond Tillich's position by arguing that self love consists in a self-understanding mediated in the person's moral conduct can offset such intuitionism because it clarifies the connection between moral being and our thinking about it. See Donald R. Weisbaker, "Paul Tillich on the Experiential Ground of Religious Certainty," *American Journal of Theology and Philosophy* 1:2 (1980), 37–44; Mary A. Stenger, "Paul Tillich's Theory of Theological Norms and the Problems of Relativism and Subjectivism," *Journal of Religion* 62 (1982), 359–75, especially 366–67; Richard Gregg, "The Experiential Center of Tillich's System," *Journal of the American Academy of Religion* 53 (1985), 251–58.

practical directives for action. But to do so, one necessarily provides the moral act with cultural contents.

Thus, in order to understand moral change we must consider the cultural creation of the content of the moral act. The ontological character of morality does not change, but the content of morality can and should change because psychological and sociological processes construct moral systems. Cultures give expression and form to morality.[71] Nonetheless, cultural relativity and the person's freedom find objective correlates in the structure of being.[72] Thus Tillich balances the relativism of moral systems with the objective and absolute source of the moral imperative. Indeed, because Tillich understands culture as the whole of human self-interpretation, the cultural content given to the moral act is a means whereby persons and communities seek to understand themselves and how they ought to live. Culture provides these contents on the basis of collective human experience. The wisdom of this collective experience is embodied in tradition, laws, and authority. Moreover, it is internalized in the individual person's conscience. Tillich affirms the soundness of such a heritage; the wisdom which constitutes one's moral universe provides a sound basis and rich resources for the decisions which actual life demands. People need such guidance for daily life.[73] So culture provides continuity among the person's moral decisions.

Tillich concedes that the command of the law may produce obeisance in an institutionalized form (e.g., paying taxes) and in that sense can produce moral action. But this obedience is a compromise and does not manifest the true nature of the moral. Moreover, because social laws and personal habits can effect action regardless of what creative justice might demand in a particular situation, "the law provides moral motivation if morality becomes a thread within the texture of premoral forces and motives."[74] Still, logically and psychologically, the law cannot motivate us to fulfill it, it cannot make us good.[75]

In order to account for moral motivation Tillich draws upon two Greek ideas: knowledge and eros. Knowledge of the good, Tillich

[71] See John McDargh, "Theological Uses of Psychology: Retrospective and Prospective," *Horizons* 12 (1985), 247–64. See also Joseph E. Talley, "Psychological Separation-Individuation and Spiritual Reunion," *Journal of Psychology and Theology* 8 (1980), 97–106.
[72] Tillich, *Morality and Beyond*, 27.   [73] Ibid., 45.   [74] Ibid., 56.   [75] See ibid., 50.

notes, was thought to effect good action. The person's basic moral problem was cognitive in character, and could be remedied by the practice of philosophy. Tillich distinguishes the knowledge which leads to action from a scientific, objective knowledge. It is, rather, the knowledge of participation. For this reason,

> knowledge of the character of wisdom cannot be considered as functioning in one direction only, as the cause of moral action, because it is in itself partly a result of moral action. Since one must be good in order to be wise, goodness is not a consequence of wisdom. The Socratic assertion, therefore, that knowledge creates virtue must be interpreted as knowledge in which the whole person is involved (insight). That is, a cognitive act which is united with a moral act can cause further moral acts (and further cognition).[76]

Being precedes action (one cannot save oneself through one's good works) and "previous action also determines present being."[77] Thus, while the religious problem of estrangement cannot be overcome through meritorious behavior, and while the participation which does conquer estrangement remains fragmentary, free moral action can contribute to moral maturity; knowing and acting are dynamically related because being and acting are dynamically related.

The second Greek notion which Tillich utilizes to make sense of moral motivation is that of eros. Drawing on the process of therapeutic healing as an analogy for moral development, Tillich notes that moral change is only partly an effect of insight and insight is partly an effect of the moral will to be liberated.[78] The Platonic conception of eros discloses the nature of love in all its qualities: it is the drive for reunion. The person is driven, attracted by the good which is the goal or proper object of the moral command. The good which is sought relativizes morality as a stage in the pursuit of a good which transcends morality. Morality has a transmoral aim, participation in the divine. The law, understood as the demand to actualize our essential being cannot motivate us; but law, understood as our essential being (what Tillich calls the meaning of law as structure) is an object of erotic longing, that toward which we

---

[76] Ibid., 58.   [77] Ibid., 14.
[78] See ibid., 58–59. Tillich employs psychoanalytic theory as well as therapeutic processes to illustrate his understanding of sanctification, the healing process of salvation. See also Tillich, *Systematic Theology*, passim.

are driven. This drive toward reunion is a gift, a grace, because it is our longing for God, given to us by God.[79] A moral act "is not an act in obedience to an eternal law, human or divine. It is the inner law of our true being, of our essential or created nature which demands that we actualize what follows from it. And an anti-moral act is not the transgression of one or several precisely circumscribed commands, but an act that contradicts the self-realization of the person as a person and drives toward disintegration."[80] Despite the unconditional character of essential being as a moral imperative, the particular moral imperatives which have been formulated to guide action are relative and the material acts which are adequate to this self-constitution do change.

Tillich eschews any simple application of law to particular situations. Because the experiential root of morality is the person-to-person encounter, morality is a matter of justice, the acknowledgment of the other person as such, without the annihilation of oneself as a person. Indeed, Tillich maintains that abstract norms are applied in such a way as to eclipse the uniqueness of the concrete situation. Hence "moral systems, just because of their intimate connection with a cultural system, have the tendency to become oppressive if the general cultural scheme changes. They tend to produce moralism as an attitude."[81] According to Tillich, each particular moral decision is bound both by the demand of the universal law and the demand of the concrete situation. Only if both of these demands are met and made effective for the situation can justice be realized.[82] Justice, however, could be understood as a matter of external actions performed with cool objectivity; but the moral imperative demands one be a person in a community of persons, and, thus, that one be involved. So justice must be taken into love, which includes yet transcends justice.

---

[79] Tillich, *Morality and Beyond*, 61.

[80] Ibid., 20. This suggests, as we saw in Rahner, that there can be a discrepancy between the moral status of an act and its coherence with particular moral norms.

[81] Tillich, *Theology of Culture*, 133. Tillich sometimes exhibits a strong resistance to systems and institutions which, in his judgment, claim too much authority. This resistance has been attributed to Tillich's encounter with the Third Reich, but also to his personal history. See Melvin L. Vulgamore, "Tillich's 'Erotic Solution,'" *Encounter* 45 (Summer 1984), 193–212.

[82] See Paul Tillich, *Love, Power, and Justice* (Oxford: Oxford University Press, 1954), 15.

For love is both absolute and relative by its very nature. An unchanging principle, it nevertheless always changes in its concrete application. It "listens" to the particular situation. Abstract justice cannot do this; but justice taken into love and becoming "creative justice" or *agape* can do so. *Agape* acts in relation to the concrete demands of the situation – its conditions, its possible consequences, the inner status of the people involved, their hidden motives, their limiting complexes, and their unconscious desires and anxieties.[83]

Tillich insists that love is not simply added to justice. Were this the case, justice as such would be impossible. Rather, he develops the idea of creative justice to express the union of justice and love as the principle of morality. Love designates life's drive toward reunion with itself, and justice provides the norm that that which is estranged should be reunited. Only love, however, can create the participation which reunion requires. Thus, justice implies love.

Even as love fulfills and realizes the justice which norms express, it relativizes and may even contradict the norms themselves.[84] Love synthesizes the absolute and the relative, the demand of the universal law and the demand of the concrete situation. This creativity which love allows, indeed, which love demands, is necessary if the person is to do what is morally demanded. Yet, recall that for Tillich in existence the creation and fall coincide. Creativity is risky business.[85]

Whichever side of a moral alternative might be chosen, however great the risk in a bold decision may be, if it be a moral decision it is dependent only on the pure "ought to be" of the moral imperative. And should anyone be in doubt as to which of several possible acts conforms to the moral imperative, he should be reminded that each of them might be justified in a particular situation, but that whatever he chooses must be done with the consciousness of standing under an unconditional imperative. The doubt concerning the justice of a moral act does not contradict the certainty of its ultimate seriousness.[86]

The risk of morality is not limited to decisions which do not conform to traditional norms. Because such norms are contingent, even decisions which cohere with them entail a certain risk. "Accepting

---

[83] Tillich, *Morality and Beyond*, 44. For more on agape, the ambiguity of law, and creative justice see also *Systematic Theology* vol. 3, 45–50 and 271–75.
[84] Tillich, *Theology of Culture*, 145.   [85] Ibid., 140.   [86] Tillich, *Morality and Beyond*, 23.

or trespassing traditional morals is spiritually justified only if done with self-scrutiny, often in the pain of a split conscience, and with the courage to decide even when the risk of error is involved."[87]

Both Tillich and Rahner reject rigid fidelity to principles and both reject moral habituation as an adequate account of moral change. Both also endorse in different ways the importance of moral acts as ways we actualize our selves by installing our selves (Rahner) and participating (Tillich) in the concrete. Each insists on the one hand that the person realize a proper intention in a suitable concrete form, what classical Christian ethics expressed in the principle *materia bene disposita*, that the matter of an act be well disposed to the intention it is to carry and embody. On the other hand, Rahner and Tillich recognize that this may require acting that violates particular norms in order to do justice to the real moral demand of a situation.

The moral meaning of acts

A contemporary account of self love should embrace the freedom and the responsibility these arguments provide for the moral agent. Yet it should avoid the voluntarism and intuitionism that dogs these arguments, both of which lead to subjectivism. Rahner and Tillich may also mask a form of legalism insofar as each insists that the agent must discern the unique and absolutely binding obligation hidden in the situation.[88]

In a hermeneutical account of self-relation the moral meaning of an act does not reside in the act apart from the situation or the agent's intention. But neither is the act neutral material that receives its moral status from her intention. Moral meaning is not temporally located or confined. A person wakes up to her decisions, re-interprets her past. Her moral acts constitute her like sacraments of re-commitment or repentance or reflection in response to others and in relation to the goods at stake. These acts are events in which her intentions, her motives, the external features of the situation, and the others and goods involved all co-determine each other.

---

[87] Ibid., 45.

[88] Finnis makes this claim about proportionalism. I do not mean here to explore whether he characterizes proportionalism rightly in this regard. See his *Fundamentals of Ethics*.

Moreover, this co-determination occurs in a personal history such that the meaning of any particular act depends in part on other acts of hers, and on social and historical consensus about kinds of actions and the degree to which the concrete act is ordered to human flourishing or not. Given the fact of sin, the murky depths of human motivation, and the unpredictable effects of any course of action, the moral meaning of any act is known ultimately in God. A range of external or concrete acts can be hospitable to a particular (set of) intention(s). But because the idea of right self love requires us to identify some acts or projects or relations as incompatible with the self's authentic good, we need to determine the parameters of this range. Because acting proceeds from knowing the good and yields such knowledge we can do this through inductive reflection on experience and through trial and error. We also need to appeal (albeit critically) to trustworthy communities and traditions, and to commit all our ventures to the mercy of God.

I can now clarify the good of embodied integrity and its relation to continuity and change in a person's identity. Recall that for Schweiker integrity results indirectly from the education of moral sensibility through self-criticism (radical interpretation) as a condition for moral acting. Radical interpretation is the process wherein moral identity arises and whereby moral change can occur. Recall as well that because integrity is logically and ontologically prior to the person's attempts to secure particular goods she may act against these goods as part of maintaining commitments to the moral project.

For a contemporary account of self love, it is important to highlight the temporal and embodied dimensions of identity by stressing its constitution in acting. Moral change does involve the education and transformation of moral sensibilities (perceptive and affective) as conditions for changes in moral acting. But moral change also occurs in acting. Moral progress and moral regress can occur pre- or extra-linguistically as the person's acting ramifies in her experience of herself. The radically reflexive character of moral acts also accounts for the person's continuity in her acting. Her freedom has a history. Indeed, the experience of being convicted of one's sin is simply a "morning after" experience – one awakens to her own misused freedom, becomes aware of what she has chosen

and done and been, all of which have led ineluctably to what she
at present is. We are, however, and happily, more than the sum
total of our acts. Our transcendence means that we can take up a
posture toward ourselves and toward the relations and contingent
factors that situate us. We are capable of reflexive self-criticism, of
a moral self-transcendence. And in this active self-interpretation
we can accept ourselves in such a way as to accept God's offer of
forgiveness. The person receives indirectly the good of embodied
integrity when she understands herself in light of, and endeavors
to make her acts and relations works of love for, God and neighbor.

Both Rahner and Tillich recognize in some measure the reflexive character of moral acts. Rahner does this in the fundamental
option, and Tillich does this in his argument about participatory
knowledge as a form of moral motivation. Actions are reflexive
because the self constitutes herself in her acting, and because in
acting she participates in or alienates herself from the goods at
stake in a given action. A contemporary theory of right self love
can recognize with Schweiker that the self appears in the space
between consciousness and acting. But the crucial issue is how the
self is to integrate her self-understanding and her acting. By what
activities can she purify her consciousness, recognize the truth and
overcome moral insensitivity? How can she express and embody
this truth in concrete acts and relations that are faithful to and
effective for it? This is the problem of right self love. Actions and
embodiment in general become important as sacraments for inner
attitudes and dispositions, even as the meaning of actions and of
embodiment cannot be grasped apart from these internal factors.
So, we cannot claim, as Finnis and Grisez do, that one may never
act against the goods that constitute human existence. But we need
to exercise caution and self-criticism in claiming that sometimes
one might have to act against them. Judgments about what kinds
of acts are or are not ordered to the self's authentic good will be
deeply personal and particular but not private. Given the self's
relations to others and to God, she will determine herself as she
negotiates these relations in the lifelong task of adjudicating her
interests and those of others. The fact that we can and do act at
odds with the beliefs and values and commitments we profess is a
given. But by construing this disparity as the problem of self love we

note both the need to evaluate concrete acts and relations through which we take up our self-relation, and the need to accept, even embrace, this disparity. Further, by recognizing the way features of our contemporary situation exacerbate this disparity and enervate us in the face of it we recoup some agency in response to them.

At this point we can grasp the importance of bringing hermeneutical theory to bear on conceptual frameworks of being in the service of moral anthropology. The reflexive structure of consciousness that hermeneutical theory contributes offsets the subjectivism and intuitionism of Rahner's and Tillich's arguments by emphasizing cognitivism. Conceptual frameworks of being can remind us of the reality of value, the moral import of our embodiment and our connections to the natural world. As heuristic devices these conceptual frameworks can elicit and guide inductive reflection on experience. This means that in the self's moral creativity she meets the moral constraints on it.

CONCLUSION

This chapter highlighted the fundamentally relational character of moral reasoning and moral acting, as well as the dialectical tension between being and doing. These insights into moral development refine the idea of right self love insofar as they highlight the role of interpretation in self-relation and relation to others.

The fundamental unity of religion and morality has lurked throughout the preceding chapters, but Chapter Six will show explicitly that the unity of the religious and the moral in right self love point to the connections between religion and morality. If this chapter explores how we are to think about the moral life, Chapter Six explores how we are to think about such thinking.

CHAPTER 6

Self love, religion, and morality

I began by noting how contemporary philosophical moral anthropologies truncate the self. This chapter explores the intimate
relation between the moral and religious dimensions of human existence. Here I argue that (1) theological (particularly Christian
ethical) discourse recovers and expresses this inter-relation and
(2) the religious relation to God relativizes morality, but religious
constructs must be subject to moral critique. A hermeneutical account of self-relation provides a way to address a number of important questions in ethics; by exploring the place of explicit faith in
right self love, we also learn something about the scope and specificity of Christian morality and ethics. This clarifies the contribution
Christian ethics makes to wider debates about the self and about
foundationalism in ethics, debates that, we saw in Chapter One,
re-cast and heighten the problem of self love.

Already I argued that formally or structurally speaking right self
love designates a form of self-relation that responds lovingly to the
divine self-offer and actualizes this response in love for neighbors.
The inexhaustible and happy particularity of persons shows itself
in the conceptual and practical resources that mediate self-relation
and relation to God, and in the material acts and relations in which
persons posit them. Explicit faith provides a set of conceptual resources and practices through which a person understands herself and the world. Are these resources one set alongside others?
Do they express and prompt relation to others and community
or do they contribute to moral subjectivism and/or intolerance?
Pursuing these questions will let me show not simply the helpfulness of Christian ethics over against secular offerings, but that
Christian ethical discourse is self-validating.

SELF-UNDERSTANDING IN MORALITY AND RELIGION

Moralities and religions are socio-cultural and historical constructs that express the moral and religious dimensions of the person.[1] They are more or less discrete systems of reflection on those dimensions. A hermeneutical approach to self-relation emphasizes and clarifies the relation between these dimensions and their conceptualization in moralities and religions. It also emphasizes and clarifies the distinction and relation between morality and religion. It presses this question: do particular moral and religious claims and practices adequately conceptualize the moral and religious dimensions of the person? This question is pertinent to self love in two ways. If right self love is a morally proper form of self-relation, the concepts and practices that express and posit the self must do so appropriately if they are to be ordered to the self's good. Moreover, they must express and orient the self's proper relation to her neighbors and the world; particular moralities and religions must not be tyrannous.

These two demands center on contemporary debates about moral realism and relativism and on contemporary experiences of diversity, fragmentation, and, unhappily, violence and oppression, ostensibly warranted by religious claims. These debates, experiences, and problems lead many to advocate moral subjectivism and to regard religious commitments as private choices to be tolerated and protected as such. A hermeneutical approach to self-relation captures the insights of these experiences and debates but avoids moral subjectivism and the privatization of religion. It places moral and religious constructs in a mutually critical relation. It evaluates moral claims and norms in relation to the objective values and goods that constitute human existence. And in Christian ethics, it evaluates them in light of the truth about the person as this is revealed in Jesus Christ. A hermeneutical approach also evaluates religious claims and practices on these same grounds, and according to criteria that are internal to particular traditions and communities.

---

[1] Some contemporary thinkers argue that religion is a modern construct and cannot be predicated of the human as such. See Wayne Proudfoot, *Religious Experience* (Berkeley, CA: University of California Press, 1985).

This chapter attempts to show all of this and, in doing so, to demonstrate the promise of a hermeneutical account of self-relation for reflection on self love and for (Christian) ethics more generally. It also endeavors to show the apologetic fruit Christian ethics bears for the problem of self love. The chapter takes up these tasks by reading Rahner and Tillich hermeneutically. This reading reaps the insights of their respective frameworks of being and avoids moral subjectivism and the privatization of religion. It also deals more adequately than Rahner and Tillich do with the moral connection between the person's religious relation to God and the moral act of self-constitution.

Let me turn to Rahner first. His position is amenable to a hermeneutical account of self-relation; such an account actually clarifies the insights of Rahner's transcendental Thomism in a way that frees us from its voluntarism and sets moral talons into the categorical dimension of freedom. According to Rahner, through religion and morality the person reflects on and thematizes the transcendental and non-thematic orientation which she experiences. Moral acts have religious import. They do not merit or earn salvation, but in her moral acts the person can express and posit her self-understanding in such a way that her acts contribute to and shape her more basic stance of faith. Rahner goes so far as to say that salvation takes place non-thematically in the moral act. According to Rahner there is only a logical but not a real distinction between a moral and a salvific act. Wherever the person "posits a positively moral act in the full exercise of his free self-disposal, this act is a positive supernatural salvific act in the actual economy of salvation even when its *a posteriori* object and the explicitly given *a posteriori* motive do not spring from the positive revelation of God's Word but are in this sense 'natural'."[2] Rahner makes quite a radical claim here – the person's moral conduct can constitute a de facto acceptance of God's offer of self-communication, even if the person's moral conduct lacks any thematic theistic reference. This is the case for two reasons.

[2] Karl Rahner, "Reflections on the Unity of the Love of Neighbor and the Love of God," *Theological Investigations*, vol. 6, 239. See *Theological Investigations*, vols. 1–14 (vols. 1–6, Baltimore, MD: Helicon; vols. 7–10, New York: Herder and Herder; vols. 11–14, New York: Seabury; 1961–1976).

First, Rahner argues that God's universal salvific will offers divinizing grace to everyone and thereby elevates the moral act. If the self is both transcendental and categorical, how is subjectivity divinized a priori? As Chapter Three noted, it is because God has already given God's self to the person as a constitutive element.[3] According to Rahner, any action categorically mediates the person's self-presence, particularly in her knowledge and freedom. Indeed, if the person is always already graced, her moral life falls within the realm of God's saving activity. A linear picture of justification and sanctification becomes inappropriate because the priority of the divine self-offer makes the person's religious and moral activity irreducibly responsive. Moral rectitude is not simply an extrinsic consequence of salvation any more than it is a precondition for it.[4] Recall that for Rahner the person's transcendental orientation toward God provides a non-thematic knowledge of God. Because God so offers God's self to the person, this non-thematic knowledge of God constitutes a metaphysical reception of revelation. It "includes an element of (transcendental) revelation and possibility of faith which also gives such an act that sufficient character of 'faith' necessary for a moral act being a salvific act."[5] When the person posits a positive moral act she accepts the transcendental condition of possibility of this act "even if the acceptance happens without conscious reflection and the object which mediates this moral decision is not necessarily grasped in a religious or 'theist' manner."[6] In a hermeneutical account of self-relation this non-thematic knowledge of God occurs in the orientation of consciousness itself. Here, too, when the person accepts herself in a moral decision, she accepts the conditions for the possibility of her acting.

Second, the religious and moral dimensions of the person connect in her sociality, and specifically in the unity of love for God and love for the neighbor. As Chapter Four showed, for Rahner the

---

3 Rahner develops this claim in terms of quasi-formal causality. See section three of Chapter Three for a treatment of quasi-formal causality. See also Paul de Letter "Divine Quasi-Formal Causality," *Irish Theological Quarterly* 27 (1960), 221–28.

4 Karl Rahner, *Foundations of Christian Faith: an Introduction to the Idea of Christianity*, trans. William Dych (New York: Crossroad, 1993), 152.

5 Rahner, "Unity of the Love of Neighbor and the Love of God," 239.

6 Rahner, "Anonymous and Explicit Faith," *Theological Investigations*, vol. 16, 59.

primary act of love for God is love for the neighbor. Hence, one can
love God in a non-explicit manner when one loves one's neighbor.
This is because "the subject's experience of himself and of the Thou
who encounters him, is one and the same experience under two different aspects, and that too not merely in its abstract formal nature,
but in its concrete reality as well, in the degree of success or failure
with which it is achieved, in its moral quality as an encounter with
the real self and with one's fellow in love or hatred."[7] Love for God
and love for neighbor mutually condition one another. It is not the
case, argues Rahner, that love for the neighbor simply follows from
love for God as a secondary moral consequence. Nor is it the case
that one's dealings with the world and with others can be separated
from one's response to God. Indeed, the person's response to God is
actualized in such dealings. So the person's unique relation to God,
her lonely responsible task, nevertheless cannot be understood as
a private affair.

The force of Rahner's position is two-fold. First, Rahner maintains that the religious and moral dimensions of the person should
be objectified appropriately. I indicated this in Chapter Five, under the discussion of internal and external acts. There I noted that
the external act is not an arbitrary concretization of a primary
internal act, but, rather, the internal act's constitutive medium.
Moral development consists in part in an increasing conformity
or suitability between the internal and external acts. The person's
religious activity ought also to correspond appropriately to the person's religious existence. Second, the elusive, inexhaustible depths
of the person as a moral and religious creature must be accepted
and embraced as such. The person is oriented toward absolute
mystery and is ultimately not at her full disposal. These two points
may seem to contradict one another. On the one hand Rahner argues that religion and morality must objectify the religious and the
moral as perfectly as possible. On the other hand, Rahner argues
that the person must surrender to and embrace the mystery that
seeks expression in morality and religion. But these two claims do
cohere. The appeal to mystery does not vitiate the task to objectify appropriately the religious and the moral. This is because for

[7] Rahner, "Experience of Self and Experience of God," *Theological Investigations*, vol. 13, 128.

Rahner religion does appropriately objectify the religious depths of the person when it articulates the person's relation to mystery. Similarly, because morality is the person's self-acceptance in her free self-disposal toward the horizon of absolute mystery, when it entails an abandon to mystery it objectifies the moral dimensions of human existence appropriately.

Christian ethics expresses this point by construing the Christian life as a paradox in which the self gains itself by losing itself. Human freedom is situated, yet open to further determination. It is ambiguous; it cannot be brought to reflection completely. Freedom therefore must surrender itself to God. This surrender is a venture of trust that unfolds slowly in the experience of freedom itself. The person is incapable of this surrender of freedom outside of God's prevenient grace. God has manifested this grace, this irrevocable decision to liberate freedom, in Jesus. In personal love for God the horizon and object of freedom are identical. Thus our freedom is realized, we are realized, when we abandon ourselves to God. So the claim that free self-actualization constitutes an act of faith or unbelief is not at odds with a more traditional construal of faith as trust in God. Faith, then, need not be confined to a discrete, explicit, and self-conscious act – indeed, it cannot be so confined. The totality of our free self-actualization is an act of faith or unbelief – the transcendental depths of categorical freedom mean that we take up some stance in relation to God's revelation, God's offer of salvation. This does not relativize explicit faith, for such faith can bring the depths of our acceptance into our semi-conscious self-understanding. Moreover, the faith posited by freedom has an inescapably cognitive dimension. This means, for instance, that the traditional distinction between *fides qua* (faith by which we believe) and *fides quae* (faith which we believe) helps to make sense of explicit faith as a set of commitments (cognitive and affective) through which persons understand themselves and the world and by which their way of being in the world is transformed. A hermeneutical account of self-relation amplifies these two points. If, as Paul Ricoeur suggests, we invent in order to discover, the moral and religious constructs through which persons and communities interpret themselves are relative without being irrelevant. Moreover, the moral and religious acts by which a person enacts her relations

Self Love and Christian Ethics

to God, self, and others ought to posit and embody as well as possible the love that should motivate and inform them. Yet, that love means that such acts cannot be tokens of self-mastery. Because religious and moral constructs and acts are the constitutive media of the self's various relations, the problem of self love captures the importance of evaluating them morally under the norms of love for God and neighbor. These constructs and acts can be evaluated with respect to objective goods of human existence as well as internally in terms of how adequately they express the self's dependence in relation to the divine and to others.

Tillich also maintains that the person expresses her religious depths in social and historical constructs. Indeed, for Tillich, religion is essentially a matter of self-understanding. Tillich broadly defines religion as the state of being ultimately concerned; when this concern has something finite such as the nation or an ideal as its object, Tillich calls this state of concern a quasi-religion. If religion is a human construct through which persons interpret themselves around some ultimate concern, then religion has an undeniable and ineradicable contingency or relativity. Yet the human predicament can only be answered by a revelation which is given to it, not produced within. Revelation, when it is received, becomes religion, and the structures of religion are cultural creations. Culture is religious, for it encompasses the totality of forms in which ultimate concern expresses itself.

For Tillich, religion, culture, and morality are ontologically related to one another as functions of spirit; the three functions each involve the entire person and, thus, never appear in isolation from one another. But, "religion must first of all be considered as a quality of the two other functions of the spirit and not as an independent function."[8] Religion cannot be reduced to an aesthetic, cognitive, moral, or psychological–emotional function, because it is the depth dimension of each of these.[9] The three functions of religion, culture, and morality are united in essential being, but due to existential estrangement, in actual life they can

Paul Tillich, *Systematic Theology*, 3 vols. (Chicago: University of Chicago Press, 1951–63), vol. 3, 96. See John. H. Morgan, "Religion and Culture as Meaning Systems: a Dialogue between Geertz and Tillich," *Journal of Religion* 57 (1977), 363–75.
Paul Tillich, *Theology of Culture* (Oxford: Oxford University Press, 1959), 5.

be and are separated and their unity appears only fragmentarily. The religious predicament of estrangement leads us to morality, because there "is not self-transcendence under the dimension of the spirit *without the constitution of the moral self by the unconditional imperative.*"[10]

Recall that for Tillich the moral imperative is the demand to become a person in a community of persons.[11] It has a religious *dimension*, its unconditional character. This refers not to its content, which is culturally created, but to its form. Tillich claims that the moral demand has a religious *source* because it can be fulfilled only by love. And Tillich recognizes a religious *element* to moral motivation because the person's inability to fulfill the moral imperative drives her to ask about the meaning of her existence, and, in doing so, to seek the grace of reunion with that from which she is estranged. The revelation that answers the religious predicament of estrangement enables the moral self-constitution of the person as a person in a community of persons. But, this revelation is received and this self-constitution occurs and finds meaning *"within the universe of meaning created in the cultural act."*[12] According to Tillich, culture provides the form of religion and the contents of morality.[13] Culture provides the form of religion because the reception of revelation is expressed in particular cultural forms such as myths, and because cultural creations in general are forms of self-interpretation in which the person expresses her ultimate concern. Culture provides the contents of morality through various attempts to specify the objective and absolute source of morality in the form of laws, traditions, and authority. Indeed, because Tillich understands culture as the whole of human self-interpretation, the cultural content given to the moral act is a means whereby persons and communities seek to understand themselves and how they ought to live. Thus Tillich balances the relativism of moral systems with the objective and absolute source of the moral imperative. This suggests that religion and morality arise through the person's self-understanding, what Tillich calls spirit, or the unity of meaning

---

[10] Tillich, *Systematic Theology*, vol. 3, 95 (my emphasis).
[11] Paul Tillich, *Morality and Beyond* (Louisville, KY: Westminster/John Knox, 1963).
[12] Tillich, *Systematic Theology*, vol. 3, 95 (my emphasis).
[13] Put differently, religion gives culture its depth and morality gives culture its seriousness.

and power. Because the person's existential self-awareness expresses itself in cultural forms it can be said that she achieves actualization through understanding.

Lest an emphasis on self-understanding be thought to foster solipsism and subjectivism, it is necessary to note that the person does not understand her predicament through solitary interpretation.

Since man can become a person only in the person-to-person encounter and since the language of religion – even if it is silent language – is dependent on the community, 'subjective religiosity' is a reflex of the communal tradition, and it evaporates if it is not continuously nourished by life in the community of faith and love. There is no such thing as "private religion"; but there is the personal response to the religious community, and this personal response may have creative, revolutionary and even destructive impact on the community.[14]

As Tillich notes, even the most private prayer depends upon language and symbols, and, therefore, upon community. Moreover, the person finds herself in a particular environment; the world which she has is also one to which she belongs.[15] Tillich notes that the person inhabits a moral universe, a tradition of reflection on the nature and telos of the person. Persons learn and use socially the concepts, symbols and practices through which they understand themselves. To some extent these social languages and practices constitute the person's experience. But they do not exhaust it or capture it wholly. By virtue of their personal histories and personalities, individuals appropriate and nuance these social resources. Because the human religious predicament requires a moral self-constitution that occurs and is given meaning only within cultural forms we must subject any religion's cultural forms, its constructs, to moral criticism. This moral criticism is undertaken in light of the person's encounter with other persons. This properly moral encounter establishes the limit or criterion for cultural ideas of personality and community and for ethical laws.[16] Thus, for Tillich the forms which

[14] Ibid., 209.
[15] The person's belongingness is expressed ontologically in the polarity of freedom and destiny.
[16] Thus, the person-to-person encounter provides a criterion for the person's moral self-interpretation. See Tillich, *Systematic Theology*, vol. 3, 158.

religion takes cannot thwart the moral task of personhood within a community of persons. It is possible and necessary to criticize the expressions and obligations that accompany organized religion and to distinguish the Spiritual Community from any particular church. These points require more development, so let me provide this by turning to the mutually critical relation of religion and morality.

SELF LOVE BEYOND MORALITY AND RELIGION

A hermeneutical approach synthesizes moral realism and moral relativism. Objective moral goods constitute human existence but particular moralities fare better and worse in acknowledging, protecting, and ordering our lives toward these goods. Christian ethics affirms these goods as providential gifts of a sovereign God who is the highest good. Just as the person's historical and social character requires her to articulate the unconditional moral demand she experiences in her being into particular norms and theories, the person's historical and social nature also requires her to construct systems to express and reflect on her religious depths; we need not restrict these to organized religions. If the relativity of morality follows from the fact that morality is a human construct, then it stands to reason that religion also entails a certain contingency. Because the person mediates the religious through cultural constructs, these constructs must be subject to criticism as well. Thus a hermeneutical account of self love should provide critical principles which allow for several things – first, for the moral criticism of the person, and second, for the moral criticism of religions, Christianity included.

A hermeneutical method in Christian ethics permits and requires a mutually critical relation between morality and religion. But this criticism does not stand or fall on hermeneutical method. Its possibility and necessity belong to the intimate relation between self love and love for God. The problem of self love drives the person beyond morality to a religious relation. Indeed, self love is a moral problem because of a fundamentally religious human predicament. I noted that Rahner understands morality as the person's free self-acceptance of his nature as the nature of love.[17] This love is "the real concern of Christian morality."[18] In this love the perfection which belongs to the person as a task (law) and the sanctity which is given to the person (grace) meet. Indeed, "morality and the fulfillment of the law always consist in one's readiness to allow oneself to be loved by God in the full measure and with all the demands on one's own love that is determined by God's love, and to enter into the experience of the radical and profound nature of this love which comes out to meet us."[19] Tillich makes a similar point by insisting that the person's inability to fulfill the moral law drives her to the transmoral conscience, the acceptance that she has been accepted though she is unacceptable.

Rahner and Tillich express an insight that is at once liberating and unsettling, joyful and grave. The moral enterprise of self love launches one into a deeper relation with God that requires the surrender of one's own attempts to be and to believe oneself to be good, that relativizes yet heightens the place of moral norms and authorities. Intimacy with God elicits a response from the person that in its existential depths and in its concrete embodiment broadens the scope of moral freedom and intensifies its demands. Intimacy with God frees the person to perceive, acknowledge, and accept her moral failings, to enter into them as opportunities for greater intimacy. And intimacy with God permits an emotional and experiential range that can include sweetness as well as struggle, communion as well as distance, humor as well as frustration. Fidelity to this God, known so personally, becomes the hallmark of one's integrity. It is a fidelity born not of self-interest or of fear, but of love. In light of this, the contemporary surge of interest in spirituality might seem a welcome response to the problem of self love. Of course, many people consciously choose to stand outside organized religions. Moreover, even those who do place themselves in a particular religious tradition run the risk of compartmentalizing their affiliation. One reason for this is the individualism that permeates much of Western attitudes toward religion and spirituality. Churches seem to be voluntary associations of like-minded people. And since the crux of Christian faith is a personal relation with

---

[17] See Rahner, "The 'Commandment' of Love in Relation to the Other Commandments," *Theological Investigations*, vol. 5, 441.
[18] Ibid., 454.   [19] Ibid., 455.

God, active participation in a church appears to be an optional accessory. Further, given the imperfection of all human communities and institutions, there can be a number of moral reasons to reject organized religion. Tillich helps us to see how right self love lies beyond religion as well as morality. But insofar as religions and spiritualities are construed as individual enterprises of self-expression and healing they prove inadequate for the problem of self love.

Because religion expresses revelation (in better and worse fashions) it is not entirely subjective.[20] Religion depends upon a reality which it does not construct, but to which it attests. But, religion like everything else, is subject to the ambiguities of life. Tillich describes two particular dangers which attend religion: profanization and demonization.[21] Profanization refers to both the institutionalization and the reduction of the holy in every religious act. In religion, the greatness of life, the holy, manifests itself in theory and praxis; yet the holy remains more than its finite appearances. When religion fails to transcend itself in the direction of the infinite, the institutionalized forms of religion (which need not accompany organized religion per se) make religion a finite object among others, a particular function of the spirit. This can happen, for example, in sets of doctrines, in the language of prayer, and when religion is reduced to forms of culture and morality. The profanizing elements in religion do not constitute an argument against its greatness, but simply disclose its ambiguity. The demonization of religion refers to the elevation of something conditional to the status of the unconditional. While the profane resists the self-transcendence which belongs to religion, the demonic distorts it. The demonic identifies a particular bearer of holiness, be it a person, a community, a symbol, with holiness itself. The demonic can also appear in culture and morality, for example as scientific absolutism.

The ambiguities of religion are conquered by the Spirit. "Conquest of religion does not mean secularization but rather the closing

---

[20] The current realism–relativism debate underlies this point. See William Schweiker, "One World, Many Moralities," in *Power, Value and Conviction* (Cleveland, OH: Pilgrim, 1998) and *Responsibility and Christian Ethics* (Cambridge: Cambridge University Press, 1995). See also Geoffrey Sayre-McCord, ed., *Essays on Moral Realism* (Ithaca, NY and London: Cornell University Press, 1988).

[21] See Tillich, *Systematic Theology*, vol. 3, 98–106. See also Walter Sundberg, "The Demonic in Christian Thought," *Lutheran Quarterly* 1 (1987), 413–37.

of the gap between the religious and the secular by removing both through the Spiritual Presence."[22] Tillich formulates this two-fold conquest of profanization and the demonic as the Protestant Principle. "It is Protestant, because it protests against the tragic-demonic self-elevation of religion and liberates religion from itself for those functions of the human spirit, at the same time liberating these functions from their self-seclusion against the manifestations of the ultimate."[23] The Protestant Principle can be operative in every church because it is not constrained to any particular church. Rather, it is an expression of the Spiritual Community. According to Tillich, the Spiritual Community is not a religious community but the "anticipatory representation of a new reality, the New Being as community."[24]

When churches are identified mistakenly as the Spiritual Community (which cannot be collapsed with any particular church), the Spirit is wrongly thought to be limited to religion in order to impact culture. In protest to this mistake, Tillich establishes the principle of "the consecration of the secular."[25] This principle can apply to groups and individuals who are openly and emphatically anti-religious; according to Tillich the Spirit can use these groups and persons to transform culture as well as churches. The second principle is the "convergence of the holy and the secular."[26] The secular operates as a necessary corrective to any claims to absoluteness which a religion might make, yet the secular is driven toward the holy because the self-transcendence of life resists meaninglessness

[22] "In so far as the Spiritual Presence is effective in the churches and their individual members, it conquers religion as a particular function of the human spirit. . . . " (ibid., 243). Moreover, insofar as the Spirit conquers religion, "it prevents the claim to absoluteness by both the churches and their members. Where the divine Spirit is effective, the claim of a church to represent God to the exclusion of all other churches is rejected" (ibid., 244).

[23] "The Protestant Principle is an expression of the conquest of religion by the Spiritual Presence and consequently an expression of the victory over the ambiguities of religion, its profanization, and its demonization" (ibid., 245). Tillich says that the Protestant Principle requires the "Catholic substance" in order to be effective. Rather unhelpfully, he simply defines the Catholic substance as the concrete embodiment of the Spiritual Presence. For Roman Catholic discussions of Tillich on this point, see Ronald Modras, "Catholic Substance and the Catholic Church Today," in *Paul Tillich: a New Catholic Assessment*, eds., Raymond F. Bulman and Frederick J. Parrella (Collegeville, MN: Liturgical Press, 1994), 33–47 and Julia A. Lamm "'Catholic Substance' Revisited: Reversals of Expectations in Tillich's Doctrine of God" in *Paul Tillich: a New Catholic Assessment*, 48–72.

[24] Tillich, *Systematic Theology*, vol. 3, 243.   [25] Ibid., 247.   [26] Ibid.

and emptiness. These two principles are rooted in a third, which Tillich calls the "essential belongingness of religion and culture to each other."[27] This principle simply expresses Tillich's claim that religion cannot express itself without culture and that culture loses its meaning and depths without religion.

Religion is not a private creation. Like all other elements of the person's life, she receives her religious existence in given material – in a community, in history – and develops her existence socially and historically. To be sure, religion must be appropriated by the person in faith and love, in a responsible, free decision. But we misconstrue the religious dimension of human existence if we regard it only as the person's subjective self-interpretation. The reflexive structure of consciousness testifies to the reality of the divine as the source of meaning and value. The conceptual resources which mediate the person's awareness of the divine orient her in the world and in response to the divine. Admittedly, religion can serve as a kind of existential analgesic, but the contingent elements of particular religions and the uses and abuses of religion do not negate the normativity of the divine–human relation. The self-interpretation which occurs in the person's appropriation of religion in faith remains thoroughly social and is to be assessed by a normative reality which the person does not fabricate. Because the person is situated in a relation with God, upon whom she depends in creaturely existence, she is not entirely at her own disposal. It follows that genuine subjectivity recognizes that something else orients and obliges her, a reality which is prior to the person's own mediation of it.

All of this leads us to the paradoxical quality of human freedom and creativity. The deterioration of secular and theistic worldviews that posit some objective reality, external to yet normative for, persons has in many respects denuminized the world. The rise of historical consciousness, the brute fact of diversity, and the modern legacy of autonomy all reinforce the fact that human beings are makers of meaning. Moreover, increasing specialization in the world – in commerce, in intellectual enterprises – and increasing technological capacities for compartmentalization and fragmentation (of the kind Chapter One noted) contribute

[27] Ibid., 248.

to the person's interior compartmentalization and fragmentation. Because of this, the person tends toward a managerial approach to the various dimensions of her existence; her personal relationships, her moral behavior, her religious activity can become mere functions of her personality, divorced from the meaning of life.[28] Ironically, however, the greater the person's control over her world and her existence, the more she experiences herself and her world as uncontrollable. The person's control over her environment has divested it of much of its mystery, but this mystery now breaks forth from the person; for this reason, the de-sacralizing of the world has a positive religious significance. This is in part because the person's increased freedom brings with it a more acute experience of the burden of freedom and the poignancy of finitude, the sober acceptance of which has religious significance. The person's experience of herself as disposing of her world and her experience of herself as being at the disposal of something other than herself belong to the pluralism of her existence. This tension comprises the task of human freedom and the paradox that one achieves freedom in self-disposal toward another.

The basic fact about the person, that her predicament cannot be resolved by her own will or effort, yet is resolved by a reality which does not violate but engages her freedom, is expressed in the Christian message of grace. Yet, the answer to the human predicament lies beyond Christianity and beyond religion as well. At the end of the previous section I claimed that a hermeneutical approach reckons with human sociality and historicity in a two-fold manner by recognizing that symbolic systems and social practices constitute the person's experience without wholly determining it and by recognizing that the reality of others provides a criterion for the person's religious and moral constructs. These two points certainly seem to encourage ecclesiological relativism by highlighting the contingent character of religions and the moral requirement to respect others. In order to gain some purchase on the contribution Christian ethics makes to a contemporary ethics of self love, let me continue.

---

[28] See Rahner, "The Man of Today and Religion," *Theological Investigations*, vol. 6. Several of his remarks remain timely and are echoed here.

SELF LOVE AND THE NORMATIVITY OF CHRIST

The ethics of self love I offer here purports to be adequate to the person as such, and thus, to be both descriptively and normatively adequate to persons across cultural and historical lines. And yet, it is a Christian ethical account, and one indebted to the theological anthropologies of two roughly contemporary German theologians. In many respects, it is highly particular. This is especially true since Rahner and Tillich argue that the human predicament is answered by the Christian message. The person loves herself rightly when she participates in, is personally related to, Jesus Christ, however unthematic such a relationship might be. This strikes many as, at best, fancy inclusivist footwork, and, at worst, an example of Christian imperialism. We will see that for both Rahner and Tillich, right self love depends upon the person's relationship with Christ, but does not necessarily depend upon any relation to or knowledge of Christianity. This position is criticized for reducing Christian revelation to anthropology or philosophy and thereby undermining the integrity of Christian ethics. This position is also criticized for failing to respect the irreducible differences and integrity of non-Christian religions. Each position, however, drives toward the importance of love. And this is why each is amenable to and may be helped by a hermeneutical approach that insists the connection between self and other is inscribed in human consciousness. A hermeneutical reading frees us from binding commitments to Rahner's or Tillich's ontologies, and this frees us to use the language of being to highlight the Christian claim that Jesus Christ reveals the meaning of human existence. It also frees us to stress a positive relation between Christian ethics and non-Christian and secular sources. This freedom in turn helps us to see the apologetic upshot of Christian ethics for self love and to consider whether and how Christian ethics can be internally self-validating.

Jesus Christ, Christianity, and salvific love

Religious pluralism challenges our thinking about the salvific import of love for the obvious reason that a belief in God's universal saving will seems to conflict with the belief that salvation comes through a justifying faith in what God has done in Jesus Christ. And while the dangers of religious imperialism and of religiously sanctioned forms of oppression remain all too present, other worries present themselves to us for consideration, namely the fragmentation and privatization of religious belief. Perhaps in response to the dangers of religious imperialism, perhaps in recognition of religious and cultural diversity, religious beliefs are regarded as altogether private, enshrined in a language of spiritual subjectivism and authenticity, and they are therefore often perceived as inadmissible in public debate and decision-making.

Various thinkers have noted and sought to respond to this problem. Kenneth and Michael Himes, for instance, argue that contemporary American culture fragments faith and social action, either denying that there is social import to religious belief or insisting that such claims cannot be incorporated into public consensus and policy.[29] This fragmentation translates the good of secularization (the separation of church and state) into a kind of incoherence or paralysis for religious believers and leaves public discussion bereft of the insight expressed in religious language and symbols. The fragmentation and privatization of religious belief comprise particular *moral* dangers. They wrongly neglect the social dimensions and implications of faith and make it difficult to criticize tyrannous and/or self-destructive forms of faith – that of others and our own.

A Christian ethics of self love confronts dual worries of religious imperialism and of discerning what is worthy of our devotion. What resonates in human experience: simply an encounter with the divine other, or the goodness of the divine? To ask whether what we worship is worthy of devotion is to note that religious claims need to be subjected to moral and social criticism. Indeed, the risks of religious imperialism and self-righteous exclusivism connect with worries over the privatization of faith and moral intuitionism in the problem of neighbor love. What explicit religious claims articulate convictions about God in a way that informs and prompts our commitments to others for their own sake?

[29] Michael J. Himes and Kenneth R. Himes, *Fullness of Faith: the Public Significance of Theology* (New York: Paulist, 1993).

Rahner may seem ill suited to meeting such challenges. His arguments for anonymous theism and anonymous Christianity may be exclusivism in inclusivist clothing. And they may exacerbate the privatization of religious belief. Rahner's transcendental accounts of human knowledge and freedom lead him to argue that human moral activity, chiefly love for neighbor, can posit a faith that is salvific even if it does not include an explicitly Christian or theistic reference. The salvific import of neighbor love speaks to the challenges of religious pluralism and to the privatization of faith. But his transcendental arguments strike many as philosophically untenable and may evacuate Christian ethics of its particularity and subsume faith into morality. A hermeneutical reading of Rahner offsets these difficulties.

The question of how Rahner relates self love and Christianity can be approached from two directions, that of the presence of Jesus Christ in non-Christian religions, and that of anonymous Christianity. The former leads to the latter. Rahner treats the question of the presence of Jesus Christ in non-Christian religions as a dogmatic question. "Such a 'presence' of Jesus Christ throughout the whole history of salvation and in relation to all people cannot be denied or overlooked by Christians if they believe in Jesus Christ as the salvation of *all* people, and do not think that the salvation of non-Christians is brought about by God and his mercy independently of Jesus Christ."[30] This dogmatic claim presupposes the universal salvific will of God. Nevertheless, if the person's salvation is to be understood as historical and social in character, and not simply confined to abstract transcendentality, Christian dogma must also presuppose that when a non-Christian attains salvation, non-Christian religions have a positive significance. Rahner contends that the dogmatic theologian can only approach this question by inquiring into the presence of Christ in the non-Christian's salvific faith.

Traditional dogmatic theology states that Jesus Christ is present and operative in non-Christian religions in and through his Spirit: the "Spirit who makes faith possible and who justifies is given in all times and places *intuitu meritorum Christi*, that is, in view of the merits of Christ. Consequently, it can correctly be called the Spirit

---

[30] Rahner, *Foundations*, 312.

of *Jesus* Christ."³¹ Rahner takes this dogmatic formulation as his starting point and asks how the grace of the Spirit, given in all times and places, might be connected to the particular historical event of Jesus' death on the cross. The Spirit and the cross relate not only in the knowledge and will of God who transcends history, but within history. God's salvific will is not the effect of the cross, but its a priori, gratuitous, antecedent cause. God's salvific will is offered for all people and "this communication is oriented to begin with towards a historical event in which this communication and its acceptance become historically tangible in this eschatological triumph."³² The historical mediation of the Spirit takes place in the Incarnation, death, and resurrection of Jesus. Thus, Rahner argues, insofar as the birth, death, and resurrection of Jesus of Nazareth are the final cause of the Spirit, the Spirit which is given to all people everywhere can be said properly to be the Spirit of Jesus. In this way, Jesus Christ is present and operative in the salvific faith of non-Christians.

At issue is the relation between a priori and a posteriori knowledge. Something which encounters the person in history, that is, something a posteriori, can only be encountered by the person given a certain a priori expectation. The concreteness of history cannot be anticipated, but this transcendental orientation of expectant hope is nevertheless mediated historically. The mediation of the person's transcendentality is the historical experience of it, and this historical experience will vary in content from person to person. According to Rahner, the mediating contents need not be religiously thematic; what is important and universal is that the contents mediate a person to herself as freely disposing of herself in a decision of ultimate validity. History is the history of freedom, and freedom, as we have seen, is the capacity to make such a definitive decision; history, then, in its very structures, anticipates decisions which move from open multiplicity to something final and irreversible. Moreover, because the person's transcendental freedom is supernaturally oriented, it searches for a decision in history about the salvific outcome of history.³³

³¹ Ibid., 316. Indeed, this claim is crucial to Rahner's entire theological method.
³² Ibid., 317.
³³ See ibid., 320–21. Rahner goes on to say that a dogmatic theologian can leave the interpretation of saviour figures to the historian of religion. See Edward J. Miller, "Inclusivist

This leads us to Rahner's concept of anonymous Christianity. Stated simply,

> man is called an "anonymous Christian" who on the one hand has *de facto* accepted of his freedom this gracious self-offering on God's part through faith, hope, and love, while on the other he is absolutely not yet a Christian at the social level (through baptism and membership of the Church) or in the sense of having consciously objectified his Christianity to himself in his own mind (by explicit Christian faith resulting from having hearkened to the explicit Christian message).[34]

Thus, Rahner attempts to account for the tension between a belief in God's universal salvific will and the belief that only faith justifies. Can salvific faith be attributed to non-Christian, even atheistic persons? This question is complicated further by the fact that God's salvific will cannot be guaranteed to persons by virtue of their nature. That is, nothing about the person requires or necessitates God's saving grace. If this were the case, salvation would not be gratuitous. This difficulty can be resolved by a return to the supernatural existential. Recall that for Rahner the supernatural existential means that God's self-communication, at least as an offer, is an abiding existential of the person. It does not belong to the person's nature as such. Rather, it designates God's offer of self-communication, the person's capacity to receive God's grace. Because the supernatural existential belongs to all persons, it accounts for the universality of God's salvific will, at least as an offer made to every person. The person can accept this offer in an explicit act of faith, or she can accept this offer implicitly in her self-acceptance as a creature oriented toward mystery. This latter response is anonymous theism.

---

and Exclusivist Issues in Soteriology: to Whom Does Jesus' Saving Power Extend?" *Perspectives in Religious Studies* 12 (1985), 123–37; Jacobus A. Van Rooy, "Christ and the Religions: the Issues at Stake," *Missionalia* 13 (1985), 3–13; Richard Viladesau, "How is Christ Absolute? Rahner's Christology and the Encounter of World Religions," *Philosophy and Theology* 2 (1988), 220–40; and Maurice Wiles, "Christianity and other Faiths: some Theological Reflections," *Theology* 91 (1988), 302–08. This article also discusses Tillich.

[34] Rahner, "Observations on the Problem of the 'Anonymous Christian,'" *Theological Investigations*, vol. 14, 283. There is a considerable amount of secondary literature on Rahner's argument about anonymous Christianity, much of it highly critical. See for example Lucas Lamadrid, "Anonymous or Analogous Christians? Rahner and von Balthasar on Naming the Non-Christian," *Modern Theology* 11 (1995), 363–84. For a defense of Rahner see Gavin D'Costa, "Karl Rahner's Anonymous Christian: a Reappraisal," *Modern Theology* 1:2 (1985), 131–48.

Does this implicit acceptance suffice for an anonymous Christianity? Because persons are saved by the grace of Christ, Rahner asks if the person's transcendental orientation includes a reference to Jesus Christ. He maintains that it does. Recall that for Rahner Christ is the goal of all creation.[35] Christ is the entelechy of the person, and she experiences this in her experience of her self as oriented toward mystery. Indeed, Rahner insists that the Christian message only makes explicit the person's own experience of herself.

"Accordingly, no matter how he wants to understand and express this in his own reflective self-understanding, he is becoming thereby not merely an anonymous 'theist', but rather takes upon himself in that Yes to himself the grace of the mystery which has radically approached us. 'God has given himself to man in direct proximity': perhaps the essence of Christianity can be reduced to this formula."[36] Because the person's orientation toward God has its goal in Christ, the name anonymous Christian "implicitly signifies that this fundamental actuation of a man, like all actuations, cannot and does not want to stop in its anonymous state but strives towards an explicit expression, towards its full name."[37] This leads Rahner to argue that the person can culpably reject Christianity. Anonymous Christianity accounts for the salvific faith of those who have not encountered the gospel or whose exposure to it has been so limited and distorted as to constitute an obstacle for the intrinsic movement toward a more explicit faith. But if a person "is offered, in a manner which is credible to him, the chance to give objective structure and shape to his being (and therefore an opportunity of supernatural elevation), and if he rejects this possibility, then he is deliberately denying his grace-filled transcendence as well. It is not

---

[35] See Denis Edwards, "The Relationship between the Risen Christ and the Material Universe," *Pacifica* 4 (1991), 1–14.
[36] Rahner, "Observations on the Problem of the 'Anonymous Christian,'" 394.
[37] Ibid., 395. Elsewhere Rahner writes, "There can be an 'anonymous faith' which carries with it an intrinsic dynamism and therefore an obligation to find full realisation in explicit faith, but which is nonetheless sufficient for salvation even if a man does not achieve this fulfillment during his lifetime, as long as he is not to blame for this. Naturally such a person would deny, both to himself in his conscious awareness and to others, that he has such anonymous faith and in consequence this doctrine is not directly available for apologetic use. But this does not prevent a Christian from holding that his non-Christian or atheist fellow human being may be an anonymous believer" ("Anonymous and Explicit Faith," *Theological Investigations*, vol. 6, 54).

possible to have 'anonymous faith' when its thematic expression in the Christian belief in revelation is culpably rejected."[38]

Rahner's argument for the normativity of Christ is related to his claim that a moral act of neighbor love may express salvific faith apart from explicitly Christian or even theistic conceptualization. Thinkers like Hans Urs von Balthasar, Edward Vacek, and Jean Porter reject this claim. The implicit faith expressed in neighbor love is not a substitute for explicit faith but its minimum.[39] Rahner's claim that a moral act can instantiate salvific faith may subsume faith into morality.[40] Indeed, Porter notes that Rahner so conflates salvific love with the moral act of charity that he empties salvific love of the content that served "to indicate the point of being a Christian, to set criteria for success or failure as a Christian, and finally to formulate guidance and to offer remedies when things go wrong."[41] We are thereby rendered incapable of making such discriminations. Vacek makes a similar point by arguing that although love for God and for neighbor are related to and lead to one another, when one loves a neighbor one is not necessarily intending to love God thereby. There is a distinctive form of Christian love, since the Christian stands within a tradition and intends something quite different than an atheist intends in loving.[42] At stake in these points is, among other things, the question of how constitutive one's intention is for the meaning of an act. If salvific love and charity are correlative with one another then, as Porter notes, there seems to be no material difference between love for God or neighbor, between faith and works. And this suggests that what I understand myself to be doing in an act or relation of love is irrelevant to what is in fact occurring.

A hermeneutical reading of Rahner can accommodate Porter's and Vacek's insights because it allows us to clarify the distinctive

---

[38] Rahner, "Anonymous and Explicit Faith," 59.

[39] Eamonn Conway, *The Anonymous Christian – a Relativised Christianity?* (Frankfurt am Main: Peter Lang, 1993).

[40] Moreover, it can clarify the distinctive natures of religious and moral acts, and the importance of the agent's intention in each. But such an impression must be balanced against Rahner's emphasis on spiritual discernment as an element of moral decision making.

[41] Jean Porter, "Salvific Love and Charity," in *The Love Commandments: Essays in Christian Ethics and Moral Philosophy* (Washington DC: Georgetown University Press, 1992), 256.

[42] Edward Vacek, *Love, Human and Divine: the Heart of Christian Ethics* (Washington DC: Georgetown University Press, 1994).

natures of religious and moral acts (even if there is an essential unity between them) by stressing the importance of the agent's intention in each. That is, while there is not a necessary relation between explicit faith and salvific faith, explicit faith would provide the epistemological principles with which Christians can "set criteria for success or failure" as Christians and "formulate guidance." This does not make explicit faith into a heuristic device; rather, explicit faith, as a mediation of self-understanding, confers a particular identity. Faith is more than intellectual assent to various propositions. Yet it is also more than an act of will. Faith must consist in a recognition of the truth. If faith is a matter of self-understanding that posits a particular way of being in the world, then explicit faith provides an account of the world and of our place within it, the means with which we interpret our existence. *These means are shown to be true when they testify to and direct us practically toward the key Christian insight that the meaning of life is found in one's self-disposal in love.* Certainly other religious symbol systems, theistic and otherwise, and non-religious sources of culture can so testify and orient us. The requirement that our interpretive "apparatus" orient us practically is one way of formulating the traditional Christian claim that one tests spirits by their fruits. This means that (1) these interpretive frameworks can and should be tested and revised so as to be made more truthful and (2) faith cannot be understood properly as a private commitment, unrelated to the demands of social justice, or as primarily affective, unrelated to how we describe the world and our place within it. There are reasons internal to Christian faith that caution against sectarian withdrawal as well as imperialism, though sadly these reasons are not always heeded. The very argument that implicit faith drives toward appropriate objectification in explicit faith requires Christians to evaluate the formulation of dogmatic claims on the basis of love for the neighbor. And that neighbor love demands due recognition of the historicity and particularity of persons and the positive significance of non-Christian religions. The demand is not for ecclesiological relativism but for mutual and sensitive criticism. Yet, if intention is wholly constitutive of the meaning of an act or relation, we undermine reflection on whether certain acts or relations really can embody and posit the intention an agent has.

So a hermeneutical reading of Rahner can offset the risk of sub-suming faith into morality. It provides for the integrity of Christian ethics as it emphasizes the status and operation of explicit faith in the Christian's self-understanding. But we must not distinguish salvific love and the moral act of charity in a way that does not account for their relation. To make their difference hinge solely on the intention of the agent can segregate them unduly. It also undermines reflection on whether certain acts and relations really can embody and posit the intention an agent has. A hermeneutical account of self-relation can render the relation of salvific love and charity within the fabric of perception and cognition that makes up human consciousness: it recognizes, with Vacek, that a Christian and an athiest may intend something different in loving but insists, with Rahner, that more is going on than what each intends. In the agent's self-understanding and acting she takes up a relation to the goods she encounters in the world and to the divine other to whom her self-awareness testifies. Too much emphasis on either the depths of freedom or on conscious intention can lead to moral subjectivism and displaces moral attention to concrete acts and re-lations. Reading Rahner hermeneutically qualifies his voluntarism and accommodates the critical insights of Vacek and Porter. More-over, importantly, this reading helps us attend to the inter-relation of (Christian) self-understanding and acting. The particular beliefs and commitments (explicit faith or not) that orient our acting can be tested inasmuch as they impel us to moral acts of charity and to explicit acts of love for God. But our acting also is not simply the fruit of those beliefs and commitments. It reflexively informs, deepens, or counters them. It sustains or thwarts, broadens or nar-rows our openness to the objects of belief and commitment. So, a hermeneutical reading can provide Christian faith its particular and proper place and yet also provide for Rahner's insight that we receive and respond to God's self-communication in Christ in ways not limited to explicit faith.

The Christ event, self-criticism, and agape

Recognizing the interpretive character of religions promotes and complicates inter-religious exchanges in various forms of dialogue,

comparative analysis, ecumenism, and criticism. It seems to promote such exchanges (which admittedly vary considerably in type
and tenor) insofar as the constructs through which individual and
collective self-interpretation occur are historically and culturally
contingent and can (and very well may) give way to other constructs
more adequate to or at least more contemporary for the religious
depths expressed in them.[43] That is, the interpretive character of religions cautions, indeed necessitates, against absolutizing particular
constructs and thereby invites (though does not ineluctably lead to)
more positive and engaged relations among adherents to various
religions. Still, the interpretive character of religions complicates
inter-religious exchanges as well. To begin, the fact that religions
are personal and collective forms of self-interpretation begs questions whether they are truthful fictions, or heuristic devices, or
consoling illusions, etc. The complexities of religious psychology
aside, the very interpretive character that reveals exclusive and
imperialistic religious claims to be historical and social constructs
may also account for the fact that history has never been shy of
them; religious claims are apt vehicles for our egoism and narcissism, providing them various lofty and noble aims and sanctions.
Religious beliefs threaten an interpretive or hermeneutical concupiscence that grafts everything into my own constructs such that my
"ultimate concern" may be and remain my self. Moreover, the interpretive character of religions is sometimes taken to indicate that
inter-religious exchanges and comparisons ought not smack of any
claims to or concerns for normativity. The socio-cultural and historical contingency of religions means for some thinkers that there
are no grounds or objective criteria with which to subject religious
claims, symbols, and practices to moral criticism. This risk is particularly grave given contemporary Western culture's embrace of subjectivism and relativism, and continuing questions about whether

---

[43] I say these constructs promote inter-religious exchanges insofar as their contingency can
be distinguished from that which they mediate – which is not confined to such particularity
though it does not appear apart from it – because I assume (with Tillich) that the fact that
religions unavoidably employ constructs does not mean that they are constructs without
remainder. As Paul Ricoeur has put it, we invent in order to discover. See his *Interpretation
Theory: Discourse and the Surplus of Meaning* (Fort Worth, TX: Texas Christian University,
1976). Such a claim cannot be defended here. Moreover, the literature on the question
whether there is some *sui generis* religious experience is massive. I leave it to others to
defend this position and to defend Tillich as one representative of it.

and how faith may be admitted into public debate and decision-making. Indeed, the increasing privatization of religious belief and the increasing conjunction of spirituality with self-help programs has in many respects severed faith from social justice and presents additional obstacles to the moral criticism of religious beliefs and practices.[44]

The prevalent worries seem to be that religions provide unwelcome, and/or unwarranted, and/or imperialistic moral criticisms. And in the face of these worries, religion is squired away and privatized. Is there a way to wrest the self-interpretation operative in religion from its privatization yet still avoid the hermeneutic concupiscence and religious imperialism it threatens? Perhaps surprisingly, such moves become possible when we turn to Tillich's claim that Christ is normative for the evaluation of religions. Initially, this can be said because Christ functions as a self-negating criterion. According to Tillich, the event on which Christianity is based is such that it provides not only the criterion for judging Christianity but for judging other religions and quasi-religions as well, simply because this particular event points beyond its particularity. By moving from the normativity of the Christ event to the principle of agape we grasp the fundamental connection of self and other as the ground for the moral criticism of institutional and personal religious constructs and practices. This connection is at the heart of a hermeneutical account. For Tillich the relation between Christianity and other religions is not limited to other organized religions, but includes secular forms which possess religious elements. According to Tillich, the pluralism of world religions is not as significant today as the encounter of organized religions with quasi-religions.[45] The appearance of ultimate concern within secular aspects of culture should not come as a surprise or as a special problem. Because profanization and demonization form a polarity between which religions vacillate, the profane acts as a necessary

---

[44] The secondary literature on Tillich characterizes the differences in his early and later work in a variety of ways, e.g., in terms of Americanization. Some contend that Tillich's early work makes him a theologian of culture, while his later writings indicate that after coming to America he became more of a church theologian. While it was not Tillich's aim to combat privatized religiosity, my extension of his project provides a means to do so.

[45] Paul Tillich, *Christianity and the Encounter of the World Religions* (New York and London: Columbia University Press, 1963), 5.

corrective to the demonic; hence, secular expressions of ultimate concern can counter the misguided, demonic elevation of finite concerns to the status of ultimacy. Tillich maintains that Christianity must value the secular realm; Christianity should express the ultimate meaning of actions in daily life.[46] Right relation with God, self, and others can be worked out within ordinary tasks and encounters, that is, without elaborate religious or moral systems and within given cultural ideas of and programs for self-realization.

This appreciation of the secular, however, is qualified by a recognition of the ambiguities of profanization. Tillich notes that "the acceptance of secularism can lead to a slow elimination of the religious dimension altogether."[47] To be sure, Christianity rejects elements of religions and quasi-religions. "If a group – like an individual – is convinced that it possesses a truth, it implicitly denies those claims to truth which conflict with that truth. . . . Consequently the encounter of Christianity with other religions, as well as with quasi-religions, implies the rejection of their claims insofar as they contradict the Christian principle, implicitly or explicitly."[48] What is this principle? It is "the event on which Christianity is based, and . . . the continuing spiritual power of this event, which is the appearance and reception of Jesus of Nazareth as the Christ, a symbol which stands for the decisive self-manifestation in human history of the source and aim of all being."[49] Although the answer to the person's predicament has been given in Christ, the person need not receive it in Christianity. Thus, while Tillich resolutely maintains the absolute and decisive character of the Christ event, he insists

[46] See ibid., 94. In this respect Tillich reveals his Lutheran heritage. Indeed, Tillich echoes Reformation Protestantism with his criticism of demonization and of institutionalized forms of profanization and his appreciation for the secular as an appropriate place for the manifestation of the holy. For a discussion of Tillich and Christianity, see William P. Alston, "Realism and the Christian Faith," *International Journal for Philosophy of Religion* 38 (1995), 37–60.

[47] Tillich, *Christianity and the Encounter of the World Religions*, 48. Protestantism, argues Tillich, maintains that the secular realm is not nearer to the ultimate than the sacred realm is. "Its positive valuation of the secular makes the relation of Protestantism to the quasi-religions much more dialectical and even ambiguous. Protestantism can receive and transform the religious elements of the quasi-religions" (ibid., 49).

[48] Ibid., 28–29.

[49] Ibid., 79. See Ruth Page, "The Consistent Christology of Paul Tillich," *Scottish Journal of Theology* 36 (1983), 195–212; Edward J. Miller, "Inclusivist and Exclusivist Issues in Soteriology: to Whom Does Jesus' Saving Power Extend?"; and H. D. McDonald, "The Symbolic Christology of Paul Tillich," *Vox Evangelica* 18 (1988), 75–88.

that Christianity should not adopt an agenda of conversion toward other religions. Moreover, Christianity must subject itself to ongoing criticism based on the criterion of the Christ event, a criterion which may manifest itself outside religion and in extremely anti-religious persons and trends. Tillich does not suggest that one negate or relinquish Christianity, or any other religious tradition per se. Rather, he argues that religion "cannot come to an end, and a particular religion will be lasting to the degree in which it negates itself as a religion. Thus Christianity will be a bearer of the religious answer as long as it breaks through its own particularity."[50] According to Tillich, the event on which Christianity is based is such that it provides not only the criterion for judging Christianity, but for judging other religions and quasi-religions as well, simply because this particular event points beyond particularity.[51] This could mean that conversion should give way to dialogue with other religions, and, moreover, that quasi-religions could be understood as an indirect path toward religious transformation.[52]

Because all (quasi) religions are (social) forms of human self-interpretation, Tillich can say that "there are [in other religions] elements in human nature which tend to become embodied in symbols similar to those of his own religion."[53] For this reason, "the decisive point in a dialogue between two religions is not the historically determined, contingent *embodiment* of the typological elements, but these elements themselves."[54] According to Tillich, a helpful comparative starting point is "the question of the intrinsic aim of existence – in Greek, the *telos* of all existing things. It is here that one should start every inter-religious discussion, and not with a comparison of the contrasting concepts of God or man or history or salvation."[55] Telos-formulas express views of reality out

[50] Tillich, *Christianity and the Encounter of the World Religions*, 96.
[51] Ibid., 82. Tillich writes elsewhere that "the unconditional claim made by Christianity is not related to the Christian Church, but to the event on which the Church is based" (*Theology of Culture*, 41). Tillich argues that Protestant Principle is mindful of this, while the Roman Catholic Church has failed to subject itself to self-criticism on this score.
[52] See Douglas O. Schwarz, "Religious Relativism: Paul Tillich's 'last word,'" *American Journal of Theology and Philosophy* 7:2 (1986), 106–14 and John Foerster "Paul Tillich and Inter-religious Dialogue," *Modern Theology* 7 (1990), 1–27.
[53] Tillich, *Christianity and the Encounter of the World Religions*, 3.   [54] Ibid., 57.
[55] Ibid., 63. "The way is to penetrate into the depth of one's own religion, in devotion, thought and action. In the depth of every living religion there is a point at which the religion itself loses its importance, and that to which it points breaks through its particularity,

of which the particular accounts of God, the human, and salvation arise and are explicated. Of decisive importance for the Christian telos-formulation is its ethical expression in agape. Agape allows for an encounter with other religions and quasi-religions which accepts them but seeks to transform individual and social structures which are against love. Because agape accomplishes what the person-to-person encounter demands and religion must be judged by this encounter, what can be considered now is the connection between the other person as a criterion or limit for my self-actualization and the Christ event as a criterion for (quasi) religions. Importantly, the principle of agape which directs the criticism of other religions and quasi-religions as well as the self-criticism of Christianity is the same principle of self-criticism that applies to my own attempts to understand myself. This suggests that the self–other connection grounds the moral criticism of religious belief and practice. Tillich's account of agape is the critical pivot that links interpersonal relations and the need to subject religions to moral criticism. Specifically, the self-negating criterion of Christ not only addresses the hermeneutic concupiscence driving religious constructs. It also addresses the privatization of faith.

Why does agape as a critical principle disclose the connection of self and other and ground thereby the moral criticism of religion? Agape seeks the fulfillment of the other for its own sake. Thus, to say that God is love is to say that God seeks the fulfillment of that which God has created.[56] Because of the connection between God's love for the person and the person's fulfillment as such, it should be noted that "divine love includes the justice which acknowledges and preserves the freedom and the unique character of the beloved. It does justice to man while it drives him toward fulfillment. It neither forces him nor leaves him; it attracts him and lures him toward reunion."[57] Divine love includes justice, which also resists and condemns that which is against love. Tillich speaks of this as love's compulsive power.[58] Tillich calls love the most radical concern. As the most radical concern, love's object must be the

elevating it to spiritual freedom and with it to a vision of the spiritual presence in other expressions of the ultimate meaning of man's existence" (Ibid., 97).

[56] See Tillich, *Systematic Theology*, vol. 1, 280–81.

[57] Ibid., 283.   [58] Ibid., 283–84. See also vol. 2, 77.

completely concrete being, the person.[59] This claim intimates the deep connection in Tillich's thought between love and morality, whereby the person's relation with God entails the moral act of establishing oneself as a person and comprises the moral imperative to become a person in a community of persons.

Given this connection of self and other, resonating in the depths of self-relation, Tillich's position can fund specific moral criticisms of religious imperialism and the privatization of religion. The previous section suggested how Tillich can fund moral criticism of religious imperialism (even if some thinkers still find some of his philosophical and religious commitments ill-suited to such a task).[60] Still, Tillich might seem an unlikely resource with which to address the privatization of religion since he risks an intuitionistic ethics. Moreover, Tillich's own receptivity to psychotherapy as a means for achieving the self-acceptance central to faith and to quasi-religions in general suggests just the interiorization and therapeuticization of faith that proves problematic. Many thinkers have noted that Tillich just as often construes faith as a self-affirmation that allows one to cope with the anxiety of estrangement as he construes it as the conquest of that estrangement in the establishment of communion with others.[61] There is merit in such criticisms – Tillich allows for but does not himself undertake the moral criticism of religions beyond the dangers of demonization and profanization. More than this, the interpretive character of religions Tillich posits proves problematic. If institutional religion runs risks of imperialism, are there corresponding personal dangers entailed in my self-interpretation around my ultimate concern? Put differently, if we agree with Tillich that religion is self-interpretation around an ultimate concern, does it follow that religious belief and its cultural forms always risk a kind of totalizing, hermeneutic concupiscence? As William Schweiker argues, "the search for fulfillment tries to complete life, make a person whole. And because these are quests or projects,

---

[59] Ibid., vol. 1, 211.

[60] Certainly, on this count Tillich needs to be read in light of his historical context. There is no denying that the events in and surrounding World War II impacted him profoundly.

[61] See for example Donald F. Driesbach, *Symbols and Salvation: Paul Tillich's Doctrine of Religious Symbols and his Interpretation of the Symbols of the Christian Tradition* (Lanham, MD: University Press of America, 1993).

power becomes central in life. It is only through maximizing power that the values of authenticity and fulfillment can be attained."[62] If this is so, privatizing religious belief fails to remove the risk of effacing others. It also fails to remove the risk of personal obeisance or devotion to an unworthy God.

A hermeneutical reading of Tillich brings resources in his argument to the fore in order to address these problems. Specifically, it mines his account of agape for its link between self and other. Agape overcomes our predicament of estrangement and reunites us with essential being by effecting our participation in New Being (Christ) in whom estrangement is conquered. For this reason, agape also accomplishes what the person-to-person encounter demands – the moral act of self-constitution as a person. And it does this in such a way that the personhood of others is respected and preserved. Since human beings only become persons in the person-to-person encounter, the other, as other, comprises a limit to my self-constitution and therefore a criterion for my self-interpretation. To understand myself and my predicament correctly, then, is to grasp my dependence in relation to being-itself and to others, and, moreover, to do so in a way that does not efface the other or surrender myself.

Agape, then, is the ethical expression of the drive and aim of being. Given love's compulsive power to destroy that which is against love, in order to do justice to the other agape requires a commitment to achieving a unity-in-difference. This respects and preserves the other's difference as well as my individuation. A hermeneutical account reveals that agape also requires a commitment to destroy that which is against love in practices or in systems of meaning-making. To fail to do so proves self-destructive as well as destructive of others. This point is important. *My self-understanding and its various expressions in religious symbols and cultural forms are true and worthy only if they attest to and impel me toward the claims of others, the demands of personhood in myself and in them.* Thus, while Tillich does not adequately undertake the moral criticism of (privatized) religion, or, say, stress the relation between faith and social justice, a hermeneutical reading of his argument can.

[62] Schweiker, *Responsibility and Christian Ethics*, 225.

The question remains, however, how to specify the relation between Christian theology and general moral reflection. How are we to understand the relations among Christian theology, general moral reflection, and particular prescriptives for action? Let us turn now to consider this relation between self love and moral thinking.

SELF LOVE AND THEOLOGICAL ETHICAL THINKING

In the remainder of this book, several tasks converge: (1) my argument culminates methodologically by showing the contributions Rahner and Tillich make to a contemporary ethics of self love and how a hermeneutical approach resolves problems in them and promises a way to confront other metaphysically indebted theological anthropologies; (2) I complete my account of self love by clarifying the status of explicit faith and what this implies for the universality and specificity of Christian morality and ethics; and (3) I show what Christian ethics contributes to secular inquiry into self love by showing how it is (to borrow Charles Taylor's term) "error-reducing" as well as internally self-validating.

Rahner and Tillich help us address the contemporary problem of self love in several respects. They broaden the problem of self love beyond adjudicating the self's interests vis-à-vis love for neighbor; self love is a matter of proper self-relation. Moreover, their metaphysically indebted anthropologies offer a heuristic device for thinking about the relation of self love and love for God and the character of (right) self love. In this respect they are, ironically, more concrete and practical than many deliberate Christian ethical treatments of self love. As Chapter Two suggested, these local debates in Christian ethics tend to operate on the terms of a reified account of love. This risks both moral abstraction from acts and relations and moralism.

Nevertheless, if I am right that (1) right self love is ultimately about an intimate relation with God that both relativizes and heightens what is morally required of the person and (2) right self love, as the proper form of self-relation requires us to evaluate morally the truth of the person's self-understanding and the concrete acts and relations through which she takes up her self-relation, then we need to understand better than Rahner and Tillich do the relation between the moral act of self-constitution and the person's religious relation to God. Both of them fail to provide adequately for the moral evaluation of the various forms self-relation can take. In order to evaluate morally the various forms which self-relation can take, it is necessary to subject this religious relation to God to moral norms. Rahner and Tillich fail to allow for this moral evaluation for different reasons.

For Tillich the moral act of self-constitution is a necessary condition for the person's religious relation to God (insofar as the moral act of being a person is a prerequisite for being in any relation), but is not constitutive of that relation. According to Tillich

> every moral act is a responsible act, a response to a valid command, but man can refuse to respond. If he refuses, he gives way to the forces of moral disintegration; he acts against the spirit in the power of the spirit. For he can never get rid of himself as spirit. He constitutes himself as a completely centered self even in his anti-essential, antimoral actions. These actions express moral centeredness even while they tend to dissolve the moral center.[63]

Tillich recognizes that self-relation can take a variety of forms, some of which are destructive and morally invalid. Because even anti-moral acts establish the person as a centered being, one can be morally vicious and yet still be rightly related to God. What could be more Christian than this message? We are saved while we are yet sinners. Still, can we say that one's moral character and (mis)deeds and relations are neatly segregated from one's religious relation to God? This hardly seems adequate to the totality of the person. Tillich may insist that moral self-determination is not constitutive of the religious relation, but he certainly argues that the religious relation impacts the moral act. Because a false religious relation threatens to dissolve the person's centeredness, it vitiates the person's moral self-constitution; it is morally self-contradictory.

---

[63] Tillich, *Systematic Theology*, vol. 1, 39. See also 284, where Tillich writes, "A finite being can be separated from God; it can indefinitely resist union; it can be thrown into self-destruction and utter despair; but even this is the work of the divine love.... Hell has being only in so far as it stands in the unity of the divine love. It is not the limit of the divine love. The only preliminary limit is the resistance of the finite creature."

But this simply returns us to Tillich's claim that even anti-moral acts "express moral centeredness even while they tend to dissolve the moral center." Tillich effectively relativizes the moral question of whether or not a given form of self-relation is destructive to the self. Thus it is not possible meaningfully to evaluate morally the various forms self-relation can take.

He attempts to resolve the problem in the following fashion:

> Why should one affirm one's essential being rather than destroy one's self? The answer to this must be that the person becomes aware of his infinite value or, ontologically expressed, of his belonging to the transcendent union of unambiguous life which is the Divine Life; this awareness occurs under the impact of the Spiritual Presence. The act of faith and the act of accepting the moral imperative's unconditional character are one and the same act.[64]

This equation of faith and the recognition of the moral imperative's unconditional character is problematic since elsewhere in Tillich this same recognition of the demand of essential being is distinguished from faith as the ecstatic experience in which this law ceases to be a law because it has been fulfilled. Here Tillich seems to operate with an understanding of faith as ultimate concern. So, Tillich's argument is confused about the relation between the moral act and relation to God, and what's more, he flounders on the very tasks of right self love, that of evaluating the various beliefs (religious and otherwise, in their affective and cognitive aspects) with which the person understands herself, and evaluating the acts and relations through which she takes up her relation to herself, to God, and to neighbors.

Like Tillich, Rahner maintains that the moral act of being a person is a necessary condition for religious relation to God. However, unlike Tillich, Rahner argues that the moral act can be constitutive of one's religious relation. This is because the moral act is divinized by grace and thereby elevated. The person's a priori orientation toward God "includes an element of (transcendental) revelation and possibility of faith which also gives such an act that sufficient character of 'faith' necessary for a moral act being a salvific act."[65] The

---

[64] Ibid., 159.
[65] Rahner, "Unity of the Love of Neighbor and the Love of God," *Theological Investigations*, vol. 6, 239.

religiously constitutive character which moral action can have is illuminated further by how Rahner understands freedom. Rahner understands moral freedom as "necessarily always also religious freedom; even if this is not expressly known, it is at least silently experienced in the fact that this freedom cannot be transmitted, in the responsibility and infinity of freedom."[66] So Rahner specifies the moral connection between the person's moral self-constitution and her religious relation to God differently than Tillich. In doing so Rahner seems to provide for the moral evaluation of one's religious relation to God. But this is not the case.

Rahner argues that any categorical object can mediate the person's transcendental experience of God as well as her response to God. Thus although Rahner argues that moral self-constitution can be constitutive of one's relation to God, the very transcendental dimension which allows him to make this argument accounts for his claim that any object can mediate the moral and religious relation. For this reason, Rahner fares little better than Tillich does when it comes to evaluating morally the forms self-relation takes. Rahner does acknowledge that the thematization of one's transcendental experience can be more or less appropriate – he indicates as much when he says that anonymous Christianity has explicit faith as its entelechy, as well as when he argues that the unique will of God in a moral situation is something the person is morally obligated to discern and to bring into actuality. Here again, the person is threatened by false and tyrannous forms of the religious relation. Moreover Rahner's argument makes it difficult to assess morally the objects and commitments which mediate the person's self-relation; surely it makes a difference whether the person experiences her transcendental relation to God through a love of wealth as opposed to love for her neighbor. Indeed, Chapter Four noted that the pluralism of human life tempts the person to center her existence on some particular inner-worldly value. Thus, that with respect to which the person centers her existence does matter morally and religiously. The difficulty is that Rahner does not bear

---

[66] Rahner, "On the Origins of Freedom," in *Karl Rahner: Theologian of the Graced Search for Meaning*, ed., Geoffrey B. Kelly (Minneapolis, MN: Fortress, 1992), 119.

out this impulse in his thought so as to argue that the thematizations of one's religious relation are subject to moral evaluation.

The person's being includes a capacity for and trend toward reflection on it (although it is never completely captured in such reflection). Because moral thinking arises out of moral being and has moral being as its object, moral thinking is fundamentally an act of self-interpretation, practiced individually and collectively; this self-interpretation is undertaken with the conceptual and practical resources persons and communities create. These resources are ways to express and respond to the values and goods they meet in the world and to the divine as the source of value. This "reflexive realism" demands moral reflection and testifies to the norms for such reflection – God and neighbor. This is why the imperative for self love is the command to love God and neighbor. Religious and moral activity are ways in which persons and communities endeavor to understand the divine horizon or ground toward which they are driven and in which they participate, as well as ways they try to guide action in accordance with the divine. Furthermore, the constructive character of religion and morality highlights these systems and institutions as arenas of human self-interpretation; but their roots in the real provide criteria by which to assess their constructive elements. The person constitutes herself relationally (in relation to others and to the ground of being) and hermeneutically (how she understands herself as constituted by these relations and whether she lives in consonance with them).

The claim that self-interpretation is mediated in the person's religious and moral activity is a formal claim about the fundamental structure of understanding and its relation to agency; this formal structure accommodates various contents. For example, democratic liberalism might mediate a person's self-interpretation, or a commitment to a particular project such as one's family or a social justice enterprise. Explicit faith confers a particular identity; it does this so profoundly that it re-constitutes the conditions for one's agency. But given the epistemological effects of acting, in one's neighbor love one can express and work out a knowledge of and love for God that is not (for any number of reasons) conceptualized in explicit faith. A hermeneutical approach shows Christian ethics and Christian morality to be both universal and particular. Certainly ethics employs particular sources, though these sources (e.g., scripture) are not self-contained. They are themselves conditioned by historical and cultural forces and have a history of effects whereby they impress on the historical consciousness of those who do not know them directly or recognize them as authoritative. Certainly Christian convictions can inform one's intentions and motivate one to act, and certainly they can yield moral and religious obligations that do not bind others. It is entirely appropriate that Christian ethics sets "criteria for success or failure" in these respects. Christian ethics is validated in ways internal to Christian communities. But this fact does not necessarily confine the truth of Christian ethics or the scope of Christian morality.

A hermeneutical account of self-relation insists that the self's relation to others is inscribed into human consciousness. Christian ethics insists that the person realizes herself in a self-disposal of love for God and neighbor. Bringing philosophical hermeneutics to bear on it in order to show the contributions it makes to the problem of self love does not mean that Christian ethics is tested and validated by an independent philosophical anthropology. Of course, a hermeneutical account does open it to secular and non-Christian resources for thinking about the self and its relation to others in the world. These resources can deepen and nuance Christian ethics, prompt it to articulate more clearly and adequately the truth about the person. But Christian ethics does this by reflecting on this truth as it is revealed in Jesus Christ. This means that there are principles and practices internal to it that can specify the "point of being Christian" and "set criteria for success and failure as a Christian" and that Christians can endeavor to love *as* Christians.

To claim that Christian faith is one of any number of commitments which might mediate self-understanding does not make it one option among other, equally valid, options. But it does subject Christian theological discourse to moral evaluation. If Christian ethics opens up human moral existence, its force and veracity as a means to do this must be established dialectically with respect to other options. It must demonstrate its claim to apprehend rightly the dignity and meaning of life before the divine, in the world, and in relation with others. The person's self-relation testifies to the reality of the divine and right self love designates a particular form of self-relation, a way of being in which the experience of the divine which underlies the self's actions and relations provides the meaning and coherence for her life. To the extent that Christian ethics specifies the fundamental structure which its discourse mediates, and keys this to a vision of life before the divine in which the person's well-being is neither divorced from nor subordinate to that of others, Christian ethics validates itself through the dynamic of self-relation.

How, then, does the account of right self love offered here fare in relation to other Christian ethical arguments about self love? Recall from Chapter Two that I argued that the contemporary literature on self love tends to begin with an analysis of love rather than the lover, evaluates self love with respect to love for the neighbor, and collapses the nature and moral evaluation of self love. This conceptual correlation of self love and neighbor love fosters relative silence on love for God (though Vacek is a notable exception) and cuts short theological anthropology. This in turn undermines moral reflection on religious accounts of the divine–human relation and on the concrete acts and relations through which persons take up relation to self, God, and neighbor in the world.

By shifting our starting point from love to the self who is to love, and by shifting our center of gravity from neighbor love to love for God, we position ourselves well to glean the insights of Christian ethical treatments of self love and to avoid their difficulties. To begin, these shifts tease apart the nature and moral evaluation of self love so that we can recognize that self-relation takes better and worse forms. The norm of self-realization does not equip us to distinguish them. But by taking love for God as our center of gravity, we avoid subjectivism and excessive reticence about normative anthropologies; love for God directs our attention to the divine as the highest good and the source of value, and to our creatureliness and to the goods that comprise it.

This point permits, for example, sympathy with and criticism of Nygren's contention that self love is thoroughly pernicious. Recall that Nygren found eros utterly opposed to Christian love (self-sacrificing agape). Nygren reminds us that self love (when it is wrong) can obstruct love for God and neighbor. His emphasis on sacrifice reminds us to transcend desire sufficiently to gauge the correspondence (or lack thereof) between desire and one's basic moral commitments, and to reform desire in the ways that we can. The ethics offered here shares these claims with Nygren. But it differs from him on the egoism of loving God as the highest good. Nygren neglects, as John Burnaby argued, the communal character of love and good in Christian thought.[67] Love for God is not a private pursuit (though it is increasingly regarded as such in our contemporary situation). It is, as the Christian doctrine of the communion of saints suggests, a thoroughly communal delight (and, in this world, struggle). And it is empowered and perfected by God's love for us, which instructs and enables us to love others and things for their sake in God.[68]

God's love for us and our love for God drive us more deeply into the world with others, a world marked by sin, and more deeply and truly into a confrontation with ourselves. So, against those Christian theologians who deem self love natural and morally neutral, the ethics offered here denounces moral indifference to the problem of proper self-relation. It insists that self love is not simply a precondition or by-product or paradigm of neighbor love. It shares with Ramsey the insight that slothful unwillingness to be oneself can be a form of pride (and with Outka that it can be a form of faithlessness). But it does not derive a duty of self love from neighbor love. Because the person is created to love God, and because this ethics has love for God as its center of gravity, it addresses and is better equipped to identify duties to the self that might arise out of love for God. Because both love for God and for neighbor are norms for self love, this account also addresses Ramsey's worries about the selfishness of mutuality.

Self love and neighbor love will conflict, though they may, episodically and ultimately, be harmonized. Therefore Christian ethics must articulate the positive, independent content of right self love if we are to adjudicate conflicts. It must offer a vision to orient us and tools to deploy so that we can endeavor to love ourselves rightly. Outka's language of structural self-responsibility is helpful.

---

[67] John Burnaby, *Amor Dei* (London: Hodder and Stoughton, 1947).
[68] Oliver O'Donovan, *The Problem of Self-Love in Augustine* (New Haven and London: Yale University Press, 1980).

The account of self love offered here fleshes out that language by grappling with our creatureliness. Reformulating ontologically indebted anthropologies assists us in this task.

The ethics offered here shares much with but also corrects Christian ethical arguments for self love as an independent duty. It does this by identifying the good of right self love as embodied integrity. Feminist tendencies to stress autonomous self-determination can collude with the immunization and privatization of desire and with contemporary versions of the mind–body split. And these tendencies contribute to rather than critically assess the norm of self-realization. Feminist emphases on love as mutuality can neglect the proper place of sacrifice and unwittingly reinforce the dichotomy of self-sacrifice and a love that seeks reciprocity. They also leave love for God out of the self–neighbor relation, or make it a by-product of the relation. Finally, feminists can undermine their concern for embodiment by an undue wariness of normative anthropologies. They therefore court moral subjectivism and ironically risk a voluntarism in which intention constitutes the moral meaning of our acts and relations. Vacek risks this, too.

In contrast, a hermeneutical account of self love construes self-realization not simply as autonomous self-determination but more broadly as proper self-relation. It highlights the unity-in-difference of self and neighbor, thereby providing a proper place for sacrifice. In a hermeneutical account self-sacrifice is limited and ordered, not valorized, by the commensurability of self love and love for God. This account provides for moral criticisms of religious accounts that would render love for God as something that exacts the self's denigration. Moreover, a hermeneutical account stresses our bodily being in a world of value. It presses and responds to the questions of whether our self-understanding is true and whether our acts and relations appropriately embody our intentions, affections, and commitments. In all of these ways, it fares better than available Christian ethical treatments.

How does it address contemporary secular approaches to (and denials of) the self and the norm of self-realization? As Chapter One noted, our contemporary moral situation exhibits problems and questions that modern thinkers endeavored to address: the relation of mind and body, the self's continuity, questions of a

stable human nature, the conditions of agency (especially freedom
and desire), the relation of the person to value, and the will to
power. These problems and questions meet in a suspicion of and
reticence about normative anthropologies, especially metaphysically indebted ones. They also express and reinforce the norm
of self-realization. I have argued that a hermeneutical account of
self-relation can treat ontological frameworks as heuristic devices
that address these problems and questions and the norm of self-
realization. It has important affinities with Christian theological anthropology that make it a valuable method for retrieving Christian
insights (e.g., the commensurability of self love and love for God)
and for responding to modern challenges. Thus, it can dispose us
well to the force and veracity of Christian ethics.

Consider, for example, the way a Christian ethical account of
freedom accommodates and corrects our modern emphases on
autonomy. Christian ethics recognizes the positive import of autonomy (it signals the non-instrumental worth of the self and the need
to resist tyranny and oppression). But it does not make the descriptive mistake of understanding the self as a "free agent" or sovereign
source of value. Christian ethics affirms freedom as established in
relation to an other who transcends it. Specifically, the difference
between God and the creature means, among other things, that
freedom emerges in an antecedent order of value. Freedom is situated, co-determined, and conflictual, and just so it is a capacity
for self-disposal or self-commitment. Freedom is not, as autonomy implies, a freedom of choice that requires independence from
all choices. Instead, Christian ethics rightly perceives the unity of
freedom in and through freedom's history.

Christian moral insight into our creatureliness also accommodates and corrects (post) modern deconstruction of the self. This
is especially true when a hermeneutical method is used to read
Christian claims about our creatureliness. Because it insists with
(post) modern thinkers that we are social, linguistic and self-
interpreting creatures, it does not require or permit a static human
nature. It does affirm the goodness and moral import of our bodily
existence. The relatively stable needs and goods that characterize
human existence provide objective reference points for moral reflection. A hermeneutical method both grants our historical and

cultural creativity in specifying their meaning and ordering our lives to them, and insists on deconstructive and liberating reflection and praxis so that we might do so in ever better fashion. Christian ethics, while not at all immune from criticism and revision, offers a vision of the human good and rich symbolic resources and practices that normatively direct us in these tasks. It also shares with (post) modern deconstructions of the self an insistence on a post-moral freedom. Its (self-) critical power prohibits complacent rest in a single system of meaning or idolatrous regard for some finite value or project. The sovereignty of God and the freedom Christ brings exact and prompt ongoing vigilance and openness to transformation. But this freedom answers rather than thwarts our aspirations for coherence. The answer is experienced in the loss or gain of God in the response we make to God's self-communication; the history of our free response to God's gracious love gives coherence to our own self-relation. We come to know ourselves (and others) in God.

This means, as well, that Christian ethics affirms our plurality without absolutizing it, affirms our complexity without compartmentalizing or fragmenting the self. The "cult of self-creation" promises ways to "fix" ourselves into versions we (and others) may love, but it is predicated on self-loathing. It also misconstrues the relation between our identity and our acting. Christian ethics insists on the goodness of our creatureliness and the freedom of self-acceptance (and its correlate, responsibility). A hermeneutical method can highlight Christian insight into our self-constitution through acting and the provisional moral meaning of those acts in the divine counsel. It accounts for moral change not by stressing Nietzschean higher overcomings or by making oneself worthy, but by describing the way faith vivifies our agency, purifies and directs desire and sets our freedom free.

In doing all of this Christian ethics responds to the privatization and immunization of desire. It recognizes the way desire is shaped and elicited (and therefore is not private). It makes sense of our experiences of conferring value and being confronted by it. It indexes desire to objective goods and to God as the source of value and the highest good; it thereby prohibits the immunization of desire. In particular, a hermeneutical method for Christian ethics requires us to consider how desire expresses itself in our concrete acts and relations.

So, a Christian ethical argument for right self love is not a gross instantiation of the will to power. Nor is it a slave morality that diminishes human life. A hermeneutical account of self-relation affirms the interpretive and perspectival character of human thought but also can re-deploy ontology as a resource for insightful self-interpretation and as an exercise of practical reason.

CONCLUSION

Persons are problems to themselves; the question of how to be rightly related to oneself taps into the deepest aspirations and anxieties of the moral life. The problem of self love concerns nothing less than one's very existence before God and in the world. This book has wrestled with the tensions between the complexity of the person and of the moral life, and the need to think clearly and fruitfully about this. Perhaps the most fitting conclusion to this work, then, is to recognize that something of the meaning and goodness of life before God is to be found in our asking about it and in our attempts to answer.

Bibliography

Adams, James Luther, *Paul Tillich's Philosophy of Culture, Science and Religion* (New York: Harper and Row, 1965).

On Being Human Religiously: Selected Essays in Religion and Society, ed., Max L. Stackhouse (Boston, MA: Beacon Press, 1976).

Adams, Robert M., "Saints," *The Journal of Philosophy* (July 1984), 392–401.

Adler, Nathan, *The Underground Stream: New Life Styles and the Antinomian Personality* (New York: Harper and Row, 1972).

Alison, James, *The Joy of Being Wrong: Original Sin Through Easter Eyes* (New York: Crossroad, 1998).

Allik, Tina K., "Nature and Spirit: Agency and Concupiscence in Hauerwas and Rahner," *Journal of Religious Ethics* 15 (1987): 14–32.

Alston, William P., "Realism and the Christian Faith," *International Journal for Philosophy of Religion* 38 (1995), 37–60.

Anderson, Benedict, *Imagined Communities: Reflections on the Origin and Spread of Nationalism*, 2nd edn. (New York: Verso, 1991).

Anderson, James F., *Paul Tillich* (Albany, NY: Magi Books, Inc, 1972).

Anderson, Ray S., *On Being Human: Essays in Theological Anthropology* (Grand Rapids, MI: William B. Eerdmans, 1982).

Andolsen, Barbara Hilkert, "Agape in Feminist Ethics," in *Feminist Theological Ethics: a Reader*, ed., Lois K. Daly (Louisville, KY: Westminster/ John Knox, 1994).

Anshen, Ruth Nanda, ed., *Moral Principles of Action: Man's Ethical Imperative* (New York and London: Harper and Brothers, 1952).

Antonaccio, Maria, "Contemporary Forms of Askesis and the Return of Spiritual Exercises," *Annual of the Society of Christian Ethics* 18 (1998), 69–92.

Augustine, St., *Confessions*, trans. Henry Chadwick (Oxford: Oxford University Press, 1991).

Bacik, James J., *Apologetics and the Eclipse of Mystery: Mystagogy According to Karl Rahner* (Notre Dame, IN: University of Notre Dame, 1980).

Balibar, Etienne, and Immanuel Wallerstein, *Race, Nation, Class: Ambiguous Identities* (London: Verso, 1991).

Beauchesne, Richard J., "The Supernatural Existential as Desire: Karl Rahner and Emmanuel Levinas Revisited," *Église et Théologie* 23 (1992), 221–39.

Bechte, Regina, "Karl Rahner's Supernatural Existential: a Personalist Approach," *Thought* 48 (1973): 61–77.

Bell, Daniel, *The Cultural Contradictions of Capitalism* (New York: Basic, 1976).

Bellah, Robert, Richard Madsen, William M. Sullivan, Ann Swindler, and Steve M. Tipton, *Habits of the Heart: Individualism and Commitment in American Life* (New York: Harper and Row, 1985).

Benhabib, Seyla, *Situating the Self: Gender, Community and Postmodernism in Contemporary Ethics* (New York: Routledge, 1992).

Berry, Wendell, *Standing By Words: Essays by Wendell Berry* (San Francisco, CA: North Point Press, 1983).

What Are People For? (New York: North Point Press, 1990).

Bossy, John, *Christianity in the West, 1400–1700* (Oxford: Oxford University Press; John Bossy, 1985).

Bresnahan, James F., "Rahner's Ethics: Critical Natural Law in Relation to Contemporary Ethical Methodology," *Journal of Religion* 56 (1976), 36–60.

Brown, Peter, *The Body and Society: Men, Women and Sexual Renunciation in Early Christianity* (New York: Columbia University Press, 1988).

Brummer, Vincent, *Speaking of a Personal God: an Essay in Philosophical Theology* (Cambridge: Cambridge University Press, 1992).

Buckley, James J., "On Being a Symbol: an Appraisal of Karl Rahner," *Theological Studies* 40:3 (1979), 285–98.

Bulman, Raymond F., and Frederick J. Parrella, eds., *Paul Tillich: a New Catholic Assessment* (Collegeville, MN: Liturgical Press, 1994).

Burnaby, John, *Amor Dei* (London: Hodder and Stoughton, 1947).

Burnham, Frederick B., ed., *Postmodern Theology: Christian Faith in a Pluralist World* (New York: Harper and Row, 1989).

Butler, Joseph, *Five Sermons Preached at the Rolls Chapel: and a Dissertation upon the Nature of Virtue*, introduction by Stuart M. Brown (New York: Liberal Arts, 1950).

Butler, Judith, *Gender Trouble: Feminism and the Subversion of Identity* (New York and London: Routledge, 1990).

Bynum, Caroline Walker, *Holy Feast and Holy Fast: the Religious Significance of Food to Medieval Women* (Berkeley, CA: University of California Press, 1987).

Cahill, Lisa Sowle, *Between the Sexes: Foundations for a Christian Ethics of Sexuality* (Philadelphia, PA: Fortress Press, 1985).

Sex, Gender and Christian Ethics (Cambridge: Cambridge University Press, 1996).

Callahan, Annice, "Karl Rahner's Theology of Symbol: Basis of his Theology of the Church and the Sacraments," *Irish Theological Quarterly* 49 (1982), 195–205.

"The Relationship between Spirituality and Theology," *Horizons* 16 (1989), 266–74.

Carey, John J., ed., *Kairos and Logos: Studies in the Roots and Implications of Tillich's Theology* (Cambridge, MA: The North American Paul Tillich Society, 1978).

Carr, Anne, *The Theological Method of Karl Rahner*, AAR Dissertation Series, no. 19 (Missoula, MO: Scholars Press, 1977).

Castels, Manuel, *The Power of Identity*, vol. 2, *The Information Age: Economy, Society and Culture* (Malden, MA: Blackwell, 1997).

Cates, Diana Fritz, *Choosing to Feel: Virtue, Friendship and Compassion for Friends* (Notre Dame, IN: University of Notre Dame Press, 1997).

Cawte, J., "Karl Rahner's Conception of God's Self-Communication to Man," *Heythrop Journal* 25:3 (1984), 260–71.

Chadwick, Owen, *The Reformation* (London: Penguin; Owen Chadwick, 1972).

Chodorow, Nancy, *Feminism and Psychoanalytic Theory* (New Haven: Yale University Press, 1989).

Chopp, Rebecca, *The Power to Speak: Feminism, Language and God* (New York: Crossroad, 1989).

Cobb, Kelton, "Reconsidering the Status of Popular Culture in Tillich's Theology of Culture," *Journal of the American Academy of Religion* 63 (Spring 1995): 53–84.

Coburn, Robert C., "The Idea of Transcendence," *Philosophical Investigations* 13 (1990), 322–37.

Conway, Eamonn, *The Anonymous Christian – a Relativised Christianity?* (Frankfurt am Main: Peter Lang, 1993).

Cornell, Drucilla, *At the Heart of Freedom: Feminism, Sex, and Equality* (Princeton, NJ: Princeton University Press, 1998).

Coward, Rosalind, *Patriarchal Precedents: Sexuality and Social Relations* (London: Routledge and Kegan Paul, 1983).

Cowburn, John, *Love and the Person: a Philosophical Theory and a Theological Essay* (London: Geoffrey Chapman, 1967).

Curran, Charles, *The Catholic Moral Tradition Today: a Synthesis* (Washington DC: Georgetown University Press, 1999).

D'Arcy, M. C., *The Mind and Heart of Love* (New York: Meridian Books, 1959).

Davis, Joseph E., "Identity and Social Change: a Short Review," *The Hedgehog Review* 1 (Fall 1999): 95–102.

D'Costa, Gavin, "Karl Rahner's Anonymous Christian: a Reappraisal," *Modern Theology* 1:2 (1985), 131–48.

de Letter, Paul, "Divine Quasi-Formal Causality," *Irish Theological Quarterly* 27 (1960), 221–28.

de Rougemont, Denis, *Love in the Western World*, trans. Montgomery Belgion (Garden City, NY: Doubleday and Company, Inc., 1957).

Devaney, Shelia Greave, "Problems with Feminist Theory: Historicity and the Search for Sure Foundations," in *Embodied Love: Sensuality and Relationship as Feminist Values*, eds., Paula M. Cooey, Sharon A. Farmer, and Mary Ellen Ross (San Francisco, CA: Harper and Row, 1987).

Dilman, Ilham, *Raskolnikov's Rebirth: Psychology and the Understanding of Good and Evil* (Chicago and La Salle: Open Court, 2000).

Donagan, Alan, *The Theory of Morality* (Chicago, IL: University of Chicago, 1977).

Driesbach, Donald F., "Paul Tillich's Hermeneutic," *Journal of the American Academy of Religion* 43 (1975), 84–94.

"Essence, Existence, and the Fall: Paul Tillich's Analysis of Existence," *Harvard Theological Review* 73 (1980), 521–38.

Symbols and Salvation: Paul Tillich's Doctrine of Religious Symbols and his Interpretation of the Symbols of the Christian Tradition (Lanham, MD: University Press of America, 1993).

Dych, William V., *Karl Rahner* (London: Geoffrey Chapman, 1992).

Eberhard, Kenneth D., "Karl Rahner and the Supernatural Existential," *Thought* 46 (1971), 537–61.

Edwards, Denis, "The Relationship between the Risen Christ and the Material Universe," *Pacifica* 4 (1991), 1–14.

Edwards, Jonathan, *On the Nature of True Virtue*, foreword William K. Frankena (Ann Arbor, MI: University of Michigan, 1960).

Erikson, Erik, *Identity: Youth and Crisis* (New York: Norton, 1968).

Etzioni, Amitai, *The Spirit of Community* (New York: Crown, 1993).

Farley, Margaret, *Personal Commitments: Beginning, Keeping, Changing* (San Francisco, CA: HarperSanFrancisco, 1986).

"Feminist Theology and Bioethics," in *Feminist Theological Ethics*, ed., Lois K. Daly (Louisville, KY: Westminster/John Knox, 1994).

Fields S. J., Stephen, *Being as Symbol: on the Origins and Development of Karl Rahner's Metaphysics* (Washington DC: Georgetown University Press, 2000).

Finnis, John, *Fundamentals of Ethics* (Washington DC: Georgetown University Press, 1983).

Flanagan, Owen, *Varieties of Moral Personality: Ethics and Psychological Realism* (Cambridge, MA: Harvard University Press, 1991).

Flanagan, Owen and Amélie Oksenberg Rorty, eds., *Identity, Character and Morality: Essays in Moral Psychology* (Cambridge, MA: MIT Press, 1990.

Foerster, John, "Paul Tillich and Inter-religious Dialogue," *Modern Theology* 7 (1990), 1–27.

Foucault, Michel, *Discipline and Punish: the Birth of the Prison*, trans. Alan Sheridan (New York: Pantheon Books, 1977).

The History of Sexuality: an Introduction, trans. Robert Hurley (New York: Random House, 1978).

Frankfurt, Harry, *The Importance of what We Care About* (Cambridge: Cambridge University Press, 1988).

Freud, Sigmund, *Civilization and its Discontents* (New York: Norton, 1930).

Fromm, Erich, *Man for Himself: an Inquiry into the Psychology of Ethics* (New York: Rinehart, 1947).

Furnish, Victor, *Love Command in the New Testament* (New York: Abingdon, 1972).

Gallagher, John A., *Time Past, Time Future: a Historical Study of Catholic Moral Theology* (New York: Paulist, 1990).

Gergen, Kenneth J., *The Saturated Self: Dilemmas of Identity in Contemporary Life* (New York: Basic, 1991).

Gilleman, Gérard, *The Primacy of Charity in Moral Theology* (Westminster, MD: Newman, 1959).

Gilligan, Carol, *In a Different Voice* (Cambridge, MA: Harvard University Press, 1982).

Goffman, Erving, *The Presentation of Self in Everyday Life* (New York: Doubleday, 1959).

Goldstein, Valerie Saiving, "The Human Situation: a Feminine View, in *Womanspirit Rising: a Feminist Reader in Religion*, eds., Carol P. Christ and Judith Plaskow (San Francisco, CA: HarperSanFrancisco; Christ and Plaskow, 1979).

Graber, Glenn, "The Metaethics of Paul Tillich," *Journal of Religious Ethics* 1 (1973), 113–33.

Graham, Elaine, *Making the Difference: Gender, Personhood and Theology* (Minneapolis, MN: Fortress, 1996).

Gregg, Richard, "The Experiential Center of Tillich's System," *Journal of the American Academy of Religion* 53 (1985), 251–58.

Grisez, Germain, *Christian Moral Principles*, vol. 1 of *The Way of the Lord Jesus* (Chicago: Franciscan Herald, 1983).

Gustafson, James M., *Protestant and Roman Catholic Ethics: Prospects for Rapprochement* (Chicago: University of Chicago Press, 1978).

Gutiérrez, Gustavo, *A Theology of Liberation*, rev. edn., trans. and eds. Sister Caridad Inda and John Eagleson (New York: Orbis, 1990).

Hadot, Pierre, *Philosophy as a Way of Life: Spiritual Exercises from Socrates to Foucault*, ed. and intro., Arnold I. Davidson (Oxford and Cambridge, MA: Blackwell Publishers, 1995).

Hallet, Garth L., *Christian Neighbor Love: an Assessment of Six Rival Versions* (Washington DC: Georgetown University Press, 1989).

Priorities and Christian Ethics (Cambridge: Cambridge University Press, 1998).

Harrison, Beverly Wildung, *Making the Connections: Essays in Feminist Social Ethics*, ed., Carol S. Robb (Boston, MA: Beacon, 1985).

Harvey, David, *The Condition of Postmodernity: an Enquiry into the Origins of Cultural Change* (Oxford and Cambridge, MA: Basil Blackwell, 1989).

Hauerwas, Stanley, *A Community of Character* (Notre Dame, IN: University of Notre Dame Press, 1987).

"Agency: Going Forward by Looking Back," in *Christian Ethics: Problems and Prospects*, eds., Lisa Sowle Cahill and James F. Childress (Cleveland, OH: Pilgrim, 1996).

Hauerwas, Stanley, and Gregory L. Jones, eds., *Why Narrative?: Readings in Narrative Theology* (Grand Rapids, MI: W. B. Eerdmans, 1989).

Hazo, Robert, *The Idea of Love* (New York: Frederick A. Praeger, 1967).

Hewitt, John P., *Dilemmas of the American Self* (Philadelphia, PA: Temple University Press, 1989).

Heyward, Carter, "Heterosexist Theology: Being Above it All," *Journal of Feminist Studies in Religion* 3 (1987): 29–38.

Highfield, Ron, "The Freedom to Say 'No'? Karl Rahner's Doctrine of Sin," *Theological Studies* 56 (1995), 485–505.

Hill, W., "Uncreated Grace – A Critique of Karl Rahner," *Thomist* 27 (1963), 333–56.

Himes, Michael J. and Kenneth R. Himes, *Fullness of Faith: the Public Significance of Theology* (New York: Paulist, 1993).

Irwin, Alexander C., "The Faces of Desire: Tillich on 'Essential Libido,' Concupiscence and the Transcendence of Estrangement," *Encounter* 51 (1990), 339–58.

Isasi-Díaz, Ada María, "Solidarity: Love of Neighbor in the 1990s," in *Feminist Theological Ethics* ed., Lois K. Daly (Louisville, KY: Westminster/John Knox, 1994).

Jackson, Timothy P., *Love Disconsoled: Meditations on Christian Charity* (Cambridge: Cambridge University Press, 1999).

Johann, Robert O., *The Meaning of Love: an Essay towards a Metaphysics of Intersubjectivity* (London: Geoffrey Chapman Ltd., 1954).

Johnson, Mark, *The Body in the Mind: the Bodily Basis of Meaning, Imagination, and Reason* (Chicago: University of Chicago Press, 1988).

Kant, Immanuel, *Fundamental Principles of the Metaphysics of Morals*, trans. Thomas K. Abbott (New York: Macmillan, 1949).

Kegley, Charles W., and Robert W. Bretall, eds., *The Theology of Paul Tillich* (New York: Macmillan, 1961).

Keller, Joseph, "Mysticism and Intersubjective Creativity," *Studia Mystica* 8:4 (1985), 36–46.

Kelsey, David H., *The Fabric of Paul Tillich's Theology* (New Haven and London: Yale University Press, 1967).

Kierkegaard, Søren, *Works of Love*, eds. and trans. Howard Hong and Edna Hong (New York: Harper and Row, 1962).

Kottukapally, J., "Nature and Grace: a New Dimension," *Thought* 49 (1974), 117–33.

Kramer, Peter D., *Listening to Prozac: a Psychiatrist Explores Antidepressant Drugs and the Remaking of the Self* (New York: Viking, 1993).

Laing, R. D., *The Divided Self: an Existential Study in Sanity and Madness* (Baltimore, MD: Penguin, 1965).

Lamadrid, Lucas, "Anonymous or Analogous Christians? Rahner and von Balthasar on Naming the Non-Christian," *Modern Theology* 11 (1995), 363–84.

Lamm, Julia A., "'Catholic Substance' Revisited: Reversals of Expectations in Tillich's Doctrine of God," in *Paul Tillich: A New Catholic Assessment*, eds. Raymond F. Bulman and Frederick J. Parrella (Collegeville, MN: Liturgical Press, 1994).

Larmore, Charles E., *Patterns of Moral Complexity* (Cambridge: Cambridge University Press, 1987).

Lasch, Christopher, *The Culture of Narcissism: American Life in an Age of Diminishing Expectations* (New York: Norton, 1979).

The Minimal Self: Psychic Survival in Troubled Times (New York: Norton, 1984).

Lauritzen, Paul, "The Self and its Discontents," *Journal of Religious Ethics* 22:1 (1994), 189–210.

Lewis, C. S., *The Four Loves* (London: Geoffrey Bles, 1960).

Lichtman, Susan L., "The Concept of Sin in the Theology of Paul Tillich: A Break From Patriarchy?" *Journal of Women and Religion* 8 (1989), 49–55.

Lifton, Robert Jay, *The Protean Self: Human Resilience in an Age of Fragmentation* (New York: Basic, 1993).

Locke, John, *Essay Concerning Human Understanding*, ed. with a foreword by Peter H. Nidditch (Oxford: Clarendon Press; New York: Oxford University Press, 1979).

MacIntyre, Alasdair, *After Virtue*, 2nd edn. (Notre Dame, IN: University of Notre Dame Press, 1984).

258 *Bibliography*

Mahoney, John, *The Making of Moral Theology: a Study of the Roman Catholic Tradition* (Oxford: Oxford University Press, 1987).

Marcuse, Herbert, *One-Dimensional Man: Studies in the Ideology of Advanced Industrial Society* (Boston, MA: Beacon, 1964).

Martin, Bernard, *The Existentialist Theology of Paul Tillich* (New York: Bookman Associates, 1963).

McDargh, John, "Theological Uses of Psychology: Retrospective and Prospective," *Horizons* 12 (1985), 247–64.

McDonald, H. D., "The Symbolic Christology of Paul Tillich," *Vox Evangelica* 18 (1988), 75–88.

McFadyen, Alistair, *Bound to Sin: Abuse, Holocaust and the Christian Doctrine of Sin* (Cambridge: Cambridge University Press, 2000).

McFague, Sallie, *Models of God* (Philadelphia, PA: Fortress, 1987).

Mead, George Herbert, *Mind, Self and Society* (Chicago: University of Chicago Press, 1934).

Meilaender, Gilbert, *Friendship* (Notre Dame, IN: University of Notre Dame Press, 1981).

Merton, Thomas, *The Nonviolent Alternative*, ed. Gordon Zahn (New York: Farrar, Straus, Giroux, 1980).

Metz, Johannes Baptist, *Faith in History and Society: toward a Practical Fundamental Theology*, trans. David Smith (New York: Seabury, 1979).

"An Identity Crisis in Christianity? Transcendental and Political Responses," *Theology and Discovery: Essays in Honor of Karl Rahner*, ed., William Kelly (Milwaukee, WI: Marquette University Press, 1980), 169–78.

Meyrowitz, Joshua, *No Sense of Place: the Impact of Electronic Media on Social Behavior* (New York: Oxford University Press, 1985).

Miller, Edward J., "Inclusivist and Exclusivist Issues in Soteriology: to Whom Does Jesus' Saving Power Extend?" *Perspectives in Religious Studies* 12 (1985), 123–37.

Miller, William Ian, *The Anatomy of Disgust* (Cambridge, MA, and London: Harvard University Press, 1997).

Mitchell, Juliet, *Women's Estate* (New York: Random House, Vintage Books, 1973).

Modras, Ronald, "Implications of Rahner's Anthropology for Fundamental Moral Theology," *Horizons* 12 (Spring 1985), 70–90.

"Catholic Substance and the Catholic Church Today," in *Paul Tillich: a New Catholic Assessment*, eds., Raymond F. Bulman and Frederick J. Parrella (Collegeville, MN: Liturgical Press, 1994).

Morgan, John H., "Religion and Culture as Meaning Systems: a Dialogue between Geertz and Tillich," *Journal of Religion* 57 (1977), 363–75.

Muck, Otto, *The Transcendental Method*, trans. William D. Seidensticker (New York: Herder and Herder, 1968).

Bibliography

259

Murdoch, Iris, *The Sovereignty of Good* (London: Routledge and Kegan Paul, 1970).

Metaphysics as a Guide to Morals (New York: Allen Lane/Penguin, 1993).

Niebuhr, H. Richard, "Faith in God and in Gods," *Radical Monotheism and Western Culture, With Supplementary Essays*, foreword by James M. Gustafson (Louisville, KY: Westminster/John Knox, 1960).

The Responsible Self (San Francisco, CA: HarperSanFrancisco, 1963).

Nussbaum, Martha, *The Therapy of Desire: Theory and Practice in Hellenistic Ethics* (Princeton, NJ: Princeton University Press, 1994).

Nygren, Anders, *Agape and Eros*, trans. Philip S. Watson (London: S.P.C.K., 1957).

O'Connell, Timothy, *Principles for a Catholic Morality*, rev. edn. (San Francisco, CA: HarperSanFrancisco, 1990).

O'Donovan, Leo J., ed., *A World of Grace: an Introduction to the Themes and Foundations of Karl Rahner's Theology* (New York: Seabury, 1980).

O'Donovan, Oliver, *The Problem of Self-Love in Augustine* (New Haven and London: Yale University Press, 1980).

O'Grady, Jane, "Emotions and feelings" in *Oxford Companion to Philosophy*, ed., Ted Honderich (Oxford and New York: Oxford University, 1995).

O'Keefe, Mark, *Becoming Good, Becoming Holy: On the Relationship of Christian Ethics and Spirituality* (New York: Paulist, 1995).

Outka, Gene, *Agape: an Ethical Analysis* (New Haven: Yale University Press, 1972).

"Universal Love and Impartiality" in *The Love Commandments: Essays in Christian Ethics and Moral Philosophy*, eds., Edmund N. Santurri and William Werpehowski (Washington DC: Georgetown University Press, 1992).

Ozment, Steven E., *The Reformation in the Cities* (New Haven and London: Yale University Press, 1975).

Page, Ruth, "The Consistent Christology of Paul Tillich," *Scottish Journal of Theology* 36 (1983), 195–212.

Parsons, Susan Frank, *Feminism and Christian Ethics* (Cambridge: Cambridge University Press, 1996).

Peter, Carl, "The Position of Karl Rahner Regarding the Supernatural: a Comparative Study of Nature and Grace," *Proceedings of the Catholic Theological Society of America* 20 (1965), 81–94.

Plaskow, Judith, *Sex, Sin and Grace: Women's Experience and the Theologies of Reinhold Niebuhr and Paul Tillich* (Lanham, MD: University Press of America, 1980).

Pope, Stephen, "Expressive Individualism and True Self-Love: a Thomistic Perspective," *The Journal of Religion* 71 (July 1991), 384–99.

Porter, Jean, *Moral Action and Christian Ethics* (Cambridge: Cambridge University Press, 1995).

The Recovery of Virtue (Louisville, KY: Westminster/John Knox, 1990).
"Salvific Love and Charity," in *The Love Commandments: Essays in Christian Ethics and Moral Philosophy*, eds., Edmund N. Santurri and William Werpehowski (Washington DC: Georgetown University Press, 1992).

Post, Stephen, *A Theory of Agape: On the Meaning of Christian Love* (Lewisburg, PA: Bucknell University Press, 1990).

Proudfoot, Wayne, *Religious Experience* (Berkeley, CA: University of California Press, 1985).

Rahner, Karl, *Theological Investigations*, vols. 1–14 (vols. 1–6, Baltimore, MD: Helicon; vols. 7–10, New York: Herder and Herder; vols. 11–14, New York: Seabury, 1961–1976).

The Dynamic Element in the Church (London: Burns and Oates, 1964).

Spirit in the World, trans. William Dych (New York: Herder and Herder, 1968).

Hearers of the World, trans. Michael Richards (New York: Herder and Herder, 1969).

Meditations on Freedom and the Spirit (New York: Seabury, 1978).

The Love of Jesus and the Love of Neighbor, trans. Robert Barr (New York: Crossroad, 1983).

Karl Rahner: Theologian of the Graced Search for Meaning, ed., Geoffrey B. Kelly (Minneapolis, MN: Fortress, 1992).

Foundations of Christian Faith: an Introduction to the Idea of Christianity, trans. William Dych (New York: Crossroad, 1993).

Ramsey, Paul, *Basic Christian Ethics* (Louisville, KY: Westminster/John Knox, 1950).

Reiff, Philip, *The Triumph of the Therapeutic: Uses of Faith After Freud* (New York: Harper and Row, 1966).

Reno, R. R., *The Ordinary Transformed: Karl Rahner and the Christian Vision of Transcendence* (Grand Rapids, MI: William B. Eerdmans, 1995).

Reuther, Rosemary Radford, *Sexism and God-Talk: Toward a Feminist Theology* (Boston, MA: Beacon, 1983).

Richard, Jean, "Theology of Culture and Systematic Theology in Paul Tillich," *Église et Théologie* 2 (1986), 223–32.

Ricoeur, Paul, *Interpretation Theory: Discourse and the Surplus of Meaning* (Fort Worth, TX: Texas Christian University, 1976).

Oneself as Another, trans. Kathleen Blamey (Chicago: University of Chicago Press, 1992).

Roth, Robert J., ed., *Person and Community: a Philosophical Exploration* (New York: Fordham University Press, 1975).

Royster, James E., "Paul Tillich's Ethical Thought," *Ohio Journal of Religious Studies* 5 (April 1977), 35–51.

Rudman, Stanley, *Concepts of Persons and Christian Ethics* (Cambridge: Cambridge University Press, 1997).

Sabatino, Charles J., "An Interpretation of the Significance of Theonomy within Tillich's Theology," *Encounter* 45 (1984), 23–38.

Sayre-McCord, Geoffrey, ed., *Essays on Moral Realism* (Ithaca, NY and London: Cornell University Press, 1988).

Scharf, Uwe C., "Dogmatics between the Poles of the Sacred and the Profane: an Essay in Theological Methodology," *Encounter* 55 (1994), 269–86.

Schlabach, Gerald W., *For the Joy Set Before Us: Augustine and Self-Denying Love* (Notre Dame, IN: University of Notre Dame, 2001).

Schrag, Calvin O., *The Self After Postmodernity* (Cambridge: Cambridge University Press, 1997).

Schwarz, Douglas O., "Religious Relativism: Paul Tillich's 'last word,'" *American Journal of Theology and Philosophy* 7:2 (1986), 106–14.

Schweiker, William, "Hermeneutics, Ethics and the Theology of Culture: Concluding Reflections," in *Meanings in Texts and Actions: Questioning Paul Ricoeur*, eds., David E. Klemm and William Schweiker (Charlottesville, VA: University of Virginia Press, 1993).

Responsibiltiy and Christian Ethics (Cambridge: Cambridge University Press, 1995).

Power, Value and Conviction (Cleveland, OH: Pilgrim, 1998).

Sennet, Richard, *The Fall of Public Man: On the Social Psychology of Capitalism* (New York: Knopf, 1977).

Sharpe, R. A., *The Moral Case Against Religious Belief* (London: SCM Press Ltd., 1997).

Shaw, Elliott, "All You Need is Love: Ethics in the Thought of Paul Tillich," *Modern Believing* 37 (January 1996), 24–30.

Sheehan, Thomas, *Karl Rahner: the Philosophical Foundations* (Athens, OH: Ohio University Press, 1987).

Singer, Irving, *The Nature of Love*, 3 vols. (Chicago: University of Chicago Press, 1987).

Singh, Sachindra Kumar, *Religious Philosophy of Paul Tillich* (Delhi-6:Capital Publishing House, 1989).

Sinnett, M. W., "The Primacy of Relation in Paul Tillich's Theology of Correlation: a Reply to the Critique of Charles Hartshorne" *Religious Studies* 27 (1991), 541–57.

Slater, Peter, "Tillich on the Fall and the Temptation of Goodness," *Journal of Religion* 65 (1985), 196–207.

Soble, Alan, *The Structure of Love* (New Haven and London: Yale University Press, 1990).

Staes, Paul, *Positive Self Regard and Authentic Morality* (Aeteneo de Manila University, 1972).

Stambaugh, Joan, *The Formless Self* (Albany, NY: SUNY, 1999).

Stenger, Mary A., "Paul Tillich's Theory of Theological Norms and the Problems of Relativism and Subjectivism," *Journal of Religion* 62 (1982), 359–75.

Stern, Karl, *The Flight from Woman* (New York: Farrar, Straus, and Giroux, 1965).

Sundberg, Walter, "The Demonic in Christian Thought," *Lutheran Quarterly* 1 (1987), 413–37.

Talley, Joseph E., "Psychological Separation – Individuation and Spiritual Reunion," *Journal of Psychology and Theology* 8 (1980), 97–106.

Tallon, Andrew, "The Heart in Rahner's Philosophy of Mysticism," *Theological Studies* 53 (1992), 700–28.

"Rahner and Personalization," *Philosophy Today* 14 (1970), 44–56.

"Personal Becoming," *Thomist* 43 (1979), 1–177.

Tanner, Kathryn, *God and Creation in Christian Theology* (Oxford: Blackwell, 1988).

The Politics of God (Minneapolis, MN: Fortress, 1992).

Taylor, Charles, *Sources of the Self: the Making of the Modern Identity* (Cambridge, MA: Harvard University Press, 1989).

The Ethics of Authenticity (Cambridge, MA: Harvard University Press, 1992).

Taylor, Mark Lloyd, *God is Love: a Study in the Theology of Karl Rahner* (American Academy of Religion Series. Atlanta, GA: Scholars Press, 1986).

TeSelle, E. A., "The Problem of Nature and Grace," *Journal of Religion* 45 (1965), 238–49.

Tillich, Paul, *Systematic Theology*, 3 vols. (Chicago: University of Chicago Press, 1951–63).

The Courage to Be (New Haven: Yale University Press, 1952).

Love, Power and Justice (Oxford: Oxford University Press, 1954).

Biblical Religion and the Search for Ultimate Reality (Chicago: University of Chicago Press, 1955).

Dynamics of Faith (New York: Harper Torchbooks, Harper Brothers, 1957).

Theology of Culture (Oxford: Oxford University Press, 1959).

Christianity and the Encounter of the World Religions (New York and London: Columbia University Press, 1963).

The Eternal Now (New York: Charles Scribner's Sons, 1963).

Morality and Beyond (Louisville, KY: Westminster/John Knox, 1963).

Tilly, Maureen H., and Susan A. Ross, eds., *Broken and Whole: Essays on Religion and the Body* (Lanham, MD: University Press of America, Inc., 1994).

Toner, Jules, *The Experience of Love* (Washington: Corpus Books, 1968).

Turkle, Sherry, *Life on the Screen: Identity in the Age of the Internet* (New York: Simon and Schuster; Turkle, 1995).

Vacek S. J., Edward, *Love, Human and Divine: the Heart of Christian Ethics* (Washington DC: Georgetown University Press, 1994).

Van Rooy, Jacobus A., "Christ and the Religions: the Issues at Stake," *Missionalia* 13 (1985), 3–13.

Viladesau, Richard, "How is Christ Absolute? Rahner's Christology and the Encounter of World Religions," *Philosophy and Theology* 2 (1988), 220–40.

Vulgamore, Melvin L., "Tillich's 'Erotic Solution,'" *Encounter* 45 (Summer 1984), 193–212.

Wallace, William A., "Existential Ethics: a Thomistic Appraisal," *Thomist* 27 (1963), 493–515.

Wallwork, Ernest, "Thou Shalt Love Thy Neighbor As Thyself: the Freudian Critique," *Journal of Religious Ethics* 10 (Fall 1982), 291–92.

Walzer, Michael, *Spheres of Justice* (New York: Basic, 1983).

Waters, Mary, *Ethnic Options: Choosing Identities in America* (Berkeley, CA: University of California Press, 1990).

Weisbaker, Donald R., "Paul Tillich on the Experiential Ground of Religious Certainty," *American Journal of Theology and Philosophy* 1:2 (1980), 37–44.

Wiles, Maurice, "Christianity and other Faiths: some Theological Reflections," *Theology* 91 (1988), 302–08.

Williams, Bernard, *Moral Luck: Philosophical Papers, 1973–1980* (Cambridge, MA: Harvard University Press, 1981).

Ethics and the Limits of Philosophy (Cambridge, MA: Harvard University Press, 1985).

Wolf, Susan, "Moral Saints," *The Journal of Philosophy* (August 1982), 419–39.

Yankelovich, Daniel, *New Rules: Searching for Self-Fulfillment in a World Turned Upside Down* (New York: Random House, 1981).

Young, Iris, "The Ideal of Community and the Politics of Difference," *Social Theory and Practice* 12:1 (Spring 1986).

Justice and the Politics of Difference (Princeton, NJ: Princeton University Press, 1990).

Zurcher, Louis A., Jr., *The Mutable Self: a Self-Concept for Social Change* (Beverly Hills, CA: Sage, 1977).

Zurcher, Louis A., Jr., and Michael R. Wood, *The Development of a Postmodern Self: a Computer-Assisted Comparative Analysis of Personal Documents* (New York: Greenwood, 1988).

Index

self-relation and 36, 107, 124, 127, 132, 168, 171, 241, 249
Farley, Margaret 52, 99
Fénelon, François 138
Finnis, John 90–91, 136, 168–69, 177, 206
Flanagan, Owen 185
Foucault, Michel 19, 68, 96–97
Frankfurt, Harry 95
freedom 6, 18, 74, 76, 86, 191
    as autonomy 13–16, 19–22, 27, 30, 40, 42, 78, 115, 248
    moral acts and 194–95, 197, 199, 211, 231, relation to God and 44–45, 77, 94, 105, 108, 113, 114, 124, 129, 132, 136, 149, 159, 185, 188, 190, 213, 218, 242, 249
    self-commitment and 35, 36, 125, 126, 135, 222, 226, 248
    as situated 29, 84, 115–18, 127, 172, 183–84
    unity of 25, 165, 170, 205–06
    see also Rahner, on fundamental option
Freud, Sigmund 7, 11, 16, 95

Gadamer, Hans-Georg 85
God *passim*
    difference from creation 81, 106, 107, 113–15, 120, 126, 128–29, 141–42, 248
    as highest good 3, 4, 39, 59, 79, 121, 133, 138, 217, 246
    knowledge of 6, 94, 109–12, 211
    moral acts and 99, 165, 173–76, 178, 180, 194, 195, 197, 198, 205, 210, 211, 234
    moral criticism of relation to 6, 10, 42, 45, 60, 77, 80, 107, 129, 140, 141, 160, 161, 166, 208, 224, 240, 242, 247
    relation to 44, 71, 82, 93, 95, 107–08, 123, 130, 135, 157, 170, 193, 213, 221, 249, 250
    as source of value 21–22, 39, 42, 87, 128, 249
    see also freedom, relation to God and; love, for God
grace 4–5, 82, 106, 112–14, 116, 117, 120–21, 127, 129, 136, 142–43, 149, 151, 158, 173–75, 177, 185–89, 196, 202, 211–13, 222, 227–29, 249
Graham, Elaine 97
Grisez, Germain 168–69, 206
Gustafson, James 147
Gutiérrez, Gustavo 152–53, 154

Harrison, Beverly Wildung 64–66, 70, 102, 144, 184
Hauerwas, Stanley 23, 180–81
Hegel, Georg Whilhelm Friedrich 11, 15–16
Heyward, Carter 155
Himes, Kenneth 224
Himes, Michael 224
Hume, David 11, 12–13

identity 2, 32–36, 69, 79, 84, 86–88, 97–98, 103–04, 125, 128, 149, 150, 182, 192, 205, 230
    body and 97–98
    Christian 35–36, 230
    integrity and 156–59, 167–71, 205
    narrative 19, 25, 180, 181
    socially constructed 2, 6–7, 19, 21, 22–31, 41, 68, 248–49
    unity of 2, 12, 18, 24–25, 31, 34–35, 163–65, 170–71, 173–74, 205, 247
integrity 84, 91, 101, 103–04, 157–58, 167–71, 181, 184, 192, 205, 218
    embodied 82, 88, 91, 92–95, 131, 156–66, 167–71, 183–84, 205–07, 247
    see also identity, integrity and
intention 71–72, 75–77, 99, 100, 103, 143, 182, 192–93, 198, 204–05, 229–31, 244, 247
interpretation 16, 17, 39
intuitionism 2, 40, 96, 106–07, 147–48, 156, 163, 190, 199, 204, 224
Isasi-Díaz, Ada Maria 152–53, 154

Jesus Christ 35–36, 59, 68, 137, 153, 187
    normativity of 223–238
    revelation in 21, 81, 82, 117, 125, 140, 161, 162–63, 184, 186, 209, 213, 244
    sacrifice of 5, 65
    uniqueness of 135–36
Johnson, Mark 96

Kant, Immanuel 11, 13–16, 38, 169, 181
Kelsey, David 162
Kierkegaard, Søren 95, 133, 157
King, Martin Luther 155
knowledge 2, 6, 11–13, 15–16, 36, 71, 82, 94–95, 100, 108–12, 115, 136, 151, 161, 164, 170, 190, 200–01, 205, 206, 211, 226

Lauritzen, Paul 24, 157
Locke, John 11, 12, 25, 157